"This is no ordinary book about the 1960s. Nor is it a left political screed. It's a jewel of a collection of US revolutionaries' memoirs that captures and recreates the period like no other. Each story is unique and mesmerizing, as well as being heartbreaking and funny, which taken as a whole clarifies overall failure of revolutionary goals while suggesting what is to be done. This is truly political literature at its best, rarely seen in the United States."
— **Roxanne Dunbar-Ortiz**, author of *Outlaw Woman: A Memoir of the War Years, 1960-1975* and *An Indigenous People's History of the United States*

"An important component of 1960s radical history, thoughtfully re-counted by the activists who lived it."
— **Max Elbaum**, author of *Revolution in the Air: Sixties Radicals Turn to Lenin, Mao and Che*

"The East was Red, and the Wind was Rising, or at least so it seemed to an astonishingly mixed bag of passionate young radicals drawn in the 1960s to the Progressive Labor Party, the Maoist-oriented com-munist group, who look back here on their radical lives. They are men and women who defied a travel ban to visit Cuba where they debated Che and played ping-pong with Fidel; Baptist Sunday school teachers who started reading Lenin and Marx; men who, on party or-ders, joined the army to 'raise a ruckus' from within; who pushed racks in the garment center to organize workers for revolution; who led successful student strikes, disrupted military recruiters, and generally put their passions into changing the world. All tell of how they fell in—and later mostly out of—love with the notion of a Red Revolu-tion. John F. Levin and Earl Silbar's collection of often soul-searching memoirs is a much-needed addition to the history of an era."
— **Tom Robbins** covered crime and politics for more than thirty years for the, *New York Daily News* and *Village Voice*

"These activists offer personal accounts of major moments in the New Left movement that peaked in the 1960s. Their memories of specific events, disputes, and personalities offer invaluable insights and guidance in understanding the emotional and intellectual vigor of that time."

— **Dan Georgakas**, co-author of *Detroit: I Do Mind Dying* and co-editor of *The Encyclopedia of the American Left*

"To my surprise, as one who avoided Progressive Labor in the sixties and beyond, and who saw little virtue in Maoism as a guide for American leftists, I recommend this collection of memoirs with enthusiasm. These accounts helped me to understand what drew young people to PL: its audacity, especially in its early years, in its 1961 trip to Cuba that challenged the travel ban, in its willingness to openly use the word 'socialism' when others in the movement avoided it, and in its early demonstrations against the Vietnam War. Furthermore, PL (and its student offshoot, the Worker-Student Alliance) focused on class and made efforts to organize workers as well as students. But PL was also internally undemocratic, dogmatic in its politics, and sectarian in its relations with other organizations—problems hardly limited to PL. Many of the essays in this book address these problems thoughtfully and insightfully. The discussion of these problems is, however, mostly focused on the damage done internally. I wish that there had been more attention to the part that PL played in the destruction of the Students for a Democratic Society, by far the largest Left/anti-war organization of the time. "

— **Barbara Epstein**, author of *Political Protest and Cultural Revolution: Nonviolent Direct Action in the 1970s and 1980s*

You Say You Want A
Revolution

You Say You Want A
Revolution

SDS, PL, and Adventures in Building a
Worker-Student Alliance

Edited by
John F. Levin *and* Earl Silbar

1741
PRESS
SAN FRANCISCO

Published by
  1741 Press
  25 Hill Street
  San Francisco, CA 94121

ISBN 978-0-578-40654-1

Printed in the United States of America

Project management and design by Hiatt & Dragon, San Francisco
Cover design: Leslie Waltzer, Crowfoot Design

Cover photo: Harvard students meeting in the Administration Building to vote on strike demands. Photo courtesy Harvard Archives.

For Joan Kramer, 1947-2017

Contents

Introduction

You Say You Want a Revolution?

John F. Levin

Today, if people know anything about Students for a Democratic Society (SDS), it is most likely as the run-up to the drama of Weathermen, a small SDS faction of two or three hundred whose story has been recounted in films, histories and a steam of autobiographies. This drama follows a familiar arc of development: frustrated by the continuing war in Vietnam and repression at home, the Weather Underground turned to revolutionary violence in the belief that their actions would inspire others to join them in "revolutionary struggle" to overthrow the US imperial state. Not surprisingly, their violence had the opposite effect, alienating and frightening potential activists. After three Weathermen blew themselves up making a bomb destined for a GI social dance at Fort Dix, the group fell apart and disappeared. This action program, while regrettable, was perfectly understandable and coherent from a liberal point of view (under the heading "frustrated idealism gone wrong"), and over the years it has become the official story of SDS.

What does this dominant narrative get wrong?

Nearly everything.

The reality was quite different. SDS at its apex in 1968/69 numbered 100,000 students, whose political views reflected a rainbow of ideologies. There were democrats and anarchists, socialists and communists, pacifists and Trotskyists, Marcuse acolytes, and Gramsci aficionados. But mostly SDSers were young idealists exploring the ideas of all of the above with a curiosity and willingness to risk everything in an effort to create that a world without war and prejudice where social justice prevailed. When SDS splintered at its June 1969 national convention, a majority of voting delegates from its chapters supported a slate of officers and a program promoted by its Worker-Student Alliance caucus. WSA argued for building a strategic alliance between students and the working class, believing such a coalition was key to forcing the US government to end the war in Vietnam and address economic inequality and the racial oppression that defined the condition of people of color in the United States.

The contributors in this book were mostly members of WSA, whose formation had been initiated by the Progressive Labor Party (PL), a Marxist-Leninist party that had been formed in the early 1960s. Here these veteran student activists recount and evaluate their participation in the major campaigns of the 1960s and early 1970s: trips to revolutionary Cuba in defiance of the State Department travel ban in 1963–64; the first mass demonstrations against the Vietnam War; the national campaigns to end the military draft; the removal of campus military training programs and end of university collaboration with the war industry. They describe their participation in the student strikes and campaigns against the war and racism at Columbia, San Francisco State, UC Berkeley, Harvard, Fordham, the University of Iowa, Brooklyn College, and elsewhere. They write about alliances they made with labor unions and community groups in fights for social justice on and off university campuses.

These accounts are both optimistic, from those still inspired, and bitter, from those now critical of their involvement. The stories they tell speak across the years, as a new generation of young activists— from Black Lives Matter to Fight for $15 to the Parkland students—face decisions about how to organize to stop wars abroad, confront racial oppression at home, and end violence and neoliberal exploitation. A recent *Nation* cover story on the Democratic Socialists of America, which has grown over fivefold since Donald Trump's election, reports an emergence of an anti-imperialist left within DSA's ranks and quotes a member saying that being Marxist-Leninist is now trendy within the organization. It is all the more reason to read the stories of activists who have been there before.

The origins of WSA lie in the early 1960s, when a group of radical factory workers from Buffalo, New York, in alliance with African American activists in Harlem and students at New York City universities, formed the Progressive Labor Movement (PLM). Almost without exception they were all former members of the US Communist Party (CPUSA) who had been expelled or resigned from the CP because they sided with the Chinese Communist Party in Sino-Soviet schism that roiled the world of international Communism. PL was neither the first group that broke with the CP nor the last, but its open advocacy of Communism and bold activism defined and distinguished PL from other CP splinter groups, who mostly focused on intellectual debates regarding the direction of a new communist movement rather than engage in hands-on organizing to create one.

Although the majority of the original PL members were in the labor and civil rights movements, there were a small group of students mostly based at CCNY, now City University of New York (CUNY). Some of their first activities were organizing support for various strikes, most notably a violent coal miners' strike in Hazard, Kentucky. They held support rallies on city campuses, collected food, clothing and provisions for self-defense and delivered them to the striking miners. They were also active in the civil rights movement, joining coalitions against employment discrimination in construction in New York City and organized material support for Robert Williams, head of the North Carolina NAACP who had called for African Americans to arm and themselves in defense against racist attacks—predating the Black Panthers' call for self-defense by a number of years.

Although these activities brought PL some notice among students and civil rights activists as well as new members, it was PL's organization of the first trip of eighty-three US students to Revolutionary Cuba in 1963 in defiance the US government's travel ban that PL had its first significant impact on the growing student activism in the US.

Ellen Israel, a nurse-midwife and international public health specialist, was a nineteen-year-old organizer of the first of two trips to Cuba in 1963: "Although those who traveled to Cuba then came from different backgrounds and had different motivations for going … many went on to become progressives, activists and even radicals either within the movements that followed or in their own work and professional lives."

Indeed, many of the Cuba student travelers, inspired by what they saw and heard in Cuba, became some of the earliest organizers of the anti–Vietnam War movement. At a conference of socialist and communist organizations at Yale University in March 1964, which was called to discuss ideological and theoretical differences, Milt Rosen, the chairman of PL, interrupted the academic-oriented plenary discussion with a call for national demonstrations on May 2 of that year under the slogan "US Out of Vietnam Now!" A committee was formed under the leadership of PL, and the subsequent demonstrations were the first national demonstration against the war in Vietnam. This led to the formation of the May 2nd Movement (M2M), a self-described anti-imperialist peace movement, primarily focused on the US involvement in Vietnam.

M2M organized demonstrations and teach-ins and was an integral part of the Free University Movement that created ad hoc schools that taught courses on imperialism, radical poetry, the labor movement, and radical theater as alternative to the ossified curriculum of establishment controlled universities. M2M published *The Free Student* newspaper, which attracted a group of young Marxist intellectuals, including Jim Mellon, Shin'ya Ono, Gene Genovese, Sharon and Alan Krebs, founders of the Free University in New York, and Anatole Anton, a veteran of the 1963 trip to Cuba, whose memoir appears in this book:

In those early days there were some special virtues of the M2M that appealed to students and academics such as myself. The most important virtue for me was that the M2M treated the Vietnam

War as an imperialist war and not as a civil war. They had the courage of their convictions in a way that other organizations didn't.

In the fall of 1964 Lyndon Johnson ran for president on a platform that pledged no wider war in Vietnam, declaring, "No American boys' blood will be shed on Asian soil," giving birth to the campaign button preferred by student activists: "Half the Way with LBJ." Students and others flocked to his campaign, rightly scared by the bellicose Republican candidate Barry Goldwater, known for his statement "Extremism in the defense of liberty is no vice."

LBJ won the election by a landslide. Then in February 1965, a short month after being inaugurated, he dispatched 100,000 soldiers to Vietnam, quintupling the number of US troops on the ground. Students, many of whom saw themselves as prospective cannon fodder, were scared and outraged. SDS, previously a civil rights and antipoverty organization, rose to the occasion and called for a demonstration in Washington. SDS leaders were hoping for maybe 5,000 participants, but more than 30,000 chanting demonstrators poured onto the Capitol Mall and SDS became the de facto leadership of the student antiwar movement. M2M printed a special issue of *The Free Student* that for the first time engaged SDS leadership in political debate about the direction of the nascent antiwar movement:

> As SDS puts it "the war is fundamentally a civil war, waged by the south Vietnamese against their government; it is not a 'war of aggression'." We appreciate the point that the war is not an infiltration or invasion from the north. But the war is a "war of aggression" by the United States against the people of Vietnam. There is virtually nothing domestic about the side of the Saigon government ... it was not American supported, it was American created.

Meanwhile, PL at its first national convention, discarded the description of itself as a "Movement" and reconstituted as a communist, Marxist-Leninist-Maoist party, governed by the Leninist concept of democratic-centralism. The convention elected a chairman, Milt

Rosen, a former member of the Communist Party's National Committee; a vice-chairman, Bill Epton, a decorated Korean War veteran and leader of the 1964 Harlem Rebellion; and a National Committee (NC), all elected by a membership that accepted "party discipline"—meaning that after full discussion and debate members agreed to abide by the party's decision regarding party line, strategy, and tactics even if they did not personally agree with the decision.

Besides being disciplined, PL also could count, and after the SDS antiwar demonstration and subsequent M2M demonstrations in late May that drew at most a couple of thousand protesters nationwide, it was clear that SDS was where the students were. After internal discussion among PL's National Committee, the party leadership instructed its cadre within M2M to dissolve that organization and join SDS. After a pro-forma discussion within M2M and over the strenuous objections of some members both within and outside PL, M2M officially dissolved itself in the spring of 1966. Some of the dissidents went along, but many severed their association with PL, believing that the decision to dissolve M2M was wrong and that they had had no voice in making it.

The 1966 SDS annual convention took place in Clear Lake, Iowa, at a Methodist family camp of clapboard cabins on the shore of the eponymous lake. Out of the several hundred students who attended, a couple of dozen at most were PL members, but their presence became a central issue of the convention. It was not at all certain that PL members would be allowed to join SDS, since a clause in the SDS constitution excluded communists from membership—a relic of the McCarthy era, when SDS was the youth group of League for Industrial Democracy (LID), a social democratic, neo-Trotskyist organization with a strong anticommunist agenda.

The anticommunist clause was antithetical to the current SDS membership, a large mass organization that prided itself in its inclusiveness and its concept of participatory democracy where all members had an equal say and decisions were made by consensus. At the first plenum session a motion was made to strike the anticommunist clause from the SDS constitution. After a debate between Steve Max and Doug Ireland, who represented LID, and Jeff Gordon and Jared Israel of PL, the convention removed the anticommunist clause from its constitution and PL student members officially became members of SDS as well. LID cut its ties with SDS soon thereafter.

PL's strategic goal was never to take over the leadership of SDS. The party recognized the fact that SDS was a mass organization representing various views and factions and even if PL and its allies could wrest control of SDS it would be a Pyrrhic victory, as indeed it was at the 1969 convention when PL/WSA became the de facto leadership of SDS. PL's strategy within SDS was to win members over to an anti-imperialist analysis of the war in Vietnam and US foreign policy as well as an understanding of the importance of an alliance with the working class in order to build an effective movement.

PL and its allies, who later became the Worker-Student Alliance Caucus, built activist SDS chapters on campuses around the country that focused primarily on the Vietnam War and all its manifestations on campuses: the draft, ROTC programs, military and corporate recruitment, and, most notoriously, Dow Chemical, the manufacturer of the napalm used in Vietnam. They organized students to engage in outreach at factory gates, support labor strikes, and defend community groups fighting for social justice. They organized and joined demonstrations in support of the African American rebellions that were raging through US ghettos. They also continued participating in quarterly SDS national meetings, arguing politics and introducing resolutions, most significantly the Student Labor Action Project (SLAP), which advocated creating an alliance between students and workers. SLAP proposed a "Summer Work-In," where students would get jobs in factories and do outreach among workers around the war and racism. Through their organizing PL recruited members both to PL and the WSA/SDS.

Internally PL continued to evolve. Its freewheeling antecedent, PLM, became a memory as the party intruded more and more into members' lives. They forbade pot smoking, urged male students to

trim their hair, and pressured couples to "regularize" their relationships in the belief that doing so would make them and their ideas more
acceptable to the working class. PL's political analysis also evolved. In
the fall of 1966 PL's National Committee criticized the Cuban leadership in PL Magazine for its alliance with the "revisionist" Soviet Union.
Shortly thereafter PL expanded its attack on "revisionism" to include
the Vietnamese Communist Party and the NLF for entering into negotiations with the US to end the Vietnam War and ultimately to the
Chinese Communist Party for following the Soviet Union down the
"capitalist road."

There was widespread and vocal disagreement within PL over these
changes in line. Members argued that they were sectarian and further
that party leadership did not engage the members in a discussion of
the new political positions. Instead, the party leaders only "explained"
the rationale for the new positions after they had been adopted, thus
violating PL's own principle of democratic centralism. But ultimately
the national leadership prevailed and the dissidents either acquiesced
or left the party. Dick Reavis, who was the leader of the WSA/SDS at
the University of Texas, described his decision to leave PL this way:

> In my ignorance of Communist history, I didn't believe anyone
> should doubt a giant like Mao and I didn't think that the global
> movement could hold together if it did. One morning at the unem-
> ployment office I questioned my *Challenge* sales partner about that.
> "But he sold out," she told me …. After a few days of mulling it
> over, I concluded that PL was an organization whose attitude was
> that "Everybody has sold out but me and you and I'm not sure
> about you" …. Two weeks later I was back in Austin, trying to piece
> my life together.

Within SDS/WSA the change in PL's positions was mitigated
because PL student cadre, with some exceptions, did not argue for
WSA caucuses and SDS chapters to adopt PL's critiques of the international communist movement. Instead they emphasized PL's continued
support for Cuba's right of self-determination and support for immedi-

ate US withdrawal from Vietnam and concentrated on the tactical battles that were raging on campus against the war, racism, and the draft.

At the quarterly national meetings of SDS where political debates
took place and resolutions on strategy where debated and voted on the
situation was quite different. Stoked by the Columbia student strike,
the upsurge in antiwar sentiment, and the "May events" in France,
where students in alliance with workers shut down their country in a
general strike, the SDS national leadership moved sharply to the left. At
the 1968 SDS convention, Mark Rudd, a leader of the Columbia strike,
and Bernadine Dohrn, later of Weatherman fame, were elected as SDS
national officers. They declared themselves to be the true allies of the
Cuban, Vietnamese, and Chinese revolutions, and they denounced PL
and its WSA allies as counter-revolutionary apostates for their criticisms. After a daisy-chain of speakers, including the spokesman for the
anarchist affinity group Up Against the Wall Motherfucker, the SDS
leadership declared themselves and their allies the "true" revolutionaries in SDS and started a chant "PL Out! PL Out!" Despite the urging,
only a small number of the delegates joined in and national leadership
backed off its efforts to expel PL/WSA. That would happen at the
convention the following year.

The student rebellions that erupted in the spring continued in
the fall of 1968 and into the following year. At San Francisco State,
the longest student strike in US history began that fall in support
of the demands made by the Third World Liberation Front and the
Black Student Union for open admissions and the establishment of a
School of Ethnic Studies. The SDS chapter at SF State embraced these
demands and was a key force in organizing support for the strike on
and off campus. Heretofore PL had supported revolutionary nationalism. Hari Dillon, a PL/WSA member and one of TWLF strike leaders, explained: "Yes, we were Third World Nationalist. But there was
another dimension to our nationalism. Our nationalism was revolutionary nationalism. Our nationalism was an affirmation of ourselves,
not a negation of others. Our nationalism was aimed at white racism,
not white people."

Then midway through the strike the PL National Committee changed PL's position to "All nationalism is reactionary." The effect of PL's change of line was profound, not only at SF State but throughout PL. Over the next several years it led to major defections from the party in San Francisco, New York, Boston, and elsewhere. Within SDS, PL's new position on nationalism was a god-sent gift to the anti-PL/WSA forces. All over the country Third World students were demanding that universities establish programs that reflected the needs of students of color, including open admissions of Third World students, establishment of ethnic studies departments, and hiring of nonwhite professors. SDS and progressive students enthusiastically supported these demands. PL no longer did, and the SDS leadership relentlessly attacked PL for it. Declaring that they were the true allies of the Black Liberation Movement, particularly the Black Panther Party, whose program PL had criticized in *PL Magazine*, SDS national leadership, now controlled by the Revolutionary Youth Movement (RYM) faction, denounced PL as racist and counter-revolutionary and made plans to expel PL/WSA from SDS at the 1969 convention in Chicago that June. And so did the FBI:

Not only did the FBI work to exacerbate conflict between the factions before the convention, they specifically advised their informants to vote a particular way. "All REDACTED informants were instructed to support the National Office faction in SDS against the PL faction." The reason? "PL control of SDS would transform as shapeless factionalized group into a militant and disciplined organization."[1]

The convention was held in a semi-abandoned convention center near the stockyards. About 1,500 delegates attended, of whom more than half were unaffiliated with either WSA or RYM. Given the widespread support in SDS for the Black Liberation struggles and the high regard in which student activists held its leaders, most notably Black Panther Party (BPP) chairman Huey Newton, it was apparent that RYM

---

1 To Director FBI 8/1/1969. New Left, Cleveland Division. Bureau File,100-449698-11. As quoted in Aaron Leonard and Conor Gallagher, *Heavy Radicals: The FBI's Secret War on American's Maoists,* Alresford, UK: Zero Books, 2014, p. 54.

had a distinct advantage. However, through their own sycophancy they managed to snatch defeat from the jaws of victory.

RYM's strategy to expel PL/WSA relied on the cooperation of the Black Panther Party. A BPP spokesman was to address the convention, denounce PL/WSA as counter-revolutionary, and declare that the Panthers would not ally with SDS unless SDS expelled PL/WSA. BPP spokesperson Chaka Walls began with a fiery, expletive-laden attack on PL/WSA to the enthusiastic cheers of the RYM militants. Then Walls veered off message and commented on the previous discussion of male chauvinism and women's liberation. "I'm for pussy power myself ... there's a lot revolutionary women can contribute and that's by getting laid."

WSA had been thrown a lifeline. "Fight male chauvinism! Fight male chauvinism!" echoed through the hall, drowning out Walls. The RYM leaders, seeing the balance of forces shifting in front of them, desperately turned the microphone over to another Panther, Jul Cook, to "clarify" Walls's remarks. Instead, Cook reinforced them. After reiterating Walls's denunciation of PL/WSA as counter-revolutionary, Cook added, "You know, I'm with the brother, though. I'm for pussy power myself." As more chants of 'Fight male chauvinism!" reverberated through the hall, Cook delivered the coup de grace to the RYM strategy: "The position of women in the revolution is prone," his words clearly audible over the chants of "Fight male chauvinism!"

RYM's opportunism had lost them the control of the convention and quite probably SDS. Two days later, Bernadine Dohrn led a walk-out of her followers, leaving behind WSA/PL SDS members and the majority of the independents, who joined PL/WSA delegates in chants of "No split!" and then "Stay and struggle!" as the RYM forces left the hall. Becky Brenner, a WSA member from University of Texas, described the moment:

> It was a joyous night because the WSA won the majority, but it was also tinged with sadness. I remember both young men and young women in tears because it was a definite turning point in

the student movement and in the leftist movement in general. WSA barely won, but we thought we could claim SDS as ours. Of course, it turned out to be only in our minds, as most people on the Left no longer saw SDS as a legitimate mass organization and it quickly lost much of its credibility.

After the RYM exodus, the convention elected a slate of new officers, including John Pennington as national secretary. With the RYM gone, PL's politics had free rein and quickly dominated the organization, with SDS adopting political positions and analyses that were almost identical to PL's. Independents, both within and outside WSA, soon came to feel that there was no place for members who did not fully agree with the PL-dominated leadership and began to drift away from SDS. At the next national meeting SDS/WSA adopted a PL-initiated proposal, "The Campus Worker-Student Alliance," which resolved that the central strategy of SDS would be to form alliances with campus workers around racism and economic issues. The CWSA initiative had some success on a number of big-city campuses, including Columbia, Fordham, and Harvard.

At Harvard there was a notable victory against the university's racism toward campus workers. Blacks were hired as apprentices in the skilled trades, but never promoted to the journeyman level after appropriate experience—a racist practice that kept Harvard's costs down. With publicity and demonstrations, students enabled workers to overturn this practice.

But overall, the CWSA strategy was a disaster. With the antiwar movement dominating national consciousness on and off university campuses, PL's strategy pushed SDS to step back from actively organizing against the Vietnam War. Independents in SDS/WSA who disagreed were marginalized and pushed out. Eric Gordon, a leader of the Tulane WSA/SDS in New Orleans, explains his departure around this and other issues:

The Boston SDS, where the national office of the WSA/SDS was located and to which our chapter valiantly clung, had fallen into a deep authoritarian arrogance. How many of those folks were PL members I don't know, but the national office made all manner of highhanded decisions for the organization, hurling insults and accusations toward anyone who questioned their tactics and puffed-up leadership. I had little interest in devoting time to reviving SDS at Tulane.

SDS / WSA continued as an organization for a few years. It engaged in campaigns against racism on campus, supported campus worker strikes and community battles against university expansion, but its isolation from the antiwar movement, which by the early 1970s included most of the country, was fatal. By the mid 1970s SDS / WSA was dissolved. A new organization, the Committee Against Racism (CAR), was formed under the aegis of PL and continues to this day as an active antiracist organization.

The twenty-three memoirs that follow are not the accounts of national leaders or media-designated luminaries. They are the voices from the guts of the student movement that swept the county in the 1960s and 1970s. They are the activists who spent their evenings writing leaflets about the Vietnam War and who were up at dawn passing them out on campuses and at high schools, subway stations, and factory gates. They are the ones who organized the campus chapters, circulated petitions, joined picket lines, faced down the cops, went to jail, and joined or allied themselves with a Marxist-Leninist revolutionary party in pursuit of creating a better, nonracist world guided by the pursuit of economic and social justice rather than maximizing profit.

Many of the contributors remain active in social justice movements today, and are keen to share accounts of their experiences, both the good and bad, in the hope that another generation of activists can learn from them as well as take heart that they are part of a grand tradition of struggle for social justice.

1

We Danced Everywhere

Ellen S. Israel

The development of student activism in the 1960s was significantly impacted by the Progressive Labor–organized student trips to Cuba in 1963 and 1964 in defiance of a US government–imposed ban on travel to the island. The Cuban revolution that triumphed in January 1959 not only confronted US imperialism in what it considered its own backyard, it inspired people to organize for their rights all over the world. That included the United States itself, where Fidel's visit to Harlem in 1960 on a trip to the United Nations emphasized Cuba's solidarity with the growing civil rights and black nationalist movements. I was one of the organizers of these Cuba trips.

How I Got Involved

I was a quintessential red diaper baby. My parents were members of the Communist Party USA (CPUSA) but left during World War II when the party told them to abandon all struggles for social justice in the US and "join the war effort."

My father, Barney Shallit, was a social worker who had helped lead the first strike for union recognition of social workers in Los Angeles. I remember joining the picket line when I was four or five and my dad defending me from an "anti" who was pushing me and yelling at me. He also worked as a social worker and advocate in the infamous concentration camps for Japanese Americans during World War II, including the worst of them, the Tule Lake Segregation Center, where the government imprisoned residents without citizenship, mostly older people and their children and families who didn't want to be separated from them. He had lifelong friendships with several internees as a result and wrote about the experiences of those in the camps.

The obvious racism (there were no German or Italian internment camps) and the clandestine theft of the Japanese farmers' rich land at little or no cost by the Western states' growers' associations, was my first stark lesson in how US capitalism uses racism to further its economic and political goals.

I was in the third grade when we moved to Oakland from Los Angeles and found housing on the edge of a segregated black community, where I was assigned to an all-black district school. My mother, Claire Shallit, was the only white mother in the PTA. I hadn't known black children in Los Angeles and for a few days I felt very different. But I started to make friends quickly, visiting their homes and hanging out with their families. My parents for their part invited those families to our house. I remember my mother at the bake sales and school events working with the other mothers, making lasting friendships, and always with her big, beautiful smile.

Getting close to these families and having them pull me into their lives with both arms gave me an opportunity to see the daily effects of bigotry, which fueled my lifelong commitment to exposing and opposing racism wherever I saw it.

My parents also welcomed and befriended the first black family to break the housing color line (the "red line") that lay at the bottom of our all-white street, which resulted in my family's total isolation from our white neighbors. As soon as the African American family moved in next door, my mother invited them over. We visited often, and my little brother became "besties" with their youngest daughter, Pookie.

In high school my parents also approved my playing hooky to attend the infamous May 13, 1960, House Un-American Activities Committee (HUAC) hearings in San Francisco's City Hall, which became known as

"Black Friday." Though no longer in the CP, my parents had expected that my father would be called before HUAC when we lived in Los Angeles, a prospect that had prompted our move to Oakland. HUAC had already destroyed the livelihoods of scores of writers, teachers, union organizers, and others.

This time, HUAC was investigating "Communist subversion" on university campuses, in unions, and in schools (25 percent of those subpoenaed where teachers). A coalition that included students, Bay Area journalists, teachers, university professors, and others formed to protest the hearings. About 3,500 people demonstrated over two days. It was my first exposure to state violence when supporters of those subpoenaed were first not allowed into the hearings (the committee was issuing "white cards" to friends of the committee to stack the hearings) and were then beaten, washed down the steps of City Hall with high-pressure fire hoses, and arrested. That brutal scene of people knocked down by the watery blasts and then tumbling over each other down the stairs was front page news in California and all over the country.

After two years at San Francisco State, where I was active in local dance and the Opera Ring Theatre, I decided to take a Greyhound across the country to explore opportunities on the musical stage. I arrived in New York City in 1962, aged nineteen, and was welcomed by my uncle and aunt, Earl and Helen Robinson. Earl, who had written "Joe Hill," "Ballad for Americans," "The Lonesome Train," and many other iconic songs, was a famous Communist composer and performer. Soon after I arrived I was introduced to Progressive Labor through a family friend, Fred Jerome, a public leader of PL (and son of V. J. Jerome, the cultural commissar of the CP), who was at that time one of my very few contacts in New York. It was a natural thing to join them because of my interest in civil rights and communism. I had read a bit about the new China, and was intrigued by Progressive Labor's critique of the Soviet Union, which had led to a split with the CPUSA and the formation of PL. Their hope was that the Chinese CP would stay on a revolutionary path and would not reverse direction like the

Soviet Union had. PL looked like a place for me to learn, to become politically active, and to have a social circle to boot. They were just forming a student group of about a dozen young men and women, mostly children of lefties, and I joined. The first thing the new Progressive Labor Movement (later to become Progressive Labor Party) did was organize support for a particularly militant United Mine Workers (UMW) strike in Harlan County, Kentucky. We collected food, clothing, and money to distribute among the strikers' families and tried to bring media attention to the issues in the strike as well.

But the focus of the PL student group soon shifted to organizing a trip of students to Cuba in defiance of a government travel ban that made it a crime punishable by a fine of up to $2,000 and five years in prison for US citizens to travel to Cuba and four other Communist countries.

PL saw the Cuba trips as an opportunity to demonstrate its commitment to revolution and communism, show its capacity to take bold action, recruit members to PL, and establish a place for itself in the growing US student movement. The idea was to challenge the government's travel ban to Cuba as a violation of our First Amendment rights and to establish that Americans could travel without restriction, seek information on their own, and make up their own minds about Cuba rather than accepting the US media version of the island as horror show.

Organizing the Trips

Our organizing for the project took us to college campuses and wherever we knew of individuals or groups who would put together a meeting of people who might be interested in going with us to Cuba. These "recruitment" meetings consisted of showing films and giving talks about Cuba's young revolution, while also explaining the constitutional challenge. We stressed the importance of seeing Cuba for ourselves and bringing back the real story to the US to counter the official media characterization of Fidel and Cuba as the Communist menace ninety miles south of Florida. We discussed how the US travel ban violated

American citizens' rights in order to shore up the anticommunist and antirevolutionary sentiment needed to perpetuate the Cold War and hide US domination of the region.

The first Cuba trip, in the summer of 1963, attracted mostly students who were already somewhat radical, including black nationalist students from the San Francisco Bay Area and activist students from Puerto Rico. Others came from the Midwest, the South, and the Northeast. Some were mainly opposed to US foreign policy, others saw Cuba as a hopeful model for other poor countries that also needed national liberation, and all were curious. While some Cuba travelers were more serious than others, most of them contributed concretely, during and after, either by volunteering to speak to various groups, sitting for press and radio interviews, writing articles, or raising money for legal defense. The purpose was to spotlight the contrast between the government's depiction and the reality of post-dictatorship Cuba, which was now run by the Cubans themselves.

My responsibility for the Cuba trips grew as I gained more understanding and skills, but I played a kind of secretarial role behind the men although I was one of the principal organizers; at the time, all of the leadership of the effort and of PL itself was male. I was assigned to "take the letters," keep up the contacts, and make arrangements with the travelers, while the men were the planners and spokespeople.

This was the first inkling of what I saw as my years in PL stretched on that the issues of women's equality and leadership were not seen as important. At the time, there was only one woman on the National Committee of PL, and women's issues were not raised when supporting or writing about various struggles unless it was unavoidable, such as supporting mothers receiving Aid to Dependent Children. None of the wives of the leaders were in PL, none of the spokespeople were women, and often the main things young women were encouraged to do was to attract promising men to the party and sell *Challenge*, the party's newspaper.

The leadership even took a stand against openly supporting abortion rights, since it was "too controversial within the working class." At one point in the late sixties, some PL women did write a piece about abortion rights and tried to start a discussion, but it was squashed by the leadership.

Getting to the island was a trip in itself. Initially, in December 1962, we planned to go to Cuba via Canada. At the last minute, however, the Canadian government, pressured by the US, refused to grant a landing permit for the Cuban airplane that was to take us. We therefore then adopted as secretive an approach as possible to avoid the government blocking us again. We met with our Cuban hosts at their UN mission and talked about our strategy with a radio blaring to drown out our conversation for the listening FBI. We openly bought tickets to Mexico as a decoy, and then secretly purchased other tickets for the actual trip. We also met with our lawyers, Leonard Boudin and Victor Rabinowitz, to plan the constitutional challenge to the travel ban after our return. For the journey, we had organized all fifty-nine students into smaller teams of five or six and went separately to the New York Port Authority to board the buses to Idlewild Airport (now JFK). We tried to act like tourists, dressed as such, and kept to ourselves. But as I looked around, I could see Feds everywhere in their signature dark suits and ties, watching. We boarded the buses, went through the process at the airport (still with Feds all around), and boarded two different planes hoping that at least one of the groups would make it. My heart was in my mouth the whole time, but when the flight rose into the sky, a cry went up all over our plane to the surprise of the rest of the passengers.

Both flights landed in England and we flew together to Paris, where we stayed overnight. Our Cuban hosts had arranged for us to go to Prague the next day to pick up the Cuban plane in friendly territory. When we reached Prague, US federal agents were waiting for us in the airport and the US vice-consul read a statement warning us about proceeding. We had briefed everyone that we were citizens traveling with valid passports and were not obligated to relinquish those passports nor did those federal agents have the authority to force us. The agents tried to stop people, telling them that they were violating US law, but most of us just moved forward. Then someone came to me and said that two of the people in my small group had been taken to a room and their passports confiscated. I was just twenty years old, but I went to the room, told the agents that they didn't have the authority to take valid passports from US citizens traveling for their own purposes—and was shocked when they actually gave them back. I left the room with the other travelers and promptly threw up once we were safely out of sight. To protect us from further interference, the Czech officials took all of us that night to the mountain vacation village of Karlovy Vary, where they put us up in an old European-style spa. It was full of vacationing high-level Russian officials, who were in sharp contrast to our motley crew sharing the ornate dining room with them. After a couple of days, we returned to Prague and with huge relief boarded the Cuban plane.

Impressions of Cuba

We arrived in Cuba and plunged headlong into learning about the revolution from the participants: university students, artists, dancers, *folklorico* performers, *campesinos*, industrial workers, and others. We visited the ballet school, which was being supported by the government, and saw *Swan Lake* performed by the incomparable Alicia Alonzo—a Cuban prima ballerina and choreographer who had lived and performed in New York, throughout Europe, and in the Soviet Union, but who returned to Cuba after the revolution to found the Ballet Nacional de Cuba. We went to a new school being built for both the performing and visual arts where students from all over the island were admitted for free if they had the necessary aptitude. We met at length with members of the National Film Institute and discussed filmmaking in the new Cuba, what revolutionary art was, and what was meant by freedom to constructively criticize and promote within the revolution, but not to be destructive of it. We visited the anthropological institute and heard about efforts to revise Cuban history to reflect the true social realities of the past—for example, regarding slavery and racism—from the people's perspective.

And along with a million Cubans from all over the country, we joined the 26th of July celebration in Havana, commemorating the rebel attack on the Moncada Barracks in Santiago de Cuba in 1953 that is considered the start of the Cuban Revolution, and listened to Fidel's address and interacted with the crowd for hours.

Leaving Havana, we traveled by bus throughout the country and met with cooperative farmers who were experimenting with hydroponics and new breeding methods, homeowners in new housing projects, and workers in both small and large plants. We visited several new schools and attended cultural events in cities and villages. And we danced everywhere we went with the Cubans, who were always dancing—after lunch, after dinner, later in the evening, and even sometimes at breakfast! It was a lovely way to interact with people all around the country. (I remember one evening in Santiago de Cuba when we heard music and saw lights moving in a line down the mountain behind the motel. Soon a traditional band of local peasant musicians filled the courtyard, attracting people from all around the neighborhood, and they played and played until everyone was completely caught up in the dancing and singing and unity of the moment.) We visited historic sites like the Bay of Pigs, where the US-backed invasion by counterrevolutionary ex-Cubans from Miami was totally crushed and spoke with residents about the effective resistance. We visited health clinics and hospitals, including a mental health facility. Not one of this latter type of institution had existed before the revolution, since the rich would simply go to other countries if they needed mental health treatment.

We traveled to the east of the country and into the Sierra Maestra where the rebel army had been based and from which it launched campaigns against Batista's army. Enthusiasm for the revolution was particularly strong in the east, considered the "seat" of the revolution, which was the poorest part of the country and had the largest concentration of Afro-Cubans. We visited schools for peasant children, for example in Minas del Frio high in the mountains, where children of the poorest *campesinos* talked about the opportunities they had to study for free, so they could contribute to the new society. We spent a day with sugar cane workers hoeing weeds in the cane fields, and learned about their lives before and after the revolution. In Santiago de Cuba we were greeted by The Mothers of the Martyrs. They told their stories and those of their sons and daughters who had died in the revolution. There was an emotional scene when some of our group rose to express their feelings of shame about the US government's role in shoring up the Batista dictatorship and contributing to the oppression of the Cuban people. The Mothers embraced the speakers and there were many tears all around.

What we found was that four and a half years into the revolution there was widespread support for and participation in the changes that were being implemented by Cubans from all sectors of society. Racial discrimination was now a serious crime. Schools were being built all over the island, including in some of the confiscated mansions of Miramar, one of the richest Havana neighborhoods of the former national elite. We visited some of these schools and loved seeing the contrast of the palatial rooms and marble staircases and manicured grounds now filled with busy young children of all shades of color in their school uniforms. We also met many, many engaged students all over the country—at universities, as well as grade and high schools, who were excited to build the revolution. We already saw the results of unprecedented efforts to ensure that students from poor backgrounds had full support to get higher education, including tutoring to address previous inequities. We had many discussions about the parallels and differences between the student movements in the US and student action in Cuba—the big difference being that Cuban youth felt part of their revolution and US youth often felt in conflict with their government. Most of the Cuban students participated in Defense of the Revolution groups, which included study, discussion, and military training to prepare for any future invasion like the Bay of Pigs. We visited a school in the countryside that offered a curriculum focusing on fishing technology as part of an ongoing effort to build Cuba's fishing industry. As in all the schools, there were many children of peasants attending with full support, including room and board.

There was a vibrant literacy campaign where students and teachers fanned out over the whole island with the goal of teaching every single Cuban—especially reaching the *campesinos*—to read and write, which resulted in close to 100 percent literacy within a few years. Another example of this collective spirit was the mass volunteering from all sectors of Cuban society to bring in the sugar cane harvest. The medical schools were beginning to churn out doctors, and health care was free to all. It was fascinating to observe, however imperfect, Revolutionary Cuba's far-reaching version of "democratic centralism." This involved the whole-scale participation of the population in regular two-part discussions. The first, specific to their workplaces, schools, and neighborhoods, covered the improvement of quality of life, productivity, and working conditions, and the second covered their ideas about the broader policies and direction of the revolution. They would send their ideas and recommendations up the established channels though the local, regional, and national leaderships, who would in turn send feedback and suggestions back down through the same channels. The discussion would then continue after these changes were made to include further ideas to be channeled up again to create a continuous upward spiral of better and better conditions and outcomes for people.

Despite the lack of resources, greatly exacerbated by the US embargo, the Cubans developed numerous strategies to improve the daily lives of their citizens—for example, hydroponics to increase food supplies; crossbreeding of local cows with Canadian bulls to improve and strengthen their stock and ensure adequate milk supplies (provided free to all children under five); and developing huge duck farms to increase available protein sources for the people.

Getting a clear picture of the problems Cubans faced was hindered by rarely finding leaders who would admit to any shortcomings. This was true of those in charge of institutions, the national press, and the government. We had discussions with lower-level managers and officials who did express criticism of the pace of some aspects of the revolution, and again, this helped us to grapple with the difference between criticism within and outside the revolution. We also met people completely opposed to the revolution, but in my experience they were from the formerly privileged class who were just no longer privileged. Later in the trip we met with Che Guevara and asked him the same questions we had asked others: Why is the wage gap still so wide? Why are so many unwilling to admit there is still strong racism in the country, that darker people were in almost all cases the poorer and most discriminated against? Why is there still so much dependence on single crop/sugar production? What is Cuba's plan for becoming self-sufficient and reducing dependency on the Soviet Union? Even, from one traveler, why provide white bread rather than whole grain bread to the people?

Che agreed with some of the specific shortcomings we had observed and discussed with us their importance and possible solutions, most notably the denial of the seriousness of continuing racism. He said it was foolish to ignore obvious racism and its effects by denying it—that, in fact, it must be dealt with strongly—but that people also need to be educated about it. He said narrowing the wage gap would take time in order to avoid a backlash from skilled workers. He said that due to Cuba's lack of cash, the US embargo, and the enormous priorities of the new nation, sugar was still the main way Cuba could earn foreign exchange to buy what it needed to advance. As to the bread question, he said that Cubans liked their white bread and that whole grain would take time to promote.

One of the black students from the San Francisco Bay Area asked Che why they didn't introduce African history in the Cuban schools. Che was dismissive, saying that it was a united Cuba now and that giving special attention to ethnic histories was divisive. For instance, he himself was Argentine, so therefore should his children need to be exposed to Argentine history in Cuban schools? The student stood his ground respectfully, saying that it was hardly the same thing, since half of Cuba's people were directly related to Africa, with many still practicing African spiritual traditions, and that the existing racism in Cuba was against Afro-Cubans, not Argentines. Che was also dismissive of a question about forming worker's councils (soviets) to provide more direct avenues of power for working people. Despite these wrinkles, I appreciated that we were in a dialogue that was different from previous encounters with those in authority.

We also met with Fidel in the coastal resort town of Varadero. Castro arrived amid a fleet of old Chevies and engaged our group around ping-pong games with lots of banter about North vs. South, détente, and imperialism. Several students played and bantered with him—and he won each time! It was a different experience from Che—Fidel offered a very human connection and great fun.

Crucial to the trip were the meetings we had among ourselves where we discussed what we were finding and our different perceptions of the same experiences. I remember the high quality and caliber of the discussions and debates as people worked together to understand what we were experiencing and how to best represent that so we could improve Americans' understanding of the Cuban Revolution. We also discussed the legal situation and possible scenarios we might face, including the US government's intention to invalidate our passports.

On Our Return

We were in Cuba for two months, though the second month was unplanned because President Kennedy had told all allied countries to forbid us from traveling through their territories. There was some worry and some demoralization, especially when the end of August came and the fall semester was about to begin. Then, unexpectedly, fascist Spain permitted us passage and we flew to New York via Madrid. We had had myriad discussions before our trip about how to respond when the government tried to invalidate our passports. When we arrived at Idlewild we sent a few people through immigration to speak to the large contingent of national and international press who were waiting outside while the rest of us staged a sit-in, demanding the government drop its intention to invalidate our passports. After several hours, with the press watching, the government relented and we passed through immigration with valid passports intact and "entered the US" stamps only. Once outside, we held a press conference that was covered around the world.

The government's next move was to subpoena several people to testify before HUAC in Washington on "Illegal travel to Cuba." Those who were subpoenaed prepared with the lawyers and the PL leadership and developed a proactive strategy. Rather than pleading the Fifth Amendment against self-incrimination, which had been the traditional approach of most people who had been called to testify before HUAC, we would explain fully and in depth why we went to Cuba, and what we had found there, which would belie the US government's propaganda about Cuba. Before the hearings, we organized as many people as we could—Cuba travelers and others—to go to Washington and attend the hearings. Our approach surprised and frustrated the committee members, who were used to being able to intimidate and bully activists into "pleading the Fifth" by threatening prosecution.

Since we had good legal arguments for having defied the travel ban, we spoke about that and all the achievements of the Cuban Revolution. The committee members alternately demanded that we answer their questions and tried to shut us up. When the continual vocal support from the audience reached a peak, the committee summoned the police, who waded in, beat people, threw them into elevators, carried them out of the building, and arrested them. Of course, this was in the press and ended up as a black eye for HUAC. (After the second trip to Cuba the next summer, another HUAC hearing was convened where the Cuba travelers took an even bolder approach, attacking the reactionary and racist behavior of individual committee members in their legislative roles.)

After the trips, the government indicted eight leaders of the Student Committee for Travel to Cuba in 1964 (myself and seven guys). One of these, a PL member named Phillip Luce, either was an informant or got scared and became one. He appeared as a government witness during the trial, which lead to a short but well-publicized stint as a paid stoolpigeon. Our case was appealed all the way to the Supreme Court, which upheld our argument that the travel ban was unconstitutional. This was a moral victory, but the government, in defiance of the Supreme Court ruling, continued to restrict travel to Cuba.

In the year following the Cuba trips, we spoke at venues all over the country about our experiences to maximize the impact of these trips on a whole new generation who were questioning US policy and actions in Cuba, Latin America, Africa, and, increasingly, Vietnam. We urged students and others to become active, either on campuses or in their communities, in the growing opposition to the war in Vietnam, racism, and continued intervention in Cuba. Two Cuba travelers, Eric Johnson and Roger Taus, took a copy of *We Are Still Here*, a film we had received from Vietnamese National Liberation Front comrades in Havana, to Portland and Seattle as part of a recruiting effort for the next Cuba trip. The student leaders there had been warned by the FBI not to allow the film to be shown, but they showed it anyway. At least 100 people attended and several signed up to go on the next trip to Cuba. The biggest event was a gathering of 1,400 people in September 1963 in New York City's Town Hall where the Cuba travelers spoke about both the issues and their recent experiences in Cuba, while outside a large crowd of counterrevolutionary Cubans protested, tussling with police. Several tried to enter the auditorium to disrupt the event, but they were stopped by our own volunteer security squad and at the end of the evening all attendees were safely accompanied out of the building and down to the subways.

Most of the more than 130 travelers to Cuba returned with a desire to make change, either by embracing radicalism and joining PL, or working with SDS or other social change organizations. A couple of the African American travelers chose to not return home from Cuba, but instead to go on to Tanganyika to try to contribute to that new revolution. One traveler wrote:

> [The Cuba trip] definitely led to my activism and embrace of Leninism just a year later. At the point when I met Sal [one of the PL organizers] in San Francisco I was dreaming of dropping out of college and making my way to India. Either that or trying to find

a way to buy some land in Mendocino. I was living in the Haight and going to SF State, taking random classes in music and poetry, hanging out with people who formed the counterculture, the acid-rock bands, experimental film, street poetry, the Mime Troupe and hiking around Tilden and Golden Gate Park on peyote. That Cuba trip and then the assassination of Kennedy were the key events for me ... the fork in the road away from the counterculture.

One of the most significant outcomes of the Cuba trips was that they became a catalyst for the anti–Vietnam War effort. While we were in Cuba, some of us met with delegates of the National Liberation Front. We were so impressed with their persistence in resisting the French and now the US imperialists that we decided to launch the May 2nd Movement (M2M) to bring an anti-imperialist perspective to the nascent antiwar movement. On May 2, 1964, M2M organized national antiwar marches, which drew over 1,000 students and others in New York City, 700 in San Francisco, and smaller crowds in Boston, Madison, and Seattle.

The May 2nd Movement ultimately suffered from the same sectarianism as PL's other initiatives. Although PL organized the trips to Cuba, which had an impact on the student and antiwar movements of the 1960s and 1970s, over the years PL increasingly prioritized public criticism of those who should have been their allies—the Vietnamese, the Cubans, the African liberation movements, and, eventually, China. This shift really stung after all we had seen and done in Cuba. Perhaps this is inevitable with a group that calls itself a "vanguard party"—to feel superior to everybody else, to desperately try to look "different" from other activist groups and movements, and, above all, to be "correct."

PL called itself a vanguard working-class party, but few workers joined PL or remained members for long. In my opinion, the leaders substituted themselves as spokesmen for the working class rather than supporting working-class leaders and activists and building broader movements. Despite all the lip service to the "democratic" in democratic centralism within PL, the top leaders decided the line and when to change it (which was often and could be a complete about-face in some cases). Ideas from those doing the work were not encouraged or were squashed, even brutally.

Although I feel that the PL leadership became more and more sectarian, isolationist, and wrong, my experiences with good people and actions in PL helped form what I became: a nurse-midwife supporting women's autonomy and rights around childbirth and health, and, later, a public health activist and advisor on sexual and reproductive health and rights, working in developing countries in Africa, Asia, and Latin America. My experiences in Cuba and building support and awareness in the US helped steer me toward that lifelong work.

The Cuba trips, along with the press and media coverage all over the country during and afterwards, provided a true portrait of what was happening in the overwhelmingly pro-people, progressive revolution in Cuba, which belied the standard tale of bleak Communist totalitarianism. This coverage raised the level of awareness about the unjustifiable US stance toward the new revolution in Cuba. What is more, many of the travelers went on to participate and even help lead the antiwar, civil rights/antiracism, feminist, climate change, and other human rights movements. One of my fellow travelers described the effect the Cuba trips had on all of us:

> We were seeing ourselves after the Cuba trip as cultural guerrillas spreading a heresy. The Cuban Revolution had panache, or so we all thought, and it made you want to try something more daring with a will to make it happen.

Ellen Israel is a nurse-midwife and international public health specialist living in Boston. She practiced midwifery for many years in the Boston Neighborhood Health System and in private practice, then worked to support sexual and reproductive health and rights initiatives in over twenty countries in Africa, Asia, and Latin America over a thirty-year period. She has written articles on rights-based women's and maternal health, HIV prevention among vulnerable groups, and abortion rights. Ellenisrael3@gmail.com

2

A Revolutionary Journey

Dick J. Reavis
(University of Texas at Austin)

If Progressive Labor were a corporation, we'd have to say that it came to Texas not by opening a branch office but by licensing a subsidiary: Friends of Progressive Labor. FPL, which I founded with my wife of the time, Becky Brenner of San Antonio, was a student organization at the University of Texas at Austin.

Becky and I, both white, had been civil rights workers in Demopolis, Alabama, during the summer of 1966, along with a half-dozen other UT students. Both of us had joined the University of Texas chapter of SDS in the fall of 1965, after I finished an earlier sojourn in Alabama.

But SDS had not been entirely to our liking, especially after our Alabama experience. It was too countercultural. It lacked the popu-list undercurrents and do-or-die determination we had experienced in Demopolis. Seeking a political home with a more working-class program, at UT I had also joined the Communist Party youth division of the time, the W.E.B. Du Bois Club. But in Austin, only four of us belonged to the Du Bois chapter. Becky and I wondered what the Left was like in Mexico and both of us spoke enough Spanish to get by, so we decided to spend the summer of 1967 there.

Our first stop was Saltillo, Coahuila, where we rented an apart-ment. Within days we made contact with local leftists. I don't recall if they belonged to a particular faction, but when they asked us to smuggle ammunition, we got cold feet. So we abandoned Saltillo and rented a hotel room in the Danky, a down-on-its-heels place near the Ministry of the Interior in Mexico City, the country's spy-on-the-Reds agency. Strolling one afternoon, we came upon a group of three or four college-age guys, each clutching a dozen or more copies of Mao's *Little Red Book* at their sides. We stopped to chat. They invited us to their destination, a bookshop called El Primer Paso, or the First Step. They introduced us to a middle-aged man called "El Ingeniero," the engineer, a professional title in Mexico. In later years, I would encounter him again and learn that he was Javier Fuentes, one of the founders of Mexican Maoism.

We were also introduced to a tall, dark man with wiry hair, Silvestre Enrique Marenco Martínez, who was in his thirties. Silvestre more or less adopted us, volunteering to guide us around town. It took me awhile to discern that his accent, which seemed a monotone to me, was Central American. He was Salvadoran, not Mexican. He'd crossed the Salvadoran–Nicaraguan border and fought with the Sandinistas, then been captured and deported to Cuba. At the end of that exile, he had returned to El Salvador and then to the hills of Nicaragua, when he'd been captured and deported again, this time to Mexico. He spoke very little but his grim demeanor impressed me.

With Silvestre we got a look at the Mexican student Left, which dwarfed anything that, to my knowledge, SDS ever achieved. The Mexican students controlled whole buildings, each with a half-dozen mimeograph machines. Almost all the lefty students were straight-out Leninists of one kind or another. Though they had to whisper their ideas in public places off-campus, they talked of making a revolution within a matter of a few years. In that atmosphere, I bought a volume of Lenin's writings in Spanish and studied it at night. I did not like what I read. It seemed to me that his plan for a party would inevitably give rise to tyranny.

One afternoon Becky, Silvestre, and I were on a streetcar headed to the outlying town of Xochimilco. In those days, I always had a bottle of Coca-Cola in my hands, part of a sugar-and-caffeine habit that I've never dropped. As I sat in the streetcar, I noted a boy of about ten staring at me. After a while it dawned on me that he was watching to see what I'd do with the Coke bottle. When I had drained it, I set it on the floor and he came scurrying to beg it. Then the car stopped in a rural area and he got out, running toward an adobe shack whose windows were covered only in screening material, no glass. In those days Coke bottles were recycled to the company, and each one was worth two or three cents. I was sure that the boy felt that he or his family needed those *centavos*

Then and there I made a decision, which I've yet to repudiate. Leninism may lead to tyranny, I told myself, but the first challenge is extreme poverty. I had no doubt that the communists would take its elimination it to heart, and the Maoists seemed to be the most militant among them. I vowed to look for them in the US, and when we returned to Texas I did.

But I had not made contact with PL before something else happened. One afternoon I ran across an Associated Press story reporting the arrest of Silvestre and a dozen others. They had established a camp in the state of Guerrero and attempted to rob a train that was carrying a payroll for Mexican soldiers. They'd escaped the scene but had been rounded up upon their return to Mexico City. My thought was that since Becky and I were Americans, the Primer Paso people probably suspected us of complicity in the capture of their comrades. We had known that they had an operation in Guerrero, but we had not known its purpose. I went to Laredo and jumped on a bus, bound for Mexico City to clear our names.

I went to several apartments of the students but couldn't find anyone. The landlady of one of them, who hailed from Chiapas, told me, "Oh, he lives here, but the police came for him about a week ago and I haven't seen him since." After a couple of days I gave up. As I was returning to the bus station that served northern destinations, walking on the street that was then called San Juan de Letrán, somebody bumped me on the elbow. I turned—and saw one of the Primer Paso students. He had not been captured. He said that he was leaving the office of the group's attorney, a couple of stories above us. He also said that his comrades knew that it wasn't Becky or I who had ratted out their plan. He gave me the lawyer's office number, and through him I established a correspondence with Silvestre, who with the others was in the old Lecumberri prison, home to generations of Mexican revolutionaries.

Upon my return to Austin, I asked, by mail, to join the Progressive Labor Party, which the Chinese Communists then recognized as their fraternal party in the US. But PL wouldn't accept members in Texas because, its leaders told me, it had no one in the state to guide us. So, over the next few months, Becky and I recruited Texans who had been with us in Alabama to form what became the Friends of Progressive Labor. What attracted all of us was that the party had a militant anti-racist line and, in its publications, praised the wildcat strikes that were then common in the US. Nor was PL afraid to call imperialism by its name. It was a stand-up group.

Before long we had a dozen in our cadre, some of them drawn from SDS. PL functioned as a faction within that group. There and elsewhere, it brought socialism into SDS discourse. I suppose we stood out in Austin, because a couple of Mexican-Americans joined and because one of us, the late Charlie Saulsberry, was an African-American native of Demopolis. He had returned with our group from Alabama.

Our chief contact with figures in PL's student section was by telephone and at national meetings of SDS. Relations never were smooth, largely because the PL leadership was drawn from a narrow circle of New Yorkers, people whose parents knew each other from their years in the CPUSA. Two or three people at UT-Austin may have been red diaper babies, but no militant socialist tradition had survived. Members of the FPL were converts. PL's student leaders were essentially political heirs. They distrusted us as newcomers and Southerners and knew very little of our circumstances.

PL's student leaders apparently decided that they should distrust me after they placed my name in nomination at a nationwide SDS meeting where a new national committee was being chosen. SDS was by then radically factionalized. In my nomination speech I argued that all of the factions served a common purpose, anarchists included. After I said that, PL's leadership sent word to the convention floor that its cadre should vote against me. I wound up as an alternate, but stuck with PL because I was pledged to party discipline.

Despite our frictions with PL's national leadership, times were good for FPL. A generation of us, especially those more influenced by the civil rights movement than the antiwar movement, were nearing graduation and didn't know what to do. Most SDSers said that they wanted to work outside "the System," not inside. Many people in SDS were looking toward business opportunities in the counterculture, or teaching, or jobs in government bureaucracies. Others were entering graduate school, merely to kill time.

PL, through its literature and the Worker-Student Alliance, brought a more promising future into view. I had been especially impressed with Wally Lindner's pamphlet on the Flint sit-down strike of 1937. It showed me a whole new plan of battle. PL told us to join the working class, go into the factories, and rebuild the trade unions. This perspective was popular enough that we Friends soon built a WSA chapter that was twice the size of our club. The only fly in the ointment was that few factories had located in Texas, and almost none were unionized.

In the months that followed, we took summer jobs in those plants we could find. But we ran into obstacles that, we believed, were unique to the South. We delivered strike support to a small factory on the east side of town. A couple of weeks after we'd begun showing up on the picket lines at the East Austin plant, its union leaders visited my apartment—to tell me that communists weren't welcome in their ranks. I was an apprentice in the carpenter's union for a few weeks, until the local's president denied me membership because someone had denounced me as a communist. (We checked into the legality of barring me and found out that the Supreme Court had, indeed, upheld the exclusion of a CP carpenter, Roscoe Proctor.)

Having one member who worked in a Student Union coffee shop, we called a boycott of the place to demand that rubber floor mats be installed in its kitchen. Insofar as the boycott was successful, however, it was because we ordered pizzas that we sold as an alternative to the coffee shop's offerings. Whether or not the workers got their rubber mats I don't recall, but the boycott did not lead to any permanent organization among them.

Our limited success did not obscure the internal strife that was always riddling PL. In late 1968 or early 1969 we received a telephone call from a "national" (New York) student leader, who told us that the party had decided that "nationalism is always reactionary" and that we should act accordingly in dealings with African American organizations. I told him that I couldn't agree with that and informed my comrades of my dissent. By that time the Friends of PL had elected a co-chairman who welcomed the new line, and I left its implementation to him.

About this time, the FBI decided to COINTELPRO me. It sent a letter to PL's headquarters alleging that I was a heroin addict. I had never set eyes on that drug, didn't use drugs of any kind, and had once pulled a pistol on a drug-dealing SDSer who had come into WSA ranks. My guess is that PL received several such letters during that period and ignored all of them, as it did the letter about me. Its adult leaders had no doubt long been familiar with McCarthyite slander campaigns.

Almost all our FPL members attended the 1969 SDS convention and witnessed the organization's split. It resulted, not from violations of parliamentary order by PLers, but from the walkout of the faction led by Bernardine Dohrn and Mark Rudd, and called, I believe, the Revolutionary Youth Movement. That faction had lost a vote and, by *Robert's Rules of Order*, had become the minority in SDS. In the aftermath of the walkout, SDS, now under PL's leadership, picked Becky as its traveler to Southern campuses. It still pains me to confess as much, but while she was making her rounds for PL back in Austin, I slept with a comrade.

This wasn't my first offense as a husband. Eighteen months earlier, I'd had an affair while on a month-long SDS tour of Cuba. This time my infidelity was brought to the attention of the leaders of PL's student section, one of whom flew to Texas to preside over my trial. Its jurors—almost all of whom I'd had recruited to FPL—found that I was guilty of "male chauvinist adventurism." According to the Stalinist logic called "sharpening," the group also found that since I was a male chauvinist, my reactionary tendencies had always predominated. I had therefore been a reactionary, even in the civil rights movement. I balked at that expansion of the verdict, but nevertheless was expelled. My impression was that, had PL held state power at the time, I would have been executed.

PL soon ordered the FPL group to transfer to Los Angeles, where it had cadre who could provide trustworthy leadership. Within a couple of months, everyone but me was gone from Texas, including a few members of the WSA who joined the army to do antiwar organizing in its ranks.

Three or four months after my expulsion, I received a telephone call from one of PL's leaders offering me a way to redeem myself. We decided that I should go to San Francisco and take up the tasks of a sympathizer. Soon I found myself living in the Mission District with two working-class comrades in their thirties. I started looking for a job but didn't have any luck, people told me, because I wasn't local. PLers kept telling me to go to the Gilmore Envelope Company, and finally I did. Its personnel manager was from North Carolina, and a week later I was at work as a "gum boy" on the graveyard shift. My first night there I learned why I'd been hired: all its low-level employees were either Samoans or "Okies," a term applied to anyone with a Southern accent. On the shop floor I met a co-worker whose parents hailed from Gotebo, Oklahoma, only miles from the town where my mother grew up.

I hung out in a neighborhood bar where, the first time I went to the jukebox, two Mexican American longshoremen, both admirers of Harry Bridges, encircled me to give me the warning, "Don't play it country." At a Sears store, when I tried to purchase hand tools with travelers checks from the Republic Bank of Dallas, a white clerk refused my payment on the grounds that "We don't accept Confederate money here."

PL kept an eye on me, too. Once I asked one of its local leaders how I could get in touch with a female comrade I'd met. "I won't tell you because she's here for the same offense as yours," he informed me. Nor was I allowed to attend PL meetings, but every weekday morning, in the company of a female party member, I sold PL's weekly, *Challenge*, outside the city's unemployment office. The newspaper sold pretty well, maybe two dozen copies a day. But a couple of guys were running a three-card monte game in the alley beside the unemployment office, where laid-off workers received their checks. I proposed that we warn people, or at least paint on the wall of the building, "THREE-CARD MONTE IS A RACKET." It seemed obvious to me that doing so would render a service to the working class. But the leadership didn't want trouble with hoodlums, and perhaps that was wise.

The most important obstacle that all of us faced was that the workers weren't ready for socialism, and less than 10 percent of PL's membership was drawn from the working class. The party encouraged its former collegians to hide their books in closets and to engage in what the Spartacist League aptly calls "workerism." Whatever the workers did, we were to imitate, wherever they went, we were to go. This practice, sloganized by PL as "build a base in the working class," had begun during the WSA, when we were ordered to leave behind our bohemian ways and adopt the attire and grooming practices of workers. In San Francisco, it meant that I spent my Saturdays at the Bay Meadows race track , watching my factory chums blow their paychecks on the ponies.

My San Francisco comrades did appreciate my regularity, obedience, and contrition; it was clear that I wanted to make things right. My sales partner told me that PL had decided that I could rejoin if I wanted.

But by then the party's circles were buzzing with talk of breaking with the Chinese CP because of Mao's posture toward events in Cambodia, if I remember correctly. I didn't really understand what I heard of the internal discussion and still don't. The plain facts were that in my ignorance of Communist history, I didn't believe that anyone should doubt a giant like Mao, and I didn't think that the global movement could hold together if anyone did. One morning at the unemployment office I questioned my *Challenge* sales partner about that. "But he sold out!" she told me.

I was a bit taken aback by her pronouncement. After mulling it over for a couple of days, I concluded that PL was an organization whose attitude was that "everybody has sold out but you and me, and I'm not sure about you." I didn't like the spectre of PL denouncing Mao any more than I had liked the broadening of the verdict that led to my disgrace. It seemed that in PL, trust could never reliably be won.

Two weeks later I was back in Austin, trying to piece my life back together. I read Deutscher's books about Trotsky and flirted with the Spartacist League, only to decide that though Lev Davidovich had spotted Bolshevism's ailments, he too failed to outline a course that would have worked. Even today, there have been no revolutions led by Trotskyists.

Not knowing what to do with my new life outside PL, I drifted to New Orleans, where a former member of the Friends of PL, burned out by his sojourn in a California auto plant, had joined an informal group of about a dozen white Southern lefties who gathered around Ed Clark, a long-time PLer who had broken with the party leadership. It was not a happy time for any of us. SDS was dead and soon the antiwar movement would be in decline. Pictures of our former rivals, the leaders of the Revolutionary Youth Movement, now known as Weatherman, were on posters in every post office, and before long the authorities would be scouring the country for Angela Davis. In the slum that then was the Irish Channel, we watched the deflation of popular support for the Left and adopted a joking name for ourselves by saying that we subscribed to the theory of "Marxism-Vegetablism." Some of us, but not me, took new "party names," "Artichoke" for Art, "Tomato" for Tom, and so on. And though some of us produced an "underground" newsletter, *The Midnight Special*, most members of the group did nothing but drink. Two of them wound up on Antabuse. In the meantime, I found a job as a machine operator in a rubber-stamp plant whose practices and conditions were from the nineteenth century. We had to work on our feet, we didn't have air conditioning—and we were paid in cash. Next door to us was a competitor's shop, which we observed through our windows. Workers there had stools and air conditioning, and, presumably, got paychecks. Still trying to build a base among the working class, I wound up playing the horses again.

Over the course of a year or eighteen months, the advocates of Marxism-Vegetablism began sorting into factions. An old friend from the FLP in Texas joined the Spartacist League, and when, during its "Free Angela" days, I joined the CP, he stopped speaking to me because I had "crossed the class line." Clark, whose leadership and stature had drawn us together, began veering toward anarchism and left for California. A couple of others joined Alcoholics Anonymous and one of us, I believe, became a pot smuggler.

My own choice, I thought, was fortunate. The CP was the birthplace of American Leninism, our family home. It was a comfortable place for me because I got along well with its Southern organizer, the late Jim Baines of Birmingham, and the up-North leadership left me alone. Beyond that, the CP was the best-integrated organization, by race, sex, and age, that I've ever seen.

In New Orleans I received my first press card, from the *Daily World*, successor to the *Daily Worker*. During a weeks-long wildcat strike by African American longshoremen, nearly every day I telephoned a story to New York, and the *World* shipped papers to us by air. Club members distributed them on the docks. I read the published versions of my stories and, from the changes that the editors made, divined the rules of newspaper journalism.

I also attended a CP convention in New York, though to my dismay found it to be a top-down, essentially local affair. Nonetheless, in New Orleans we did not receive phone calls announcing sharp changes in the party line or orders to reform our personal behaviors and tastes. Compared to PL, the CP was a Caribbean vacation, and I remained a member until the late 1970s, when I quit because I'd become a reporter for the mainstream press.

Six years after their imprisonment, the Mexican supreme court ruled that the offenses of the Primer Paso crew carried a maximum sentence of only a year, and Silvestre, whom the Salvadoran government wouldn't readmit, was deported to Paris. There he married a local and became a French citizen. With his new passport he was able to gain entry to El Salvador and in early 1974 he visited me in New Orleans. But a few weeks after his return, his letters stopped coming. In the last of them he told me that what we came to call death squads were operating there. It has been my assumption ever since that they killed him.

Later that year I became a reporter in the small Texas Panhandle town of Dumas, and because I welcomed them and spoke their language, I became the de facto patron of twenty-two families of Chilean *Allendista* refugees whom the UN had freed from prison and a Catholic service had dispatched to Texas. After three years there I returned to Austin, where I began writing for magazines, especially *Texas Monthly*. One of my first short reports was about a soccer game between the Dumas Chileans and a team of Vietnamese refugees. The Chileans chanted "Ho, Ho, Ho Chi Minh!" at their rivals. My first lengthy story, also a gift from my past, was a 1977 narrative about a group of Mexican guerrillas who called themselves the Partido de los Pobres Unidos de America, or PPUA. While coursing the hills of Oaxaca with them, I ran into El Ingeniero, who at first denied ever having known me. But after a few hours of discomfort, he confessed to remembering me and told me his story, which essentially was that he had been an adviser to every peasant rebellion in Mexico since the early 1960s. He had spent most of the interval between our first and second meetings in China, where he'd met Florencio "El Güero" Medrano Mederos, the PPUA's leader.

The PPUA recruited supporters on both sides of the border and, months after my story was published, it invited me to join. But I demurred, first, because following the defeat of Mao's forces in China, the PPUA had chosen Albania as its Promised Land. Second, I feared that, like all Mexican peasant movements, it was doomed. But, nevertheless, during the last months of its existence I smuggled its newspaper, which was printed in San Antonio, across Laredo's international bridge. From time to time, I delivered a pistol as well.

The PPUA's demise came swiftly after El Güero was killed in a shoot-out with the private army of an Oaxacan planter. Though I still maintain contact with a couple of veterans of the PPUA, all of us lost hope then. In 2004 I became a professor in North Carolina, and for a couple of years I belonged the Workers World Party there, not because I recognized WWP as the proverbial vanguard, but because I stood in awe of its activists. In any case, I did not fit in. I was thirty-five years senior to the oldest of them. They met at night in Durham, eighteen miles from my home in Raleigh. During the dark winter months, I couldn't see to drive there.

Today, retired in Dallas, which is bereft of Leninist groups, I have adopted the life of those the McCarthyites termed "fellow travelers." I sometimes attend demonstrations, I read, and occasionally send a check to Leninist publications, especially those produced by the historians at *Workers Vanguard*, the Spartacist newspaper. The people whom I most admire and trust are members of Leninist organizations or those, like me, who once belonged and haven't totally repudiated their pasts.

Looking back on my disgrace in PL, my chief misgiving is about me, not about my comrades. I was out of line. I don't think that at the time I could have resisted sexual temptations, but that pointed to a flaw in my hormonal balance and also in my character. PL's judgment of me, on sexual grounds, anyway, was necessary and therefore just. I was not fit to be a leader, even in a party of dogmatists. Ever since I came to recognize PL's essential, if outsized wisdom—perhaps a decade too late—I have shied away from leading roles. Some people are better as back-benchers and I'm happy enough in their ranks.

I am nobody's comrade today, and if the truth be told, I still have doubts about our project. It seems to me that party discipline, while necessary, should be tame and lax at the onset of a prerevolutionary era and should tighten only as conditions mature. I have also observed that the more extensive a party's program is, the fewer followers it attracts. I once knew a husband and wife who divorced because they differed about whether their party should praise or condemn Vietnam's invasion of Cambodia. Ideological or programmatic disputes like that aren't worth the trouble they cause.

A once-familiar figure in the Texas Left, the short, beefy late labor organizer Franklin Garcia, used to boast that he was a communist, then follow that by saying, "and when the Revolution comes, I'll be the first person you shoot." At seventy-one, it's now clear to me that however near to execution I thought I was when I was expelled from FPL, I'm not now going live long enough to face even that ironic, if entirely revolutionary, fate.

Dick J. Reavis is a retired Texas journalist who lives in Dallas.

3

My Sister, Lynn

Paula Campbell Munro
(University of Texas, Austin)

I first got involved in SDS through my sister, Lynn Jones McCray, in 1969. I was nineteen and Lynn was twenty-three. My husband, Steve Campbell, was away in basic training with the Marine Corps. Lynn had moved to Austin that year and was living in College House, going to classes at the University of Texas and working in Robert Kennedy's campaign. Since she was something of a hippie, we went to headshops and psychedelic music concerts when I went to visit her and sat around with her and her friends who were smoking pot. Since I didn't smoke, it was pretty boring for me being the only one who wasn't stoned.

Lynn and I grew up in a working-class family. My mother was a waitress most of my childhood and then worked as a clerk in a hospital. We lived in Mineral Wells, Texas, where my father was a clerk at the Baker Hotel. Daddy, who battled alcoholism off and on for most of his life, had been fired from his job as a lineman at AT&T for drinking on the job.

Mineral Wells is small town a few miles west of Fort Worth, Texas. One of its claims to fame is Crazy Water, a lithium-rich mineral water that was the basis of spa health treatments at the Crazy Hotel in the early twentieth century. My dad and his sister Imorene both worked at the soda fountain at the hotel when they were in high school. There was also an army base, Camp Wolters, four miles northeast of town.

My grandmother on my father's side was a licensed practical nurse at the Nazareth Hospital, where I was born in 1949. She used to steal bed linens and penicillin (she gave us shots when we were sick). My grandfather hauled cattle to market for small ranchers.

I'm not sure why, but when I was in the second grade we packed up in the middle of the night and moved to Corpus Christi. My mother started waitressing and my father worked in hotels until he became a firefighter. I give this background because our working-class origins made Lynn and me unique in SDS in Austin, where most of the members came from more economically stable families. We thought they were rich. The next time I visited Lynn in Austin she had joined SDS. She sat me down and explained to me that the capitalist system was the reason for all the problems and brushes with poverty that our parents had experienced. She explained the economic theories of Marx and identified our parents as belonging to the working class. Bang, like that, the whole theory made sense to me, and I decided I was a communist too. I was living at home, and by April 1969 Steve was in Vietnam. He was a crew chief on a chopper and was shot down and killed in June. Nothing could have made the theories of class war and anti-imperialism clearer to us than our own personal experiences. Studying Marx, Engels, Lenin, and Mao in study groups strengthened our worldview. When we told our parents what we were involved in and why, they were naturally concerned, but they supported us because they said they had raised us to think for ourselves and couldn't get mad at us when we did.

Lynn was at the SDS convention in Chicago in 1969 and when she got the news about Steve's death, her comrades came up with the money to buy her a plane ticket home. She spent the whole summer helping me cope with my grief. When she went back to Austin, I followed shortly after to go to UT on my newly acquired GI Bill benefits.

My sister died in November 2015. By telling how I got involved in SDS/WSA, I'm also trying to tell Lynn's story at the same time. If she were here to write the tale herself, it would be very animated and full of adjectives and superlatives. I'll do my best to tell it for her. I never joined Progressive Labor, but we were like two halves of one person, and I lived her experiences in PL with her.

I think she got involved in SDS when she met Dick Reavis and Becky Brenner, leaders in SDS at UT Austin. By then she was deeply involved in the movement. At the 1969 SDS Convention, Becky had been appointed Southern Coordinator for PL/SDS and was planning a trip through the South to hook up with other people in SDS and try to bring them into the fold of the WSA faction. Lynn was going with her, and they invited me, the newly widowed twenty-year-old, to come along. That trip was tremendously exciting, fun, and educational for me as I listened to Becky and Lynn talk politics with the people we met. Becky Brenner has written a terrific account of that trip in her chapter of this book, so I won't repeat it here.

When we got back to Austin, I started classes at UT but dropped out to work for Southwestern Bell after a disastrous first semester where I cut classes to sit in the Chuck Wagon talking politics and planning strategies for actions in the antiwar movement. I started going out with Ian, the man I married, who was a teaching assistant at UT and a friend of Lynn's in SDS. We're still together, forty-eight years later. My sister deserves all the credit.

I worked in the Worker-Student Alliance, trying to sell *Challenge* to teaching assistants and campus workers. I attended a few meetings of Vietnam Veterans Against the War and saw how damaged they had been by their tours. There was no name for PTSD then, and the vets self-medicated with drugs and alcohol. I sat vigil with them at a demonstration in support of the activities of the Winter Soldier movement. When I first joined SDS, I was questioned twice about how I felt politically about Steve's death in Vietnam. PL made sure that I understood my tragedy in terms of US imperialism, and that gave me a framework for understanding other such events in our nation's history.

In 1973 we hosted Inti-Illimani, a Chilean folk music group stranded outside of their country after the Pinochet coup. We became involved with a Palestinian woman and worked with her to educate people on campus about Zionism and the occupation of Palestine. We, along with exiled Iranian students, tried to shout down Meir Kahane, leader of the Jewish Defense League, when he spoke on campus. To this day we're active in the movement against the occupation of Palestine. The Palestinians never give up. How can we?

SDS meetings became more and more influenced by PL. We didn't agree politically with the Socialist Workers Party's single-issue approach to the war. We believed that the antiwar movement should be viewed in terms of class struggle and anti-imperialism. We still participated in the huge protest marches and rallies, but always had leaflets with lengthy statements of PL's views and principles about the war to hand out to the misled participants. WSA was in full swing, and members were told to get working-class jobs and try to build a base with the workers. We were told to dress like workers dressed, not like hippies and anarchists, and to drink beer, the workers' beverage of choice. Cohabitating partners were urged to get married like workers did. Dick Reavis even suggested we all learn to bowl because it was a working-class pastime. There was also a strict antidrug policy in PL. I remember a couple of times when Dick was really patronizing to me. I bought a new outfit to wear to a party and he commented on how working class that was, like "how sweet." Another time he made the same kind of comment when I dressed up nice to fly to Jamaica to visit Ian. My sister and I were endearing that way.

PL's formation of the Worker-Student Alliance urged students to become actively involved with real workers in the university commu-nity as well as outside. This was good, since it gave students the chance to interact with working-class people. My sister worked as a maid in a large women's dormitory on the UT campus. She became good friends with her co-workers, but none were recruited to PL.

We supported strikes and the lettuce and grape boycotts by leaf-leting at grocery stores. There was a big Safeway store in West Austin where we regularly handed out leaflets about the United Farm Work-ers boycott of table grapes and iceberg lettuce. We were pretty well received there. Austin was a liberal town, and this was something they could easily support. My sister, always the more militant one, would

recruit people to go into the store and fill grocery carts with grocer-
ies, grapes on the bottom, then leave them in the aisles to ruin the
fruit. The strike lasted so long that I got out of the habit of buying
grapes and iceberg lettuce, and I rarely do so even now. There was
also a Texas Farmworkers Union, and we supported their strike against
onion growers in the Rio Grande Valley. We met with their leader,
Tony Orendain, a former UFW officer who had relocated to the Valley.

We had an informational picket line in front of a General Motors
dealership in Austin to support the 1970 United Auto Workers strike.
There were probably ten of us. The Austin *Statesman* reported on our
demonstration and made a sarcastic comment about us driving away
in my Chevy Nova, a GM car.

We noted members of the Red Squad, the plain clothes officers
from the Austin police department assigned to track radicals, watching
and taking pictures. They always took down license plate numbers
from the cars parked in front of Ian's house when we had meetings
there. We assumed our phones were tapped. That may have been more
than paranoia because in 1984, a year after we were married and had
our daughter, Margaret, Ian, a Canadian citizen, applied for permanent resident status. Our separate interviews at the INS focused on our
radical activism in the 1970s. It took him six years to get a green card.

My sister loved to sell *Challenge* and was actually good at it. She
could have been the Minister of *Challenge* Sales for the Southwest. She,
I, and her best friend, Dick Johnson, used to drive down to San Antonio
to sell *Challenge* to people on the streets around the Alamo. We especially targeted and tried to sell the paper to personnel from the military
bases around town. PL thought that the military should be organized.
No one was more antiwar than the people who had served in Vietnam.
They clearly understood anti-imperialism. I can't remember specific
conversations, but many of them were against the war. Dick and I
didn't have the skills that Lynn had in selling *Challenge*. Sometimes
we'd head off to our assigned corners and dump most of the copies in
a trash can and go have coffee until time to meet up with Lynn. Once
she found boxes of unsold *Challenge*s under my bed and was disap-

pointed that Dick and I weren't really selling them on campus. Until her death, she chided me for it on the one hand and apologized on the other for forcing Dick and me to try to sell them.

My sister moved to Houston and worked with PL under the leadership of Stevie Eisenberg. The two of them sat me down for a meeting when I was visiting and asked me to donate some of the insurance money from my husband's death on active duty in Vietnam to PL. I was using the money to buy property for our parents in the Texas Hill Country, but they wore down my objections and I gave them $400. I wrote an article for *Challenge* about the coordinated efforts of workers from all over the state to help restore services in Corpus Christi after Hurricane Celia. It was edited beyond recognition to reflect what they called "revolutionary enthusiasm." It was a pretty straightforward article about the numbers of IBEW (International Brotherhood of Electrical Workers), CWA (Communication Workers of America), and Plumbers union workers who came from other parts of Texas and volunteered time to help restore services in the aftermath. I said it was a show of working-class solidarity with the people of the city. The edited version inflated the numbers for no explainable reason. I was getting tired of PL.

At the direction of PL, Lynn became a student at Texas State University, a traditionally African American college in Houston. She was building a base there among the student body. Her friends came to her defense several times when she was selling *Challenge* on campus and was physically harassed by Brothers of the Nation of Islam.

At some point in late 1969 or early 1970, Lynn broke with PL over the China question, the national question, and their position on gays. She was a strong Maoist and disagreed when the party criticized China. She and I read party documents together and this criticism of China, along with their criticism of the Black Panther Party for nationalism and their opinion that gays should not be admitted to PL because homosexuality was anathema to the working class, tipped the scale against them. Her best friend, Dick Johnson was gay. (He died of AIDS in 1985.) As a student at TSU, she had become close friends with members of People's Party II. PPII was made up of young revolutionary black men, led by Carl Hampton, who were doing Black Panther–style community organizing and community service from their headquarters on Dowling Street in Houston's Third Ward. When she left PL, PPII gave her sanctuary because Stevie Eisenberg and other PL members pursued her so relentlessly to try to get her to come back.

My husband was a teaching assistant at the University of Texas at the time and wanted a PPII member to speak to his English classes at UT. Steve Edwards, minister of defense of PPII and a friend of Lynn's, agreed to come. Due to intense police scrutiny at PPII headquarters, we took two cars: Steve and Ian in one car, and Lynn and I in the other. Lynn and I were stopped by the police as we drove away from headquarters and Ian picked up Steve and went on to Austin unnoticed. The police searched our car and tried to say that my knitting needles, tucked in a ball of yarn in a bag, were a weapon. They didn't know much about needlecraft.

In Austin, Steve spoke in Ian's classes and the classes of one his associates. He punctuated the point that "power comes from the muzzle of a gun" by pulling his revolver out. Ian and his associate were promptly fired. They were also spearheading an effort to organize teaching assistants into a union at the time, so the university had plenty of reason to try to get rid of them. Their students and other teaching assistants organized and rallied against the administration, and they were reinstated in their jobs shortly thereafter.

In late 1970 Lynn was invited to be part of a radical students delegation to China organized by Bill Epton. Bill had been vice-chairman of PL and a longtime Harlem civil rights and union activist who had joined PL in the early 1960s. He was arrested and charged with "criminal anarchy" when a PL-sponsored antipolice rally began to march on 125th Street in Harlem. He was expelled from PL in the late 1960s because he disagreed with PL's position that all nationalism was reactionary, including the Black Nationalism of the Panthers. He stayed active as a revolutionary and helped found the A. Phillip Randolph Labor Council. He died in 2002.

Adding Lynn to the trip rounded out the goal of the delegation to have activists of both genders from all regions of the country. I've tried to find anything written by members of the delegation on the internet but don't know the names of most of them. My sister's letters to me have been lost. The delegation visited Mao's birthplace and had shooting practice with the People's Liberation Army. They visited other sites and had many talks with members of the Communist Party, including an informal gathering with Zhou Enlai and members of the Gang of Four, who held power in the party at the time.

After she returned from China, Lynn and I had a meeting with Michael Klonsky to talk about the October League. They were trying to recruit her. I didn't want anything to do with them because they were antigay. Lynn declined the invitation, or else was not invited to join after that meeting. Lynn gave a lot of talks about what she saw and heard on the trip to China. While she was away on the trip, Carl Hampton, chairman of People's Party II in Houston, was targeted and killed by police snipers in a shootout on Dowling Street near their headquarters. He had tried many times to get PPII recognized as a chapter of the Black Panther Party but was told that the BPP was closed to new chapters.

In 1975 I worked with a Chicano group agitating for open admissions to the University of Texas for African Americans and Hispanics. John Herrera was the leader of the group. There were more foreign students at UT, a state university, than from the minorities who composed a substantial part of the state population. Our slogan was "Open it up or shut it down." We had demonstrations on campus, and five or six of us occupied the office of the president for eight hours, negotiating with administrators who were trying to understand our demands and to get us to leave the office.

There were police outside the door and in the hallway. The office was in the tower that housed many administrative offices. There was a big balcony behind the office where we hung a banner with our slogan, "Open it up or shut it down." A big crowd of students and activists outside the tower rallied in our support. Activist leaders were giving speeches and people were chanting, "Open it up or shut down." We didn't get open admissions, but we were smart enough to negotiate amnesty for ourselves for the occupation. We spoke at rallies and to the Board of Regents of the university, which included Lady Bird Johnson. I was standing right next to her when I gave my speech and kept my hand on my stomach because I was so nervous that I thought I'd throw up. We spoke about more representation on campus of the black and Hispanic population. When one of the Hispanic students called them "Pendejos" (stupid people, in Spanish), they thought he was making some kind of threat. I explained that it was just a harmless comment. I think the only result was that they named a building after a couple of black and Hispanic scholars.

After her trip to China, Lynn and I, our husbands, and several other friends from SDS worked in the US–China People's Friendship Association. The organization worked to build connections with China and support for normalization of relations with the US. Lots of Maoists and other leftists worked in the organization. We organized trips to China sponsored by our group and China Travel Services. There were also Taiwanese and Hong Kong students who supported the People's Republic of China in the group.

In 1978 Ian got a job at a small college in Kansas City, Missouri, and we moved there. I worked with an anti-right-to-work committee of the United Auto Workers the first year we were there. Since we had been active in the US–China Peoples Friendship Association in Austin, we were contacted by an administrator of Wuhan University in Hubei, China, with an offer to teach there. Fortunately, Ian's college gave him a leave of absence and we worked at Wuhan University for two years. Ian was a "Foreign Expert," teaching the first class of graduate students of English at the university since the Cultural Revolution. I worked in various positions at the university as "Spouse of Expert" at half the pay.

We got to Wuhan in early summer and were sent to the Jinggan Mountains. We had an interpreter who gave us Chinese lessons. A group of veterans of the revolutionary war were staying at the same place and at mealtime they told us stories about being on the Long March with Chairman Mao. It was an amazing experience for us to meet them.

Another English teacher and I did a closed-circuit TV class for non-English majors. The whole campus watched it, and many students I had never seen before approached me on campus and in town to say, "You are teacher Paula. You are my English teacher." I also met regularly with a group of middle-aged teachers who had formerly taught Russian and had switched to English after the split with the Soviet Union. I helped them prepare lesson plans. Our relationship with the university faculty and students ebbed and flowed with the political policies of the Party in regard to visiting foreigners. This opportunity was a clear result of our work with US–China People's Friendship Association, which in turn resulted from our status as Maoists in the student movement. Everything Lynn, Ian, and I did after the fragmentation and dissolution of the Left was framed by the worldview we adopted during our time with SDS/WSA/PL.

Lynn did union work for twenty years until she had to leave on disability with PTSD caused by her abusive boss in CWA. She was a member of CWA in Austin, Atlanta, and New York. She was a chief steward in the huge local that represented AT&T workers in Manhattan from the mid 1980s to 1990. In 1990, after the breakup of her marriage and the death of our father, Lynn returned to Texas be near our mother. She started working for CWA in Austin as one of two lead organizers in their branch union, the Texas State Employees Union (TSEU).

Since Austin is the capital of Texas, there were thousands of state workers. She and her fellow organizers worked to save state employee jobs from a move by the governor to privatize several agencies. They saved many state workers' jobs by lobbying progressive members of Congress and filing suits through a loophole they found in the privatization legislation. Even though TSEU had no standing to do so, they sat grievances for the workers in many disputes with the state. Management didn't seem to know that they didn't have to recognize grievances filed by TSEU. Lynn managed other organizers, but when she was in the field she signed up more new members than anyone else. She was an extraordinary organizer. Her experience in the Left was an excellent training ground, and she had a gift for the work.

In 2000, Lynn, suffering from severe PTSD caused by years of abuse by her boss, Danny Fetonte, left CWA with full disability and a large settlement. He was director of TSEU and often took her aside and yelled and screamed at her, finding fault with even the successful things she did. He was furious if she acted on things that weren't his idea. Even when the campaign was going well, he berated her over the numbers of members signed by her organizers. He and Lynn's male counterpart in the union ganged up against her and thwarted her ideas. The legislative work done by her and one of her organizers had to be kept secret because Danny disagreed with it. Lynn fought every day for her position as a woman in a male-dominated workplace, just as she had fought to be heard by the male chauvinists in the movement. After she left CWA she continued to have flashbacks and relive her fights with Danny. She would become agitated and shaky. He had destroyed a strong woman's self-confidence. Her mental and physical health continued to decline, and she died in November of 2015 in Kansas City, where we lived.

Ian was a college professor for forty years, teaching African, Caribbean, and other world literatures to try to bring different worldviews to his students. I worked for AT&T and worked in CWA for twenty years. At AT&T, my friend Catie Olivares and I founded the Hispanic Employees Association to help address Latino issues in the workplace. An example was pay differential for bilingual employees who were pulled from their jobs to interpret without compensation for that additional skill and service. Then I taught high school Spanish for another twenty years. I always included imperialism in the Third World in my Spanish classes. With other educators, I got to spend a month in Ecuador in 1999 and ten days in Cuba in 2001.

Being active in the Left in the late 1960s and the first half of the 1970s shaped our lives and worldview in a huge way. It led us to stay active in community work. Many of our friends are still active in progressive/revolutionary groups. I volunteer as an interpreter for Spanish-speaking patients in a free clinic. Lynn and I have young friends who are carrying the torch, but the "Movement" is fragmented now and is hardly recognizable as such. In fact, our young Marxist friends call it "liberal reform work." Lynn struggled bitterly with our friends over the dangers of sectarianism that splintered the Left in the 1960s and 1970s and broke up relationships, friendships, and families. I remember a meeting with some non-PL SDS people where we argued theory for hours. The meeting broke up abruptly when Lynn told them that come the revolution, it was obvious that "we would end up on opposite ends of the gun." I didn't experience criticism/self-criticism, not being a member of PL, but Lynn told me stories about it. She believed in it as a Maoist concept, but in PL it had devolved into a kind of bullying to get people to follow the party line.

It has been amazing to reconnect with old friends we worked, studied, and struggled with in those days. Even though it was a short period of time before we all went in different directions, they were intense times and we formed strong bonds. My experiences in the Left, as well as those of all my sisters in struggle, were often governed so much by an all-male leadership and the professions of our partners or husbands. Many of us went where they went and did what they did, although feminism and equality for women was always a part of our struggle in the movement, in the unions, and in our relationships. This struggle, as well, is ongoing.

Paula Munro is a retired Spanish teacher who lives in Merriam, Kansas (a suburb of Kansas City). She spends her time hanging out with her friends, reading, doing some art, volunteering as an interpreter for Spanish-speaking patients at a free clinic and going to the many demonstrations and marches that are coming together in the wake of the Trump Tsunami. She lives with her husband, Ian, a retired college professor and their schizophrenic cat, Charlie Dax.

4

I Was More Baptist Than John the Baptist

Becky Brenner
(University of Texas, Austin/Columbia University)

It was 1966 in Austin, Texas, and we were young white college students who had just returned from the experience of a lifetime, being civil rights workers in the very small rural town of Demopolis, Alabama. Demopolis was thirty miles from Selma and another world from where I had grown up in an affluent neighborhood in San Antonio. We returned to Austin feeling like outcasts—and we *were* outcasts! We no longer fit into mainstream college culture.

Ours was a self-induced isolation. We were the original hippies of the 1960s—adamantly against materialism and racism—and we definitely did not approve of the elitist and racist fraternity/sorority culture that dominated the University of Texas at that time. The leftist alternative Austin newspaper, *The Rag*, was hot off the press every week, and it was the center of our counterculture society. The frat rats, as they were called in our world, would beat up male hippies just for walking down the street looking like hippies. This same year (1966), a young man named George Vizard, who was in Students for a Democratic Society and was also a member of the youth group of the Communist Party, was murdered by the Minutemen (a group similar to the Ku Klux Klan) in Austin late one night while working at a convenience store. George was a well-known activist. I remember being in a march in his honor after his murder. His wife, Miriam, had to go into hiding because the Minutemen had made threats against them both. This was 1966 in Austin, Texas. One more thing—I was a twenty-two-year-old young woman.

My name is Becky (Rebecca Adolphina) Brenner, Miss Goodie Two Shoes and runner-up for the San Antonio Miss Youth for Christ of 1963. If that wasn't enough, I was chaplain of my high school sophomore, junior, and senior classes and chaplain of student council. In addition, I was also a Sunday School teacher—all in all, I was more Baptist than John the Baptist. You see, I and many others found ourselves involved in the civil rights movement precisely because of our religious convictions. I believed in the Christianity of love, that I was my brother's keeper, and I was trying to make sense of the contradictory position that Christians held on materialism and the love of money. I wanted to make the world a better place (whatever that meant), which is something that I have always known from a young age.

In 1966 America still lived under the oppressive shadow of McCarthyism. Communists were the devil on earth. I remember being literally scared to physically pick up a communist pamphlet—and I wasn't the only one. I don't know what I thought might happen. They even talked about the evils of communism in my church. So you can only imagine what a shock it was for us in the civil rights movement to be called communists! And you know what? We just decided to look into that! Someone had a copy of the *The Little Red Book* by Mao Zedong, and we read and we talked and we read and we talked and, sure enough, we decided that indeed we were communists! Thanks for that insight, you right-wingers! You really steered us in the right direction—or, actually, the left direction.

The only other people who seemed to support the civil rights movement in Austin at that time were people in Students for a Democratic Society, which was mainly focused on opposition to the Vietnam War. They were hippies, and they lived a counterculture lifestyle. We joined SDS, but even early on there were differences among the membership. We only understood those differences as various events unfolded.

Those of us who came out of the civil rights movement had a different outlook. For instance, SDS members were generally into marijuana and hallucinogenic drugs. Since we were community activists and had also just been immersed in the black community, we were not into drugs at all, largely because that community was strongly opposed to all drugs in their neighborhoods. On top of that, we had just risked our lives every day in Alabama, and we came back in a very serious frame of mind. We were used to being followed by the police, having our phones tapped, and getting each other out of jail. It sure wasn't about getting high. Of course, the other SDS members, to their credit, were seriously committed to antiwar activism and were every bit as angry at society as we were. They just came at it from a different direction. At any rate, we were young and the tensions were there, and they later played out in a very political and personal way, as if the seemingly nonpolitical cultural differences, if you will, defined who we would later become.

It wasn't until we began to participate on a national level that we could see the beginnings of the deep divisions within SDS. The first national SDS conference that we attended was in the winter of 1967 in Madison, Wisconsin. Like hobbits on an adventure, we filled our VW bus with our SDS friends and drove straight through without stopping to sleep anywhere. We had snow inside the bus that didn't melt until we got back into Oklahoma! People allowed us to "crash" wherever there was space on the floor to put down a blanket and pillow. An important discovery we made at the conference was that the differences among the SDS membership in Austin were mirrored on a national level. This was a political observation that continued to surprise me for many years, until I realized that this was the way it pretty much always is: when an idea is out there in the political universe, it is occurring all over the country, as if someone had dropped those same seeds in the ground everywhere to one extent or the other. I suppose you could argue that it was true worldwide because the Chinese Revolution led by Mao had energized people all over the world on every continent to fight against their own oppressive governments.

At the Madison SDS conference, there were the antiwar hippies and the community-focused organizers and anarchists (who called themselves the "Up Against the Wall Motherfucker"). They wore all-black and did demonstrations from the stage on how to efficiently break a brick in half with your bare hands. I never was sure why that was important, except perhaps to illustrate that they were the original bad asses. There were a few people from Austin who aligned with them. Those of us who focused on the community felt an affinity with the Progressive Labor Party's youth affiliate, the Worker-Student Alliance. We didn't dress like hippies, so even visually you could begin to tell what faction someone was in. Those in the WSA were trying to fit into the working class. Therefore, we dressed more working class—or so we thought.

Some of us went on to officially join the Worker-Student Alliance. We read *Challenge*, PL's national newspaper, and everything by Mao that we could get our hands on. PL was closely aligned with the People's Republic of China at that time. We read political writings by Marx, Engels, Lenin, and Stalin. Back in Austin, we started a study group. We were encouraged by the WSA leadership to get jobs, and we all tried to get jobs while we attended school—I got my first job ever as a worker in a flower shop. Our goal was to learn from the working class as well as try to get new members to join our group.

Within three years, SDS had developed into clearly defined factions. There were the Weathermen, Revolutionary Youth Movement I (RYM I), Revolutionary Youth Movement II (RYM II), and the WSA. At the 1969 SDS National Convention in Chicago, SDS split. It was a joyous night because the WSA won the majority, but it was also tinged with sadness. I remember both young men and young women in tears because it was a definite turning point in the student movement and in the leftist movement in general. WSA barely won, but we thought we could claim SDS as ours. Of course, it turned out to be only in our minds, as most people on the Left no longer saw SDS as a legitimate mass organization and it quickly lost much of its credibility. I was elected to represent the South, but to say that I was elected is not completely accurate. Actually, we were selected by PL's leadership, but the membership of WSA did have a vote, for what that was worth.

I must weave my personal story in with the political story, as the two were so intricately connected. I think, as a woman starting out in SDS, that my personal life most often dictated my political life, but over time it reversed. The leader of our small group of civil rights workers from the University of Texas was Dick J. Reavis. He and I were married after that summer of 1966. When I first met Dick, he thought that he might become a Baptist minister. I was thinking of becoming either a youth director or a missionary. But after that summer in Alabama, where the religion of the Ku Klux Klan was Southern Baptist, neither of us ever wished to associate with the Baptists. That was the end of our involvement with the Baptist church, except for working with black churches that were active in the movement.

In the beginning, I saw myself as the good religious woman who stood behind her man and was his helpmate, but my comrades in Austin began to encourage me to speak up in meetings and to read the political philosophy for myself. I was just tiptoeing into this at the time of the 1969 Chicago SDS National Convention. When they won the majority at the convention, WSA took over SDS and a leadership slate was suggested by PL. When Dick and I found out that I had been suggested by PL to represent the South on the national WSA governing board, Dick was upset that he wasn't picked and argued that he would do a better job. After all, he was the one who understood the various positions that PL had adopted. Back then, those SDS members who could argue politics were considered our "leaders." They were eloquent and charismatic. Each faction had at least one of these leaders who people looked to for guidance. I also thought Dick would do a better job than I would. He was the one who could argue politically, and people looked to him for leadership. I was just someone who could help organize people into action. I was, after all, Dick's wife, not a political person in my own right. That is how I thought back then.

I've often wondered if PL picked me because they thought that I would follow right along with whatever the party line or position was.

If that was the case, it was later to backfire big time for PL. As their representative, I was to take a trip through the South with the purpose of trying to persuade people to follow PL's version of SDS. The proposed trip created tension between Dick and me, but despite that, off I went in the summer of 1969. I took my best friend with me, Lynn Jones (formerly Lynn Weathersbee), and her little sister, Paula (Weathersbee) Campbell (currently known as Paula Munro). We were in our early twenties, and Paula had become a widow just weeks before when her husband was killed in Vietnam. Lynn was also in WSA, and she had left the Chicago SDS Convention when she received the news about Paula's husband. Lynn wanted Paula to come on our trip to get her mind off her loss. Lynn and Paula were very close—the kind of closeness that any two sisters would desire for their relationship.

We began our trip with a list of names and phone numbers that we had been given by PL. Our goal was to find these people and try to talk to them. It was a somewhat dangerous trip, since our purpose had to be kept secret from people we casually met along the way. Anticommunism was rampant, and we would certainly be classified as "outside agitators" at least, if not "dirty commie rats." Since we were traveling through the South, we decided that we might as well head up north to Tennessee to spend a night with Lynn and Paula's aunt and uncle. They were, however, very conservative and our real purpose had to be hidden from them. We arrived late at night and the aunt was kind enough to fix us some pancakes.

This trip, you have to understand, was somewhat overwhelming, since we felt pretty clueless about what we were doing. Imagine our sitting at this table, tired, very uptight, and then, in an effort to stop the syrup pitcher from dripping off the spout, I tipped it back in the wrong direction without noticing and soon found myself with a lap full of sticky liquid. Their dog really loved this and we were in hysterics at the dog and the incredible mess. It was one of those situations that can still make you laugh until you cry decades later. Early the next morning, however, when Lynn noticed that the aunt had somehow found a copy of *Challenge* (maybe in our car), and had underlined the word "communism" multiple times, along with some other passages, we realized it was definitely time to leave.

Some of our contacts were simply the names of leftist bookstores and some were actual people. We didn't have the benefit of technology, and if someone didn't answer the phone we didn't make contact. We tried to find people in Jackson, Mississippi, and at Duke University in North Carolina. We did make contact in Birmingham, Alabama, and it was one time I wished we hadn't. People in Birmingham had us come to speak at someone's house. There were maybe ten or fifteen people there. They said that someone else just happened to be passing through town and that they would be over to debate us. The person who was traveling through was none other than Anne Braden, famous civil rights activist, journalist, professor, and a leader of the Southern Conference Educational Fund (SCEF). At the time, I had no clue who she was and what an honor it was to meet her. Although my memory of this event is hazy, I do remember that I couldn't really defend PL's positions very well.

We continued our trip and headed to Gainesville, Florida, where we looked for a contact. The trip was hot as hell. We had no air conditioning in our car and we would periodically stop at any gas station and use their water hose to drench ourselves before getting back into the car. It was such a crazy trip, full of pranks, like driving off and leaving each other in a parking lot, just for the fun of it.

Somewhere in Florida, in the midst of the stifling humidity, we started to hear about an approaching hurricane. It was heading right for us! We canceled our plans to go further into Florida and headed back into Mississippi—and so did the hurricane. We ended up in a little town where the eye of the storm was headed and we couldn't find any place to stay. As the storm approached, every available accommodation was filled up with people equally desperate. Motels even rented out their linen closets to people. We drove to the courthouse/police station, where a taxi driver saw us and came over to ask if we needed a place to get shelter from the storm. He offered us his little camper trailer. We were afraid he was a serial killer, but with the storm bearing down on us we had no choice. We spent a very long and sleepless night in this tiny camper, which rocked back and forth as gusts of wind would slam against it and lightning would temporarily illuminate our surroundings, darkened when the electricity had gone out. If all that wasn't bad enough, for some reason the storm brought ants to the surface and we were inundated with them inside the trailer. This storm happened to be Hurricane Camille, second only to Katrina in strength, with winds up to 175 miles an hour. We found out the next morning at daylight just how much damage there was all around us. Trees and power lines were down everywhere. We slowly wove our way around debris and out of there. The destruction stayed around us for the entire day and in fact all the way back to New Orleans. It was a killer storm, and 259 people had lost their lives the night before. We were truly lucky to be alive.

When the three of us finally arrived in New Orleans, I called PL people up north and they wanted me to fly there for a national meeting of the leadership of WSA. Lynn and Paula drove back to Austin without me and thus ended our trip through the South. Although we had a memorable trip laughing our way across the South, it was almost a complete failure as far as convincing people to join PL's SDS. I was unprepared theoretically to defend PL's political positions, and this was related to how education was conducted within PL and the WSA.

As I wrote earlier, we had WSA study groups where we studied *Challenge*, as well as theoretical writings from the Russian and Chinese revolution. We did not read opposing positions from other US leftist organizations or international revolutionary movements. I have come to believe that there is no way to deeply understand any political position without reading some opposing views on that subject as well. This error of limiting education and discussion to only those writings that support the "party line" was one of the fundamental errors that were made across the Left in the 1960s. It led to the implosion of organizations instead of their growth through political dialogue.

Among all leftist organizations focusing on their particular viewpoint to the detriment of others, PL was one of the worst. This was one of the most destructive errors in the movement. Not only were we discouraged from investigating other positions, but any other groups or governments on the Left—in fact, the entire international Left—were, according to PL, also all wrong. By some unexplained enlightenment, PL was the "sole keeper of the Truth and the Way," except for China and the deceased founders of Marxism-Leninism. All others were considered to have sold out, been bought off, or were just plain wrong and revisionist. To this day, it still amazes me how arrogant white Americans can be. But then again, many white Americans consider themselves to be part of the "chosen people" (Jewish) or "born again" Christians who are just lucky enough to be the only ones going to heaven out of the entire global population. Is it any wonder our politics would reflect this same exclusivity and superiority?

Dick's and my marriage ended within a week after that trip through the South. It was a turning point in my life. Not only did I decide to move to New York City, but I was, for the first time in my life, really on my own. In the fall of 1969 I joined PL in New York. I lived on the Upper West Side of Manhattan, and I got a job as a worker on the Columbia University campus, where I was to help organize the strategy of the Campus WSA. Because I had a Southern accent, people in New York thought that I was a "hillbilly," and that actually helped me get a job on the campus as a cafeteria worker, where I was the only white worker and the only one who spoke English as my first language.

With me working on the inside and the WSA on the outside among the students, we organized a boycott of this cafeteria when the supervisor tried to lay off an elderly survivor of the Nazi concentration camps. The students supported the boycott, and the lady with the deathcamp tattoo on her wrist was hired back. This was a good example of how the WSA operated. The supervisor tried to goad me into saying or doing something that would give him grounds to fire me, but I stayed quiet and kept cutting pies and fixing salads in little bowls. There were even better examples that came later after I left PL and joined a collective of campus workers.

The political contradictions in New York City were much sharper than they had been in Austin. The Black Panther Party was strong and visible all over New York. They hated PL because PL opposed the concept of Black Power and charged that their leadership had "sold out." For PL, it was all about fixing economics, which in turn would fix all other problems. They were under the illusion that changing the US government to a socialist government would automatically make racism go away. This is wrong, wrong, wrong—in so many ways. Yet many on the American Left continue to downplay the fact that racism cuts across more than just economics. There are no guarantees that racism, sexism, or other forms of discrimination and oppression would be abolished because someone changed the economic order of things.

At any rate, it was so tense in New York that PL members selling *Challenge* on the street would be beaten up by Black Panther Party members. This got our attention. We didn't understand why PL was hated so much. In 1970 we in WSA began to question PL's positions on racism, black nationalism, and Black Power. We began to study and question even though internal discussion was severely discouraged. Almost our entire group of young college students in and around WSA in upper Manhattan realized that PL's position was wrong.

At least half, or maybe even three-fourths, of the WSA in New York City left PL at the same time. Bill Epton, the vice-chairman of PL and a well-known African American activist in Harlem, and Jerry Tung, who was highly respected in PL and who later became the chairman of the Communist Workers Party, had already left a few months before, and this was a contributing factor for many of us in making the decision to leave PL. We were labeled cops, agents, and enemies of the people. This was to be only the first political disappointment for me as the years would go by. Other organizations on the Left treated internal discussion and differences in much the same way, and this even led to violence between organizations that should have been able to work together. We didn't value unity very highly, and we treated ideological differences between comrades and organizations as though anyone who disagreed with us was our mortal enemy.

Huge egos and individuality were disastrous elements of capitalist relationships within the movement. Just as racism would not automatically go away, capitalist relationships between people will not automatically go away if not consciously confronted. This includes not only racism but also male domination and the oppression of the LGBT community. PL was adamantly opposed to gay rights, and gay people were not permitted to join the organization.

In spite of the personal attacks, most of us did not drop out of the movement. Instead, we organized ourselves into a collective around our opposition to PL and its positions on racism, etc. I was elected the leader. Who would have thought?! Certainly not PL, and certainly not me!

We really did believe in the concept of a worker-student alliance. After leaving PL and leading the group on the Upper West Side of Manhattan who left PL together, I was asked to join a Maoist collective of campus blue-collar Columbia University workers. This group was led by the president and vice-president of Local 241 of the Transport Workers Union on campus. Bill Lyons, the president, was an older white man and an electrician, and the vice-president, Nessie Dean, was an older black man and a janitor. This union included plumbers, security guards, carpenters, and shipping and delivery workers— everyone but the clerical, medical, and cafeteria staff. These workers were members of Local 1199 of the National Union of Hospital and Health Care Employees. I was a member of Local 1199.

These two unions worked together and in alliance with student-led actions on campus. Many of the Columbia University actions were led by the campus workers and, in particular, by this Maoist collective. We won every single struggle that we took on. The university was absolutely blocked from laying off any campus worker. This small collective of maybe five people was led by Bill Lyons, who, upon discovering the writings of Mao, took his vacation days and simply read Mao's *Collected Works*. Being a part of this collective was one of the most amazing political experiences I have ever had. I would watch in awe, because they knew just what to do and say.

Our activities reached beyond trade union issues. In May 1970 the Nixon administration declared that it had expanded the war into Cambodia and was bombing that country. Over 700 campuses around the country went out on strike. Students had been shot and killed at Kent State and Jackson State Universities. Columbia's students, staff, and workers declared a strike and totally shut the school down, and the faculty voted to give "passing" (as opposed to letter) grades for that quarter on transcripts. Many of us took over different campus buildings and chained ourselves inside as part of the strike. One moment from that strike I have never forgotten is the image of the famous poet Allen Ginsberg late one night, standing outside the building that I was locked in and his reading poetry to the people inside our building. We were on one of the upper floors. It was such an amazing show of his solidarity with us.

It was a time of intense political activity. We organized busloads of people from the community and campus to go to one of the giant antiwar demonstrations in Washington, DC More than once campus workers and staff, students and community people marched through the streets of Columbia's surrounding neighborhoods in angry rock-throwing, trash-burning demonstrations against the war and weapons research on campus. It was beautiful. Progressive Labor Party could claim to have planted the seeds through its WSA project, but they were unable to carry it out because of their incorrect positions on racism and internal struggle, and because of the party's general arrogance. These were wonderful times in many ways for me. Even so, by 1972, I was ready to come back home to Texas to be around my political friends and my family. One can be surrounded by people in New York City and still be lonely. I missed trees and grass!

There were some very good things about PL and what it brought to the movement. One of the best things about PL is that it linked up our antimaterialism, alienation, commitment to justice and equality and longing for a better society to a worldview that made us question capitalism for the first time. PL introduced us to socialism, communism, and political theory. PL encouraged us to work in communities and to be pro-union. Many of us, for the first time in our lives, got working-class jobs, and we learned wisdom from the people. PL introduced us to an anti-imperialist internationalist viewpoint, even though it arrogantly saw itself as having wisdom, knowledge, and commitment superior to all others. For this reason, PL was hated by the Left, but it took us a few years to comprehend this and to understand why. To our credit, we finally got it and got out.

Looking at how we organize ourselves now, this idea of internal differences being a menacing and threatening thing and something to fear and discourage is fundamentally incorrect and may even be what has destroyed socialist societies. If society is constantly changing, and we know that it is, then how can an organization that claims to want to lead a society not thrive on debate? How can it lead if its leaders are rigidly and fearfully holding on to views that have perhaps already become obsolete?

This relates very closely to democratic centralism, which is how most of the revolutionary groups in the 1960s and 1970s were structured. We say that we trust the masses and that they are to lead, but then we organize ourselves in a top-down, centralized way in order to protect ourselves from the masses, which is no different than a capitalist-corporate view of the people below. Democracy is thrown out of a skyscraper window. This is a deep-seated attitude and contradiction that I think each of us will have to tackle. Society does not change in a smooth and gentle way. We need to embrace that struggle and trust that, even when there are ebbs and flows, society will, in the end, continue to move forward. I do believe that with all my heart.

The truth is that we now need to go further and move in a more holistic way toward a new society than did the old Marxist-Leninist governments. As Mao stated many years ago, "If you don't hit it, it won't fall." This applies particularly to racism, sexism, and how we view the balance between leadership and those at the grassroots level. Fighting solely for economic socialism is inadequate. The Left movement continues to move forward in a holistic way with or without state power, and that is a beautiful thing that we are currently witnessing.

The 2017 Women's March on Washington demonstrated a new kind of egalitarian leadership where there were no superstar leaders. The Women's March was very inclusive racially, and it modeled gender equality. It was multigenerational and multi-issue. None of this should be taken for granted. The Left movement took a leap forward, turning a corner with this march, but it was because we have learned better through years of struggle.

When I first became involved in the Movement, it seemed that, as I wrote earlier, most, but not all, women in the Movement were connected to a man. I sensed this and remember thinking that I would just get "lost" if I were on my own. Besides, it was scary to be on my own with the Left culture being so free and open in so many ways, which was so different to me. I was indeed intimidated by this openness after living the life of a strict Southern Baptist and would not have known how to navigate through this as an unattached woman.

What someone reading this might not understand is what a radical rupture it was for me to join the Left. I lost most of my high school friends and gave up my high school fiancé, Maurice, to get involved in the movement. My parents did not approve of the movement or of Dick at the time. I didn't get invited to my friends' weddings and baby showers. Not even my sisters approved. Of course, over time most of this changed and I became respected and respectable, but certainly not back then. This was true for all of us who grew up in the South. At first I was being "duped" by communists. At some point down the road I became the duper. I was sad but at the same time at peace with being an outlaw from society. I stopped wearing makeup, setting my hair, and painting my fingernails. Scandalous, for sure, back then!

My experiences in WSA and PL taught me to stand on my own two political feet. I and other women had to struggle to be heard in a meeting. Anything we said was not taken seriously, and very often the men would simply ignore the woman talking and have side conversations among themselves. It was an uphill battle to be really heard, and often we got emotional in our attempts to be heard. This was true within PL as well as WSA, but at least we were taken in as members and there was some encouragement to develop our own political skills. So, all in all, I owe PL a lot. I don't know if I would have gone on to get active in SDS without PL's presence there because the other factions were so far removed from my lifestyle and my focus on the community. I think PL gave birth to many of us on the Left.

After I moved back to Texas, I went on to join one of the other opposing factions of SDS, RYM II, which had evolved into the October League. I founded the October League in Texas and also opened a bookstore in Houston, Texas. The bookstore was located near Texas Southern University, a historically black university. I called it Prairie Fire Bookstore, named after a quotation by Mao: "A Single Spark Can Start a Prairie Fire." At that time, Texas was without a political bookstore that represented the New Left. I organized a collective to run the bookstore, and almost everyone in it joined the October League. I had truly embraced the need for education on the Left, but I was still slow to truly appreciate open debate and discussion, since the bookstore was aligned with the October League and they encouraged me to not sell the publications of other US organizations. It took me awhile to figure that one out and why that was incorrect. We did, however, sell books and periodicals from international Left movements.

Many of us in the October League left the organization after Mao died and the leadership in China disavowed many of the contributions that had been made during the controversial Great Proletarian Cultural Revolution. We valued the barefoot doctors who were sent out to the countryside and many other reforms that were aimed at lessening class distinctions over time. The October League followed the leadership in China, and it was one of the deciding factors for us, along with internal contradictions such as the lack of internal open debate. After leaving the October League (and having the same experience again of being treated as the enemy for bringing opposing views to the predominant "party line"), I joined the Communist Workers League in Los Angeles. This was a brief membership, since my husband at the time and I had two small children and the Communist Workers League and another organization were beating each other up on the street.

The atmosphere was too crazy and immature for us as young parents.

As I write this, I am now seventy-two years old. I still live by Mao's philosophy. "Serve the People" and "Combat Liberalism" (in relationships) are two essays by Mao Zedong that I have used as guides throughout my life. I had gone to jail once in Alabama and once in Austin during the civil rights movement. This changed my life forever. While in county jail in Linden, Alabama, I discovered something that helped to shape the rest of my life. I had been arrested for telling the chief of police of Demopolis, Alabama, that he was the best liar I had ever met. This happened to take place in a courtroom, where they had just found Dick guilty of sixteen counts of vagrancy (not having a job) and driving without an Alabama driver's license (even though he had a Texas license). He had been arrested off and on all during the summer as a form of harassment. I was found guilty of contempt of court and given five days in jail and a $50 fine. That same day they arrested our lawyer from New York, Don Jellinick, for practicing law without a license, even though he was a famous New York attorney. And, last but not least, that same day they arrested Charlie Saulsberry, a black activist from Demopolis. His charge was being in a white neighborhood after dark.

The male prisoners were on the lower floor of the jail and I was by myself upstairs except for one woman in the next cell down the hall. I got the woman next door, a black woman whose face I never saw, to join me in flushing our toilets all day, except for when we heard the jailer coming. Anything to cost them money, right? As a teacher later in life, I would remember my actions as students would do destructive things in the classroom to get back at the educational system they hated. You could say that the universe stepped in because, when I wasn't flushing the toilet, I realized that there was a bar of soap in my cell and that I might be able to do something with it to pass the time away. I started to carve it with my fingernails and a straight pin like you use in sewing that I also found in my cell. I carved a likeness of Dick's head and discovered that I could do art! That turned out to be a huge gift to my life. I later became an artist and an art teacher and had a twenty-year career working with inner-city youth. I set the stage for them to discover what beautiful and powerful beings they were and what magic they could create. This was my way to give back to the universe again.

One of those five days in jail was a Friday, and I could hear a football game off in the distance that Friday night. I had been popular in high school and always performed with a dance group at halftime. As I heard the band playing, I made a promise to myself that I would never go back to my old life, where I was not involved in what was happening in the world. That was in 1966, and I am writing this in 2017 to tell you that I have kept that promise to myself all these years.

I am a staunch supporter of open debate, democracy within an organization, women's and LGBT rights, and Black Power—and I have kept the focus on organizing in the community, wherever that has taken me. As a high school art teacher, I became the faculty sponsor for the Gay-Straight Alliance on campus. I fought against institutional racism within the College Board Advanced Placement Test for World Art, which actually included only 10 percent of art from the rest of the world besides the US and Europe. I was a staunch supporter of equal rights in the schools that I taught in, both in Seattle and in San Antonio, whether it was backing a student or a good administrator.

When I first entered the Left, my personal life to some extent defined my political life by who I could relate to the most on a personal level. As I look back on my life, I would say that my political life now defines my personal life. I have been married three times—to Tom, Dick and, not Harry but Gary (really, but not in that order). All three husbands were in the movement to one extent or the other. This has been a necessity, as I find that many men do not really want a strong, busy activist for a partner unless they appreciate and respect that activism themselves. I live in Texas now, and finding a like-minded man my age is beyond difficult. I have been single by choice for the last twenty years, although I am forever an optimist. My closest friends most often, but not always, have a similar world outlook to mine because it's not much fun to have to get into a debate, about racism for instance, when you're trying to take some time to relax and just enjoy life.

They say that life is stranger than fiction, and I guess I would have to agree. As I try to find my way through a rapidly changing society in every way, I'm still living life out loud. No day is long enough, and I am never bored. My mantra is "Stay healthy to be able to fight another day."

I am retired now and am doing my own art. Currently, I'm working on a painting that is about racism and the interlocking relationship of humans and nature. I am an active member of the SNCC Legacy Project/Black Power Chronicles national group in San Antonio, Texas. I am also on the Executive Board of the San Antonio NAACP. I should be more active in electoral politics, but at this point it is still hard for me to be a believer in a process that seems so rigged toward keeping the wealthy in control of the government. I believe that lifestyle needs to change along with economics, and I think that the factions opposing PL understood this first. WE MUST MODEL AND LIVE THE VALUES OF A NEW SOCIETY, as well as opposing the oppressive capitalist government. Progressive Labor Party missed this point entirely. The younger generation on the Left seems to know this and to have embraced this as essential in fighting for a better society, so much so that they are now voicing a preference for how the movement functions without "guru" leaders, as seen in the 2017 Women's Marches around the country. The marches were a beautiful example of exactly this. Onward to a better society in EVERY way, not just economically!

Becky Brenner lives in San Antonio, Texas. She is currently an activist in the black community, as well as an active supporter of the Native American and immigrant struggles. She is working on a painting about what is most important to her—racism, spirituality, and our unity with nature.

5

My SDS Activist Years in New Orleans

Eric A. Gordon
(Tulane)

Yale's SDS chapter sent a bus down to Washington, DC, for the first national march against the war in Vietnam on April 17, 1965, and I was on it. I didn't know anyone in the chapter, though, and I had no involvement with it for the remaining year-plus of my undergraduate career there. For graduate school, I got a National Defense Foreign Language fellowship to continue toward a master's degree in Latin American Studies at Tulane. Upon arriving in New Orleans in the fall of 1966, I attended a South-wide antiwar conference with about forty people and met the essential leftwing leadership in town. The main impression I came away with was factionalism. I found the Trotskyist Spartacist League particularly unhinged, endlessly agitating to establish a new Communist Fourth International.

Ed Clark lived in New Orleans, a nicotine-drenched guy I had met a couple of months previously in New York at a gathering sponsored by the Progressive Labor Party; he was the Southern representative for PL and I got to know him well. For the next three years or so, although I never joined (and Ed didn't try to recruit me), PL offered broad ideological guidance. PL helped me to concretize the concept of class, helping me to understand my own role in the class struggle and ask what sacrifices I was prepared to make for a socialist future. In those days you were either part of the solution or part of the problem.

My professors at Tulane, and classmates as well, cringed whenever I uttered the word "imperialism." By way of further characterizing Tulane at that time, the university had just started admitting African American students a couple of years before. But I only intended to stay there two years to get my master's degree. Thinking about a thesis topic that could get me a travel grant to Brazil for the following summer, I hit upon the opera in nineteenth-century Rio de Janeiro.

At my first demonstration in New Orleans, I joined twenty-five people in the Vietnam Committee at the airport Hilton picketing a speech by Secretary of State Dean Rusk, who was speaking for prowar Democratic Congressman Hale Boggs (whom we dubbed Bale Hoggs). A picture of me in that demonstration appeared in the *Times-Picayune* on October 19. The local right wing turned out as well, picketing Boggs for being too liberal! My new friends in the antiwar movement advised me that one way to make sure my New Haven draft board would be uninterested in my doing military service would be to show a committed history of political activism, so I welcomed every item added to my avoid-Vietnam-at-all-costs résumé.

The Vietnam Committee in New Orleans understood the connection between the war and rising costs at home. A January 1967 vote in the city asked people to decide if they wanted an additional percentage point on sales tax (from 4 percent to 5 percent), or a 1 percent income tax, a choice, as we put it in a flier distributed in poorer neighborhoods, "between hanging yourself and slitting your throat." Extra money for running the city's business could easily be gotten instead by taxing the port or industrial profits. Our objective was to sharpen class awareness.

Sporting a new name, the New Orleans Committee to End the War in Vietnam picketed on January 26 in front of International House in downtown New Orleans for welcoming the ambassador of apartheid South Africa as a speaker. Our February newsletter carried an unsigned item about Tulane that powerfully indicated that campus activism should be my natural place. It spoke of the "coincidence" that Tulane President Herbert Eugene Longenecker, Ph.D., D.Sc., LL.D., also belonged to the Institute for Defense Analysis. Vietnam, which had no record of bubonic plague before 1961, was then the only country in the world where an epidemic of it was occurring, and Longenecker was a biochemist by profession and on the advisory panel for biological and chemical warfare in the Office of the Assistant Secretary of Defense for Research and Development from 1953 to 1961, the same year the plague first appeared. One way university students could be effective against the war machine was to use their research skills to uncover and expose these corporate-military-university ties.

All around the country Students for a Democratic Society was taking campuses by storm. In March 1967, friends and I drove for twenty-seven hours to and from Norman, Oklahoma, for a weekend regional gathering of SDS. We represented our group, called Movement for a Democratic Society (MDS), a loosely structured nonstudent, non-campus-based chapter of SDS. Up to this point there still was no campus SDS chapter in New Orleans. We concluded that our level of anti-imperialist political consciousness in New Orleans was far higher than any other group represented at the Norman meeting.

The war and the draft: the two inescapable co-factors of sentient life in those days. In early 1967 SDS started encouraging the formation of local draft resisters unions. If any member was called for his physical, he and his fellow members would go down to the draft board with literature, start raising a ruckus distributing it and talking to the other draftees about the war in terms radical enough that the draft board would find the individual "physically unfit." Indeed, I knew several guys in New Orleans who had been declared 4-F owing to their anti-war activism. Inductees who were caught reading the *Little Red Book* by Chairman Mao were speedily de-inducted!

In New York, the huge April 15 Mobilization against the war attracted some 125,000 (according to the police, so attendance was possibly substantially more). SDS did not actively promote the Mobe, however, on the grounds that these big twice-a-year demonstrations represented top-down leadership not committed to creating a lasting movement of the poor, people of color, and workers and students for radical change. In that sense we separated ourselves from the pacifists, the Communist Party, the Socialist Workers Party, and liberal Democrats. At the time I must have agreed with this line, but I disagree with it now. The immediate demand on the front burner was to end the war, and for that any and all sectors of the population that could be mobilized to march, protest, write letters, etc., should be engaged, even if not all reciting the same radical catechism. Signs of our fatal sectarianism in SDS could be seen already.

On April 1, 1967, our local lefties sponsored a series of demonstrations against Anastasio Somoza, the Nicaraguan dictator, first outside a downtown hotel where he spoke at a business council meeting, and then on the Tulane campus, where the university administration welcomed him as an honored guest. Tulane officials were shocked by the outpouring of hatred for this man. The university's many Latin American students all came out to join our city-wide Left to make his visit memorable and embarrassing. They claimed that Somoza wouldn't have dared set foot on any university campus in Latin America, and certainly not in his own country. I will never forget hearing the Latin Americans screaming out the word *"asesino!"*—murderer!—and felt for those thrilling few minutes that we had been transported to some militant Latin American capital like Havana or Bogotá.

On the following day, students at school told me they had seen me interviewed on local television. A few days later, New Orleans Mayor Victor Schiro declared on TV that the picketers had been paid (Somoza's claim, no doubt). I wrote to the TV station that every night read a letter to the editor over the air—and part of mine was read, saying how despite the mayor's cynical insinuations, our only reward had been the moral satisfaction of opposing dictatorship.

While personally I had no moral objections to marijuana, peyote, or LSD, we already had a police spy in our movement who ratted out drug use and at least twice got some Tulane students arrested. Cases of police entrapment were familiar to us. It was just politically stupid to do drugs, because we would only be punished for our politics. This thinking came from PL, I believe, because it was hardly universal everywhere in the movement.

That May I joined the Southern Student Organizing Committee (SSOC), based in Nashville, a group in solidarity with the civil rights movement, and with student issues on Southern campuses. I got a membership card with a letter that opened with "SSOC IS A WHITE TORNADO!"—an expression which would prove later on to bear some significance. At SSOC's convention in Asheville, NC, May 5–7, which our MDS-PL comrade Ed Clark attended, the organization appeared to step out in a bold new direction of trying to build a revolutionary labor-oriented movement, not merely position itself as (in Ed's damning words) "left of the KKK and right of SDS."

I did win a research travel grant to Brazil that summer. En route I stopped over in Guyana, where I had introductions from a dear friend and former CP member to Cheddi and Janet Jagan. Cheddi had been prime minister of pre-independent British Guiana from 1957 to 1964. I spent hours with them and other members of their People's Progressive Party and saw how slowly and patiently a popular Marxist movement had been built over the course of years. My "Letter from Guyana" appeared in the August *MDS Newsletter*. Compared to our inchoate, divisive, and spontaneous movements at home, I saw up-close a well-functioning radical party truly preparing to hold the reins of state power, which they eventually did.

Upon my return to New Orleans, I discovered that our movement, or a segment of it, had been infiltrated. A 150-page report had been issued by the Louisiana state HUAC, based on the testimony of three cops who had joined the Spartacists. But most of us in the larger movement were mentioned.

With all the ferment boiling over around the country, I resolved to do something finally at Tulane. I called a meeting for political action, and about seventy-five students turned out on September 28. That marked the beginning of Tulane SDS. I was elected president. The student newspaper, the *Hullabaloo*, reported on the meeting, quoting me as to what kind of American society I envisioned: "We should not dismiss the writing of Marxist thinkers in the formation of an ideology." We began the tortuous process of getting recognition as a student group on campus. By mid-October *Hullabaloo* started covering SDS regularly: in one issue three of the four front-page articles reported on SDS. Tulane pulsed with excitement that it could now count itself among the prominent American universities with SDS chapters.

The draft loomed ever larger for me now: I would not be a registered student as of the spring, since my master's program was a three-semester degree. My fight against the draft lasted many months, although I did have options: dismissal on political grounds, as a conscientious objector, or for the disqualifying medical reason of a lifelong skin condition, atopic dermatitis.

MDS remained active on many fronts. Our newsletter had almost 500 subscribers, mostly in the South, and carried articles of broad interest. One trade union campaign supported the women of Blue Ridge, Georgia, on a wildcat strike against Levi Strauss. MDS appealed to store owners not to order, stock, or sell Levi Strauss products for the duration of the strike and sponsored a public Labor Day burn-in of Levis in City Park.

Another issue that roiled campuses around the country involved career recruiting, specifically for the military and the CIA, and for privately owned companies, such as Dow Chemical, that profited obscenely from the war machine. November 6–7, 1967, saw SDS demonstrations against CIA recruiting on the Tulane campus. I wrote a spirited protest letter to *Hullabaloo*, complaining about the university's invitation of members of the Intelligence Division of the NOPD to monitor our peaceful on-campus activity, since dossiers downtown or in Washington had frequently been used to damage the careers of protesters. In the next round of career recruiting, a month later, the United Fruit Company was on the recruitment roster, so I started preparing for them. It may have enhanced our big, bad image that the university denied official recognition to SDS because I would not, as the group's coordinator, promise not to hold disruptive demonstrations. I made sure to pick up extra copies of the *Hullabaloo* issues that featured my writings or reportage about me to send to my New Haven draft board!

I started probing Tulane's connections to the CIA, Big Business, and imperialist politics. It became clear that Tulane's emphasis on Central America, in its Latin American Studies Department, had everything to do with the United Fruit Company's support for the university. So when United Fruit recruiters made their anticipated appearance at career day, SDS went into action. We published a three-page document that led off with Pablo Neruda's great poem about the Nicaraguan dictatorship and its subservience to the company. We mentioned that the president of the university lived in a mansion adjacent to campus that had been donated by Samuel Zemurray, longtime head of United Fruit. Zemurray also donated a dormitory hall, a significant collection of Mayan artifacts, and an endowed chair in Middle American Research.

In the early 1950s, a former president of Tulane, Rufus C. Harris, was an attorney for United Fruit. He also sat on the board of the National Planning Association, which in 1958 published a whitewash entitled *The United Fruit Company in Latin America*, only four years after the company, along with the CIA, had been implicated in the overthrow of Jacobo Arbenz, a democratically elected reformist president of Guatemala (John Foster Dulles and his brother Allen both had strong ties to United Fruit). Finally, we traced the interlocking membership of Tulane board members with various banks (Hibernia, Whitney, Chase Manhattan) having United Fruit connections. "Now here's a curious note," our SDS leaflet read: "There is every reason to believe that the William Gause who appeared on campus November 6–7, 1967, recruiting for the CIA, is the same William Gause who was the United Fruit Company's Southern Passenger Traveling Agent back in the late 1930s."

This kind of research flourished among SDS chapters around the country. I surmised that various government contracts with Tulane professors to study unions, political parties and processes, legal developments, rural conditions, etc., in Central America, had to be CIA monies laundered into academic respectability. I later found out that the head of my department was keeping a political file on me. The kind of work I and others in SDS did directly threatened to blow the cover on collaborating professors and departments.

Tulane SDS began getting national attention, first of all in *New Left Notes*, the SDS newspaper; and we were mentioned in the December 25 issue of *Newsweek* in a lengthy article on the new generation of college newspapers. The editor of the Tulane *Hullabaloo* resigned after being threatened by the administration over an article about SDS's antiwar activities on campus.

Some of the local MDS folks had started an earnest draft counseling project, which I later helped to run. One of the leaflets we distributed mentioned American deaths so far: 19,000. And it asked, "How many years will it go on?" It sickens me that before the Vietnamese finally defeated the US in 1975, our country had lost *three times* that many of our young people.

The FBI naturally trailed my every move, continuing "to follow and report subject's activities which may constitute a violation of the Selective Service Act of 1948." Helpfully, I can cite from my file, which I obtained years later under the Freedom of Information Act, the many specific dates on which I demonstrated in front of the Federal Building in New Orleans. We signed our leaflets with the name Draft Resisters Union Local #3—we just added #3 to suggest that we formed part of a much larger project. My file reveals FBI coordination with the NOPD and my draft board, and access to my student record at Tulane. FBI special agents devoted several reports to the use of obscenity in our handouts (the words "bullshit," "big-assed," and "shit-eating") and actually went to the trouble of obliterating the words in their copies of the leaflet and overlaying them with the word "obscene." My, the FBI were a prissy bunch, weren't they?

Factional infighting had become very abrasive, particularly between PL and the Communist Party. The struggle became especially acute when Gene McCarthy started running in the Democratic primaries, and the local liberals and the local CP representative supported his campaign. Ed Clark and Fred Lacey, both of them PL members with substantial influence in MDS, wrote a scorching attack in our newsletter on the CP politics of always supporting Democratic candidates, but only by being "anti" the Republican. "A Communist" replied in the next issue, refuting some of their arguments. I was too embedded in the politics of "my side" to notice how ugly and counterproductive all this had become. A lot of our fights in those days boiled down to differences over the questions, How soon can we make a revolution? and What does it take to get there? In its seasoned experience, the CP saw *no* revolution waiting around the corner, so they tempered their enthusiasm, trying to brace people for a long, slow lifetime of struggle demanding an almost inhuman patience.

That spring the issue started heating up between SDS and the Southern Student Organizing Committee. SDS had few chapters in the Southern states, but we felt that our politics were better than SSOC's. SSOC had chosen to work with white students, leaving black organizing to groups such as the Student Non-Violent Coordinating Committee, and other broad coalition work to the Southern Christian Educational Fund (SCEF). (To be fair, SDS did most of its organizing among white students as well.)

Finally, in March, our Tulane chapter applied for formal SDS affiliation. The five constituting members included myself, Ed Dubinsky (our faculty adviser), Carol Kates, Cathy Cade, and Lee Walker. That month Tulane rose up in great numbers, some 2,000, to protest arbitrary censorship of the *Hullabaloo*. More and more, students came to realize just who owned the place. (Fun fact: Newt Gingrich, graduate student in history, participated in the anticensorship movement.)

In early 1968 President Johnson escalated his demand for 200,000 more American troops in Vietnam, and deferments became harder and harder to secure. My war with Selective Service had become nearly a full-time job.

On April 4, 1968, Dr. Martin Luther King, Jr., was shot down in Memphis, while supporting the city's striking sanitation workers. Riots broke out in response across the country, and a gray pall of smoke hung over the Tulane campus. Despite my political rhetoric, I admit that my attention had been so intensely focused on the war and the draft that I had not truly related much to people of color, the civil rights movement, or with working people on the job. That was a limitation of SDS and the student movement, and a reflection of my own class background. But MDS did sponsor an April 10 demonstration protesting the Tennessee Life Insurance Co., as responsible for the plight of the Memphis sanitation workers, who won their battle after a sixty-five-day strike.

In those same weeks, SDS folks avidly attended the trial of H. Rap Brown, chairman of the Student Non-Violent Coordinating Committee since May 1967, who was being held at a downtown courthouse on federal firearms charges. Brown had traveled to Cuba and North Vietnam, and SNCC had turned left, embracing revolutionary anti-imperialist politics alongside its domestic civil rights agenda. With his fiery rhetoric, and with his announcement that the organization he headed would drop the word "nonviolent" from its name, he had become a lightning rod for government attention. Our MDS newsletter carried regular updates on his case.

The summer of 1968 found me in Europe and North Africa. That year saw revolt among workers and students in Paris. It was also the year of Prague Spring and the Soviet troops marching in to crush the indigenous Czech movement toward liberalization. That incident dashed to pieces many people's hopes for "socialism with a human face." The Soviet Union seemed unreformable and just as imperialistic as the US. *New Left Notes*, the national SDS newspaper, published my impressions of Paris. A brief excerpt:

> "France will never be the same again," everyone says. That depends on what you mean by "different." I do not see any reason to believe that the basic relationship of the French worker to his work will be any different in the foreseeable future. One of the posters put it succinctly. It showed a hand with a piece of chalk conjugating De Gaulle's new verb: "I participate, you participate, he participates, we participate, you participate, they profit."

My biases showed in that assessment. I could not imagine a revolution of only youth and students, a position that soon would become an influential line of thought in SDS. As those divisions started appearing, I placed myself firmly in the Worker-Student Alliance camp.

At long last the draft board scheduled my preinduction physical for Friday, October 25, at the Armed Forces Examining and Entrance Station on Canal Street in New Orleans. My MDS and SDS comrades turned out in the still-dark hours of early morning with picket signs, leaflets, and chants. At the appointed time I lined up with the other guys and we filed into the gray stone fortress. Aware that I was still governed by civilian law, I never shut up as the queue moved along, ranting about the war, capitalism, the killing. "The general reaction by these other inductees," reads my FBI file, "was to laugh at GORDON's comments." As soon as we got into the waiting room inside, I opened my shirt and removed a stack of anticorporate, antiwar leaflets and started handing them out: "The real fight is here at home—the fight for a decent life for the working man in America. That means better wages and better working conditions; unions that struggle for what we want; free medical treatment for everyone; inexpensive and adequate housing; good schools...." The ever-handy FBI file indicates the following:

> GORDON checked the following items on this form which showed that he had a medical history of the following: dizziness, ear trouble, sinusitis, hay fever, skin disease, pressure in chest, leg cramps, intestinal trouble, history of broken bones, cyst, appendicitis, painful urination, boils, gonorrhea, back trouble, foot trouble, depression and homosexual tendencies.

> Item 29 on this form asked the question, "Did you have difficulty with school studies or teachers?" to which GORDON responded in writing, "During junior, senior high school, college and graduate school; I have had difficulty defining an anti-imperialist ideology against pro-capitalist textbooks and teachers."

By 10:15 a.m. I was released, with a statement that read, "Found not acceptable for induction under current standards." I received a new classification as I-Y for the "documented recurrent and chronic atopic dermatitis and GORDON's history of psychiatric treatment," but I-Y also applied to most of the politicos the military didn't want. Either way, a happy result for me at last, but it took me a very long time to forget some of the faces I saw down on Canal Street that day. I hoped they all made it back home safe and sound.

The country felt completely demoralized with the electoral choices before us that November. Often those on the Left felt they had to vote for, and even work for, the lesser of two evils merely to get an uninspired, rightwing Democrat into office. Despite whatever progressive history he'd brought from the Minnesota Farmer-Labor tradition, Hubert H. Humphrey excited no enthusiasm whatsoever. As Johnson's vice-president, he was a fervent advocate of ever more war; crowned in Chicago at a violent party convention, he had relinquished all credibility, even against Richard Nixon. Across the country, SDS demonstrated on Election Day. I remember a kind of grim, ironic Southern satisfaction some of us in New Orleans SDS felt when we saw how well racist Alabama Gov. George Wallace did. Even though for the wrong reasons, voters rejected the Democrat in this first outing of Nixon's "Southern strategy" to peel off the South for the GOP. In the late fall of 2016, as the race between Hillary Clinton and Donald Trump tightened, I read memoirs from fellow lefties from that period regretting that they had not just held their noses and voted for Humphrey.

In the spring of 1969, Louisiana HUAC came out with its report on SDS at Louisiana schools, and I was the star of that show. They had surely been in touch with the FBI and all the other federal, state, and local agencies that tracked Red activity. "Investigation has determined," says my FBI file, "he is a dedicated Marxist and thus an interview with him could cause embarrassment to the Bureau," and that "the United States government and this society are not acceptable to subject, that he believes there will be a violent revolution in this country, and that he has stated he will be in the vanguard of this revolution."

That spring, with the draft behind me now, I threw myself back into my master's thesis to get my degree, which would put me in a better position to get a teaching job. Also, it seemed almost criminal to have done all that original research and then not offer my findings to the world. I documented significant public sentiment expressed in Rio in the 1850s to the effect that opera was designed to entertain the rich, while the poor had to pay for it. My thesis broke new ground in Brazilian musicology. My very last footnote cited Chiang Ching, *The Revolution of Chinese Opera* (Peking, 1968), a product of the Great Proletarian Cultural Revolution, my own little joke and protest concerning bourgeois culture, bourgeois universities, and bourgeois degrees. I had my oral exam on the thesis at the end of May. It was approved, and I received my degree in August.

I attended the SDS National Council meeting in Austin in late March, my first national SDS gathering, as the MDS delegate. One resolution that our WSA got passed at the Austin NC became one of New Orleans MDS's proudest moments. For years national SDS had been dismissive of the South, unsure how to organize in such an unfamiliar milieu, and it largely left white student organizing to SSOC. We in SDS got to know SSOC well and did not appreciate their essential "liberalism" and worse. In part, this dispute arose from certain old ties between SSOC and the CP. A kind of "guilt by association" tainted SSOC in the eyes of PL-oriented SDSers, who considered the CP hopeless revisionists, but there were also legitimate issues on which we disagreed with SSOC.

We demanded a national commitment to "Build SDS in the South." As the capstone to our argument we had merely to point to SSOC's logo: a pair of hands shaking, one white and one black, against the background of a Confederate flag! As if to say that black and white could accept the legitimacy of that flag so hated by everyone who supported the civil rights movement. (I was told by former SSOC members, much later, that that logo was tried out only briefly in some chapters before being abandoned, but that is distinctly not my recollection.) SDS won the day, and new chapters opened up in more areas of the South, although rather belatedly, as it turned out, for the movement was already in decline because of intense factionalism.

Not long after arriving in New Orleans, I had resumed psychoanalysis with a new doctor. I had been on the couch four or five days a week all four years at Yale, the underlying issue being my latent homosexuality, for which the field had no dispassionate, empathic vocabulary. Believing it would be judged a bourgeois indulgence, I kept my analysis strictly secret from my new movement comrades.

Now I came to a momentous, if unplanned decision. I wanted to reschedule one session with my psychoanalyst for another day so that I could attend the NC meeting in Austin. He refused. I felt challenged by his overbearing attitude and got angry. He responded, "You don't have to just lie there and shout at me. It's a free country, you know—nothing's keeping you here." I said, "You're right. I'm leaving," and on the spot I got up from the couch and walked out.

My career with psychoanalysis, really from its beginning in freshman year at Yale, was a contradiction in terms. Psychoanalysis posits that we can resolve our problems in an individual way. In my case, I often felt joyless, morose, and isolated. But what exactly was I supposed to achieve under psychoanalysis? The analyst responds that that is not his business, but only to help me do what *I* really want to do.

"My" problem was not so different from most people's problem: few radicals that I knew were happy with their work. Actually, how many people in general are happy with their work? Really, what is there to be happy about if happiness means a healthy adaptation to the world around you? Yes, we must *see* the world as it is, but who would want to *accept* it that way? Only the evidence that elsewhere in the world people's lives are better in many respects, where social welfare states are in place, and that there are movements of hope and change, including here in the US, gives a person a fighting chance to even imagine being at peace with the world.

And so, at long last, I identified psychoanalysis as an inadequate vehicle by which to process my fundamental alienation from capitalist society. Given the decline of psychoanalysis in subsequent years, this may be a more universal response than I realized at the time. Some, though not all, communists or Marxists historically expressed skepticism about psychoanalysis, fearing that under repressive conditions analysts might reveal names and other information that would endanger lives, careers, and movements. But I think the real objection is precisely to an individualist approach toward problem-solving, which, by leaving the collective outside and behind, was untenable and likely to fail.

And so, after four years in New Haven and another two in New Orleans, my psychoanalysis came to an unanticipated but timely end. But there's more to say, and I'll jump ahead a bit to finish up this thread. I don't fault my analysts especially, because almost no one in those days did any better. Nowadays it is easier to recognize a person's basic homosexual inclination and have a productive, rational, empathic conversation about it. That language did not exist then. The fact that I did have some moderate success in heterosexual relationships obscured my essential sexual identity, which never occupied front and center place in my treatment. (In those years, would anyone have even used the phrase "homosexual identity?")

Since I was already a political radical, after the 1969 Stonewall Rebellion, when the modern gay movement emerged, I had little trouble transferring my activist inclinations over to the gay movement. Finally, by 1971 it had become clear that there were others like me. I was not sick, did not require treatment, and only needed the reassurance of solidarity to find myself. Many of my new friends I found outside the Left, much of which remained essentially homophobic for years.

With all my SDS involvement, I had become something of a public bête noire around town. I tried to remain relatively anonymous on my block, and I stayed particularly clear of my immediate neighbors, a family that could be accurately (though politically incorrectly) described as poor white trash. There was a sullen wife surrounded by three or four barefoot brats always in need of a good scrubbing, and a loud, hard-drinking man with unidentifiable means of support.

Decals pasted on the front door glass said it all: the Playboy bunny and a Confederate flag.

One day I returned home in my Volvo. It was still light out, and my neighbor spotted me as I drove up. He emerged from his shotgun bungalow and approached. I wondered if he was packing heat. "Coupla guys round here lookin' for you today," he offered.

"Oh?" I answered, as evasively as possible, yearning to bolt myself in the apartment as quickly and securely as I could.

"Yeah. Drove up together. One stayed in the car and the other went up to all the neighbors askin' questions."

"Huh!" I choked. "Wonder what that's about," I said, fearing the worst, feeling my Jewish nose get larger as we spoke.

"Listen, buddy, I seen how them boys operate. Federal agents, ya know." (As if I didn't.)

"Look, I dunno what you're doin' or anythin', but don't worry, I didn't tell 'em nuthin'. You're safe with me. I'm in the Klan."

I truly appreciated the comradely support, if for no other reason than the fact that I have retold that story many times since.

Not a registered student for the spring semester of 1969, I remained active as a visitor to the campus and as more or less the *éminence grise* (at twenty-four) of Tulane SDS. Tulane hosted a city-wide SDS conference on March 1 that was attended by SDS National Internal Education Secretary Fred Gordon (no relation). That season, liberal activists took the lead on the Abolish ROTC! protests that roiled the campus. Independent researchers uncovered revelatory information about the relationship between Tulane and the Institute for Defense Analysis (IDA), a Defense Dept. think-tank tasked to provide scientific and technical support to the Pentagon in developing new weapons. The IDA Board of Trustees comprised the presidents of twelve top American universities, which included our own Herbert E. Longenecker. These individuals lent their prestige to recruit scientists to conduct research on "incapacitating" gases to drive the enemy from huts and tunnels, tranquilizing darts and adhesive glue to immobilize demonstrators, and a computerized central monitoring system and data bank to store information on all American citizens. For conducting this "search-for-truth," scholars received top grants, a leave of absence from the tedium of teaching, and the promise of future grants. These IDA revelations proved that the public image presented by Tulane and other universities was (and remains) largely irrelevant to what had become their most important function—the development of the scientific, technical, and managerial knowledge necessary for the administration of a stable but inhuman society.

In the wake of the Tulane anti-ROTC struggle, several people were expelled, another few suspended for a year, and others reprimanded. SDS's faculty advisor, Ed Dubinsky, went on trial by a kangaroo court of his "peers" and was fired from the university. I was not involved legally: the university would surely have nabbed me, except they would have had to bring civil charges against me, since I was not allowed to be a registered student until the summer semester when I would receive my degree. The editor of the student yearbook wrote a letter to Longenecker, saying how unfairly the administration had handled the whole thing, and the first thing he knew he had been charged as well!

SDS responded to Tulane's draconian judgments with a bombastic leaflet, "The Punishments Are Too Harsh! Or the End of Liberalism," saying that administrative channels served as a ruse, a mechanism for containing protest, and that our only option was to take more militant, effective action. In a few short paragraphs we laid bare the complicity between the university, its governors, the government, and the military, and their global corporate impact on workers, peasants, and students. We demanded complete amnesty.

Increasingly, my politics turned eastward. I thought that the USSR had completely sold out, and that China was the only place where anything existed resembling my idea of socialism. I had thought highly of the Cuban Revolution, and still appreciated the Cubans' tremendous advances. But I found myself critical of "revisionist" tendencies there—a word the Cubans had effectively stricken from their vocabulary. The flow of Soviet aid had stifled Cuba's growth and potential.

On the other hand, the Cultural Revolution in China seemed like the correct way to purify the Communist Party there and return it to proletarian control.

I am embarrassed today by that ideological stance. I had been caught up in a worldwide fervor surrounding the impending cataclysm we all knew was coming. What models did we seek for guidance out of the morass of war, poverty, and exploitation? The CP looked to the USSR, of course; the Maoists looked to the Cultural Revolution that would cauterize corruption and adherence to old ways. Now it all seems so naïve of us to tail the Chinese, no more creative ideologically than tailing the Soviet line. We rejected peaceful coexistence as a sellout to imperialism. All this thinking strikes me today as "un-American"—not anti-American, but simply alienated from the daily concerns of our own multiracial working class, its aspirations and needs. The curse of American revolutionaries (and others around the world as well) in their search for perfection and ideals in the historical arc of other countries has severely damaged our credibility at home. Ideology trumped analysis, the lazy reach for easy answers and the shorthand of slurs like "revisionist" substituting poorly for patient, historically rooted materialist study.

And yet in a world where US imperialism was inflicting so much more damage than the Soviets or the Chinese ever could, we saw ourselves "in the belly of the beast." Our ideas and movements were repressed, our leaders jailed and assassinated, Nixon's and J. Edgar Hoover's COINTELPRO program was in full swing, with an onslaught of extraconstitutional measures to demoralize us and destroy dissent. We did not always enjoy the luxury of armchair research and analysis. The times called for action and moral witness, and we responded the best we knew how.

The SDS National Convention took place at the Chicago Coliseum in June 1969, and it would be the organization's last hurrah. The split between PL's WSA on one side, and RYM on the other, with its Weatherman subfaction embracing "revolutionary violence," took final shape.

To speak of debate at that convention is laughable. The language of argument had more the character of vituperation and rage, as in a messy divorce. The two sides seated themselves opposing each other across the aisle. At a certain point, one side got up on their chairs facing the other, and with their *Little Red Book* of Chairman Mao in their hands gesticulated toward the others, rhythmically yelling, "Bull shit! Bull shit!" In response, the other side stood on their chairs, also holding their *Little Red Book*, and waved them back, screaming, "Fuck you! Fuck you!" To this had come our mass student movement against war, capitalism, and imperialism.

One result of the breakdown was that we in New Orleans started a rigorous study group to hash out our ideas. First we tackled the national question, always a troubling issue on the Left, which tends to explain the world more in terms of class. What is meant by "nation?" What is a colony, a neo-colony, self-determination? What does it mean to "support" a struggle? How critical can one be? How uncritical must one be? Some of this inquiry came about because of serious reservations we entertained about the Black Nationalist movement (and other nationalisms), and about the experience in revolutionary China of all-class unity in the war against Japan. What does Marxist theory suggest for developing a political line in the US? And whose Marxist theory?

In August 1969 a new hotel opened in the French Quarter. A few of us in MDS applied for jobs at the Royal Sonesta on Bourbon Street to see if collectively we could make an impact there, and maybe start a hotel workers' union. I started on the night shift at the front desk. By that fall, Tulane SDS had practically fallen into the memory hole, and a general demoralization had set in around movement circles. Most of the MDS comrades had left New Orleans by then, and some had completely dropped out of the movement. The SDS chapter at LSUNO (now the University of New Orleans) still showed some promise, and when I could I tried to show up at their demonstrations and offer a hand despite an LSU systemwide ban of SDS from its campuses.

By January 1970, having turned twenty-five and contemplating my mortality, I had had about enough of a front desk clerk's life. My pay was $97 a week gross (actually one of the highest-paying jobs below the managerial level), but I got no paid sick days and no benefits to speak of. I had achieved no success in organizing a union, nor had I the faintest idea how to do so. And I had no aspirations of rising in the hotel industry.

So I considered applying to the Tulane History Department for the PhD program. During the year of my absence from campus the Latin American faculty had transformed itself. I could now have intelligent, informed, and dispassionate conversation with the new professors about Marxism, socialism, and the Left. Michael Hall, the Brazilian history man, was a studious, ironic, and solid leftie who specialized in Italian immigration. The graduate school accepted me back for more coursework toward a PhD starting in September, with a tuition waiver. I already started talking with Mike Hall about a doctoral dissertation on some aspect of Brazilian working-class history, which overlapped with his own interests.

One Friday night that January when I got to work, the NOPD Red Squad was waiting for me in the hotel lobby. They arrested me on the spot, in relation to a demonstration at LSUNO a couple of days before, where a few dozen students and supporters showed up to support an SDSer the administration was trying to expel. An NOPD intelligence officer whom I recognized was inside the dean's office, and I saw him through an open door, at which point I called everyone over, pointed him out and stated who he was and why he was there. When the pig gave me a "V" sign I shot him back the bird and told him "Fuck you." Result: State charges of "obscenity."

Off I went to central lockup to be booked and fingerprinted and to wait until $100 arrived for bail. I worked the rest of my shift that night after I got back. I wasn't fired, though; perhaps because I might have been hard to replace on the night shift. My bust was not at all isolated. Aside from the guy the school was trying to kick out, another SDSer, Gi Schafer, was also arrested on campus for "trespassing" while handing out leaflets about the Panthers and about the school cafeteria workers. (More on Gi later.)

The FBI, knowing where I lived, "interviewed" me a couple of times. Here's one excerpt from my file:

On April 30, 1970, ERIC GORDON was interviewed by Special Agents of the FBI, at 1130 Valmont Street in New Orleans. He was asked his knowledge of CATHLYN WILKERSON. GORDON refused to permit the Agents to enter his residence and advised he did not wish to talk with police or the FBI. He displayed a hostile and offensive attitude toward the Agents.... He also said he did not know the location of any of the SDS activists mentioned. GORDON was advised of the provisions of the Harboring Statute. GORDON replied laughingly that he would call the FBI if any information came to his attention regarding the locations of those persons.

The folks the FBI asked about were Weathermen, my opponents, who had embarked on an adventurist course of violence, terrorism, and mob action. At first, after the 1969 convention, they numbered probably no more than three or four hundred. By early 1970 they were talking about "strategic sabotage" against police and military facilities. No wonder the FBI was looking for them! In the late 1960s, and into the 1970s, the Black Panther Party also adopted a hyper-militant cast, urging black people to arm themselves against the pigs—who were, after all, gunning down black leaders with virtual impunity.

This kind of thinking recalled the early twentieth-century anarchists, a few of whom embraced the "propaganda of the deed"— stunning, daring acts that by their sheer audacity and bravado would awaken the masses to revolt. Anarchists at the time, such as Emma Goldman, did not defend such actions, but tried to understand the rage and impotence in people who believed they had run out of other options for change. That's much how I felt. But however much I disagreed with Weatherman or Panther politics, I was not prepared to provide information to the authorities. One entry in my FBI file says that in April 1970 I was identified as the "SDS National Finance Manager." This was, of course, preposterous, but if they somehow thought it was true, that would have constituted a powerful reason to interview me then.

Elements of the student Left (RYM and its offshoots) developed the theory of "white skin privilege," to which there is admittedly some validity. But to others of us on the Left—PL, the CP, and the more traditional Marxist formations—Panther rhetoric and the "white skin privilege" theory aimed to throw overboard the whole issue of class in favor of analysis based on race or nationality. These had figured among the issues we in MDS New Orleans had been struggling with as well. The image of white student radicals mouthing self-deprecatory support for even the wildest of Black Nationalist demands struck me, and others in my circles, as another kind of "tailism" meant to enhance your own standing as supposed militants. Trying to turn whole populations against whitey certainly would fail as a strategy for building socialism.

My court case surrounding SDS at LSUNO now came up on the docket. On a Monday in April I was found guilty, with sentencing scheduled for April 27. Although I had originally appeared in court on my own recognizance, once the judge found out the circumstances of the demonstration at LSUNO he had me post $250 bail until sentencing. During this period, students at Tulane had virtually taken over the campus, mostly around student-power demands. The demonstrations seemed to be inspired by a talk at Tulane by Chicago 7 defendant Rennie Davis. The Tulane campus woke up the next morning to find that an old, unused building formerly occupied by ROTC had been burned to the ground by a fire "of unknown origins." At another demo at LSUNO around the question of SDS getting university recognition, four people were busted—Gi Schafer, Ed Clark, and two students there. The judge before whom I appeared had to have been aware of the insurrection erupting in a good ole Southern town that had been relatively sleepy until not many years before.

All this campus activism came to a head at the beginning of May when, after years of mass protest against the Vietnam War, President Nixon widened the war by attacking Cambodia. Students shut down universities all over the country, enraged that no one was listening to the American people. The world remembers the four students killed by the National Guard at Kent State University in Ohio, but African American students were killed also at Jackson State in Mississippi. Students at Tulane burned an effigy of Nixon, and that photo made the front page of the *International Herald Tribune*. The federal government had seemingly declared war on its young people.

The judge sentenced me to twenty days and I did my time in early September, before the fall semester began. My twenty days would be reduced to ten for good behavior. I might have appealed the sentence, but I had a certain sense of pride or even moral superiority in going to jail for my beliefs, even if the formal charge was public obscenity.

New Orleans Parish Prison was not renowned as a hellhole crawling with violent sociopaths, so I did not particularly fret for my personal safety. I shared a cell with a young black fellow who provided amiable company. He had with him a volume of short stories by the Russian writer Lermontov, and when he finished his sentence, I begged him to trust me with the book, which I would return to the library immediately upon my release. I devoured those stories hungrily, bending closely over the pages in the dim prison light.

What became obvious very swiftly was that the system of "letting you" cut your sentence in half by working for the city was merely a grossly contrived manner of obtaining free work for the city. We cleaned police schools and district bureaus, as well as court buildings, stables—the least obnoxious work, for at least horses can't clean up after themselves—and the jail itself. Some two hundred prisoners with me there were available for eight hours of work per day. Think of the money the city saved! The work was far easier, but in principle it was just an old Southern chain gang.

Memories of those ten days include metal cafeteria trays with tasteless, minimally nourishing food, stationary benches and tables in the dining hall, shuffling, resigned prisoners—not quite a scene out of Dostoyevsky, but no picnic either. No incidents, no outbursts of fighting, no weapons, no discussion of politics. The bus trips out to our daily worksites relieved the tedium. I achieved one minor coup. In a police office one day, cleaning up with a pail and a mop, I glanced at the bulletin board and saw WANTED posters with the names and mugshots of some of my former SDS friends in the RYM faction. Out of an elemental sense of solidarity I removed these posters from the wall, crumpled them up, and threw them out with the trash.

Our MDS *Midnight Special* regularly carried articles by the activist couple Jill and Gi Schafer, both listed on our editorial staff. One by Gi in the September issue, "The King and Us," reported the events of August 14, when President Nixon came to the French Quarter for a parade and speech. SDS greeted him with a ten-foot banner reading, "NO DEALS! US GET OUT NOW! SDS." As Nixon spoke, we began chanting, "US Out of Southeast Asia! Cops Out of the Ghettos!" Newspapers and TV across the country showing photos of the president almost all included our banner.

Boston SDS, where the National Office of the WSA/SDS was located and to which our MDS chapter valiantly clung, had fallen into a deep authoritarian arrogance. How many of those folks were PL members I don't know, but the National Office made all manner of highhanded decisions for the organization, hurling insults and accusations toward anyone who questioned their tactics and puffed-up leadership. I had little interest in devoting time to reviving SDS at Tulane. However, I do note that by this time SDS discourse had just begun to take the women's liberation movement to heart, and the gay movement as well.

I've mentioned Gi Schafer as one of our activists in New Orleans SDS. Gi was a bit of a loose cannon, with several arrests already under his belt (though no convictions). More than once he proposed some heavy-duty action, like breaking store windows, that no one else wanted to do. But one thing he suggested, in the fall of 1970, did excite us, and involved no violence or threats against property. Down in the French Quarter, the owners of jazz clubs, like Al Hirt and Pete Fountain, were telling the police that the open visibility of hippies, homosexuals, and cross-dressers was interfering with the tourist business.

Out-of-towners just didn't like seeing that kind of thing on the streets. Mind you, this was New Orleans, one of the few cities in America with a relatively open gay and lesbian population. So the police had actually started arresting women on Bourbon Street who were wearing jeans! Over a four-month period, the cops had made some eight hundred arrests. Gi proposed that SDS show some solidarity with the gay community, so we took ourselves down to the French Quarter and joined the protests. No other SDS chapter in the country had done such a thing. These actions constituted my first gay liberation demonstration, and perhaps they were the first in New Orleans. The police eased up: a fleeting success story.

We of the *Midnight Special* group aimed for a national readership, feeling that the politics we represented, a kind of purified SDS, was simply the healthiest political thinking in the land. We believed that the natural path of communist parties and movements inevitably led toward abusive leadership, which nevertheless did not preclude political action on our part. But though we worked collectively on the magazine, we had drifted far from anything one could call a mass base, so we wound up as a little, self-referential groupuscule of the kind that we lefties often make fun of.

The explanation for how such a thing happens lies in the complete unresponsiveness of the system to our cries and demands, now shared by an ever larger number of Americans, against the war that still dragged on, now expanded even beyond Cambodia into Laos. If nothing succeeds, people desert mass work, and those lost souls who remain naturally go to ever further extremes to find workable theories for moving forward. In their isolation they go a little crazy, acting out in fits of narcissism and depression, and sometimes anger and violence.

As mentioned, our MDS group had started looking at questions surrounding nationalism, and the contortions Marxist movements are forced to make to satisfy understandable national longings without endangering the larger socialist project. By the end of the year my infatuation with China as the upholder of the antirevisionist banner was beginning to fray at the edges. Its foreign policy looked very unsocialistic—supporting reactionary Pakistan and building up Prince Sihanouk into almost a god, although communists in Cambodia had always fought against him! And I balked at the way Mao had come to be worshiped, his image and writings forced down the throats of the masses. It was clear, too, that the people in the European social-ist states did not really run their countries. Frankly, I considered the recent rebellion of Polish workers over rising prices of 17 to 20 percent the only justifiable action against government policies.

So what were we left with? Disillusion with the "actually existing socialism" of the Soviet or Chinese variety, profound doubts about the peaceful Allende road to socialism (seemingly confirmed by later events), and revulsion against the organizations at home I had once felt close to. How do communists create a revolution that is no more authoritarian and undemocratic than the system we replace? It was time for some new ideas!

SDS held its first campus meeting in December, in preparation for a few of us going up to the national convention (of the PL/WSA-dom-inated SDS remnant) in Chicago. My travel to the convention was memorable. Gi Schafer, our quirky MDS member, took the last of his required practice flying hours, passed his test, and that afternoon, Christmas Day, he and I, with a sixteen-year-old SDS high school girl, took off in a tiny, rented three-seater so loud we had to shout to each other to be heard. We flew at about 1,000 feet, which gave us a mag-nificent aerial perspective on the whole Mississippi River valley going north. Since we had left so late in the day, and Gi was not yet qualified for nighttime flying, we spent the night in a Mississippi motel before proceeding in the morning to Chicago. Gi would have loved to shack up with the girl, but fortunately, for her sake, I was present. So Gi and I shared the double bed and she slept on a rollaway. We made it to Chicago without problem, and back, spending New Year's Eve in a motel in Vandalia, Illinois.

The convention ratified the self-proclaimed national leadership, effectively did away with chapter input, further painted SDS into a tight ideological corner out of reach by most students, and heightened the idolization of workers in a guilt-ridden morass of correct, "base-build-ing" jargon. Across the country, the movement had become demor-alized, managing to mobilize only the most perfunctory response to the expansion of the war into Laos. After that convention, our collec-tive concluded that SDS no longer served a mass constituency, and we dropped the SDS affiliation on our magazine's masthead. Ed Clark, ever the soapbox orator, but still a powerful influence among us as we witnessed his political views evolve from PL to anti-PL to anti-SDS, honed his revolutionary purism into a broadside against the National Liberation Front of South Vietnam for being sellouts.

I had begun questioning heroes, leaders, and ideologies, and finally even the officially sanctioned system of sexuality. The influence of the Stonewall Rebellion began to trickle down, awakening a sense of pos-sibilities. As I became more attuned to the inequality between men and women in society, I felt able for a time, during my coming-out process, to cover my basic homosexual inclination with the political proposi-tion that same-gender relationships were inherently more egalitarian because of the gender imbalance. I looked forward to a revolution that would help eradicate our fear of touch and intimacy, even with members of our own sex.

A few years later Gi and Jill Schafer outed themselves as longtime FBI agents. Finally I understood why he had been arrested so many times—he *sought* to get arrested—and then mysteriously got off each time. And why he so often advocated violent RYM-like tactics that none of the rest of us in MDS could embrace. As skilled undercover agents, they caused their share of damage to the movement, and to myself. But I survived them.

At some point the US Senate Internal Security Committee released a book-length report on SDS and campus activism, replete with graphs and pyramids of our power structure. I burst with uncontainable pride at the fact that my photo appeared on that pyramid, even though the schematization of our organization on the printed page resembled nothing that I knew in person. We were no Mafia family, and cer-tainly no multinational banking conglomerate, and we did not report to higher-ups with authority over us. We were merely some naïve but earnest kids who had drunk deeply of the ideals of American democracy, and knew in their guts that there had to be a fairer, more humane way. Tulane made it among the Top 10 activist campuses in the US, and I believe the only one in the South, predicted for a major blowup—an additional source of personal pride.

After a number of years wandering about as an anarchist, and long after the USSR crashed, in 2009 I joined the Communist Party USA. With no Moscow line to "tail" any more, I now find these folks the most compatible to me politically. SDS was a great cauldron of experience and ideas whose impact on me has been incalculable. Through its ranks, and the people I knew in it, I became the permanent activist that I remain.

Eric A. Gordon lives in Los Angeles and is a staff writer for the People's World *focusing on culture, religion, and labor. He has published biographies of composers Marc Blitzstein and Earl Robinson. His memoir is adapted from a political autobiography in progress. ericarthurgo@gmail.com*

Cuba: students arriving at a rural village to help the sugar workers with hoeing weeds in the cane fields.

Fidel engaging students during ping-pong matches. Fidel beat everyone.

Ellen Israel going over the schedule with Larry Phelps, left, and John Thomas, right.

Fidel dominates the ping-pong table at Varadero Beach.

"We danced everywhere we went with the Cubans—after lunch, after dinner … and even sometimes at breakfast!" Wayne Combash, left, showing off his moves..

Cuba travelers preparing to depart from Havana Airport for their journey home. Anatole Anton is on the far right.

Cuba traveler Luria Castell sampling a fine Cuban cigar.

Touring a government store.

Meeting with Cuban university students in Havana. The picture between the two flags is of Camilo Cienfuegos, a hero of the Cuban Revolution.

John Thomas talking with a group of students during a tour of a Cuban secondary .school.

Che meeting with Cuba travelers. In the discussion one of them said that she was studying political science. Che replied, "Politics is an art, my dear."

It is not enough to be for peace...

153025

"We, the undersigned, are young Americans of draft age. We are opposed to United States intervention in the war in south Vietnam. United States participation in that war is for the suppression of the Vietnamese struggle for self-determination and national independence. We herewith state our refusal to fight against the people of Vietnam."

While you are reading this statement, the Declaration above is being circulated on more than 100 University campuses across America by the May 2nd Movement. With this Declaration, which all the world will know and see, we shall match, name for name, those thousands of unknowing young Americans that our government has transformed into murderers and shipped off to Vietnam.

Hundreds of young Americans have already died in the jungles of southeast Asia, and thousands, if not hundreds of thousands more will die there in an enlarged war, unless the American government pulls out of Vietnam now. Senator Wayne Morse (Oregon) has stated: "We should never have gone in, we should not have stayed in, we should get out..." 5,000 University teachers have signed a petition calling for the neutralization of Vietnam, and leading intellectuals, religious and professional figures have signed public appeals calling for negotiations. And while you are reading this statement "our" napalm bombs continue to burn out peasant villages, "our" chemical poisons defoliate their forests, destroying their crops, killing their cattle. And "our" artillery and machine guns, manned by "our" troops (advisory), are killing their patriots.

The May 2nd Movement is a radical student peace organization.

Radical because we are not merely embarrassed by "our" role in this war—we renounce it. The war in Vietnam is not our war, and we shall in no way be party to it.

Opening of the organizing call for the May 2nd Movement.

Progressive Labor Party contingent at an early anti–Vietnam War demonstration in downtown San Francisco.

Photo: Tom Levin

Columbia contingent marching down New York's Fifth Avenue as part of an antiwar demonstration in the fall of 1966. Mike Klare marches with his hands cupped in front. John Levin is smoking a cigarette is behind him.

Becky Brenner, SDS regional traveler, hamming it up on the road, 1970.

SDS literature table at the University of Texas-Austin; Howard Hertz, left.

Dick Reavis, just back from civil rights work in Mississippi, speaking on the Texas campus. Chester Wilson stands behind him.

Paula Campbell Munro, front, and her sister, Lynn.

M2M's *Free Student.*

M2M call for a rally against the Vietnam War, New York, November 11, 1965.

Demonstrators confront Gen. Maxwell Taylor on his way to address the Commonwealth Club, San Francisco, 1966.

Spark, PL's West Coast newspaper, denounces police violence.

May 2nd Movement demonstration against US intervention in the Dominican Republic, spring 1965.

Blocking munitions shipments, Port of Oakland, 1966.

Grape boycott picket line; Cuba traveler and Bay Area leader Chris Raisner, second from left.

Photo: El Puente de Claudio

San Francisco: Mission Tenants Union demonstration linking antiwar movement with tenants rights.

John Harris, a PL organizer indicted for criminal syndicalism for organizing protests against police brutality during the 1965 Watts rebellion.

Photo: El Puente de Claudio

Antiwar picket linking the Vietnam War to the Watts rebellion.

Photo: El Puente de Claudio

May 2nd Movement antiwar demonstration, New York, 1965.

Photo: El Puente de Claudio

Progressive Labor Party chair Milt Rosen speaking in front of the New York Federal Building.

New York, 1965. Levi Laub, PL student organizer (left); Russell Stettler, student at Haverford College and M2M organizer (right).

Photo: El Puente de Claudio

National Guard occupation of San Francisco during the black rebellion, fall of 1966. PL demonstrated at the San Francisco Armory in the Mission District. Here PL member Jay Frank confronts the troops.

Progressive Labor lit table on the UC Berkeley campus, 1966. Stewart Albert, left, later a leader of the Yippies, and Steve Hamilton, later a founder of the Revolutionary Union.

Free Bill Epton button, supportin the 1966 Harlem Rebellion.

6

"On Strike! Shut It Down!"

John F. Levin
(San Francisco State, Columbia)

It began on a sunny afternoon in the spring of 1965, the last semester of my junior year at Columbia. Crossing campus on the way home to my $40-a-month apartment on 12th and Avenue B I heard rolling down from the steps of Low Library the rhythmic and soon-to-be-familiar chant "No war in Vietnam! NROTC off Campus!!" About fifty demonstrators were picketing the entrance to Low, where the graduation ceremony for that years' NROTC class was to take place. Why not? I thought, and I joined the picket line. I didn't know any of my fellow demonstrators, but when about half of them locked arms to block the library entrance, I joined them. At some point the cops were called. I don't remember whether they were city or university but in any case they attempted, without using their batons (imagine that!), to clear the entrance. When they failed to dislodge us, the Columbia administrators decided not to escalate the situation and postponed the graduation ceremony.

Only after a jubilant group of my fellow demonstrators adjourned to the West End Bar for a victory celebration did I realize that the new comrades with whom I had locked arms were mostly members of the Progressive Labor Party or May 2nd Movement (M2M), PL's student organization. I was intrigued. I had been to a couple of M2M demonstrations and had heard of the "Maoist" Progressive Labor Party over the previous few years, as they were very much in the news. I admired their militancy, and their swashbuckling style ("Absolutely, we're communists and proud of it!") and their activism: PL's vice-chairman, Bill Elton, organizing a march down 125th Street during the Harlem Rebellion to protest the killing by an NYPD cop of an unarmed black teenager, the student trips to revolutionary Cuba in defiance of the US government travel ban, the subsequent hearings before HUAC at which they reduced the bloviating congressmen to blathering idiots with their denunciations of US imperialism—all had me cheering.

By the mid-sixties, I was an angry young man. I had been raised by left liberal parents who believed that US democracy had been saved by the defeat of fascism in World War II, who voted for Henry Wallace, who taught their children never to cross a picket line, and who believed that the civil rights movement proved that the system worked. But the times were changing. My first vote, in 1964, was for Lyndon Johnson because he promised to keep the US, and my ass in particular, out of Vietnam. A few months after being elected, LBJ did an about-face and ordered a massive troop call-up to widen the war, and then, after a cooked-up incident in the Gulf of Tonkin, began a daily carpet-bombing of North Vietnam the accounts of which, broadcast on WBAI, brought me to tears. My country, which I basically believed in, had reared up in front of me like a demonic flasher, buck-naked, fangs out, vomiting napalm, and shitting cluster bombs on a defenseless people. I attended demonstrations where the speakers pleaded for LBJ to be reasonable ("Don't Bomb, Negotiate"), and I signed petitions that came my way and commiserated with like-minded friends. But mainly, head down, I worked on a novel under the watchful eye of my senior seminar professor, which I planned to submit for a fellowship that would (hopefully) launch my life as a writer.

After I graduated in June 1966 my plan was to head for San Francisco, the city of my dreams, where I would live in North Beach, hang out at the jazz clubs on Fillmore Street, attend poetry readings at Ferlinghetti's City Lights Bookstore, and listen to Lenny Bruce at the "hungry i." My role models were not Che Guevara or Chairman Mao but fellow Columbia alumni Jack Kerouac and Alan Ginsberg. Things change. I didn't much care for the people in the Columbia PL club—I found them a dreary dogmatic bunch—but on the Lower East Side, where I lived, I met PLers who were veterans of the Cuba trips and the HUAC hearings who were more to my liking and style. One of them, Roger Taus, a poet and editor of *Free Student*, the M2M newspaper, lent me a copy of Lin Biao's "Long Live the Victory of People's War," a slim pamphlet that put forth the thesis that the final conflict was afoot in the form of the rebellions taking place all over the Third World, which would inevitably coalesce into an immutable force that would encircle the First World powers, bring their collapse, and give birth to world-wide socialism. Of course, this did not come to pass, but Comrade Lin's roadmap made a lot of sense and when I was invited to a PL meeting, at Jeff Gordon's apartment on East Houston a few weeks later, I went. It turned out that it was a PL recruitment meeting—which I thought a little weird as I had done little in the way of political activity except attend demonstrations. I was almost "saved" from communism by a wanker from the Columbia PL club, who denounced me in front of those assembled as a rank individualist and unfit for a revolutionary communist party. I was in fact inclined to agree with him, but as I left the meeting another PL cadre intercepted me and told me not to pay attention to her fellow comrade and assured me that I was more than welcome to join PL. Shortly thereafter, I did. The fact that she was an attractive, leggy California gal, with a lovely smile who I had started dating had nothing to do with it....

How I Became a PL "Leader"

After graduating in June, I packed my rucksack and left for the Coast. My plan was to enroll in the MFA program at San Francisco State (now San Francisco State University) and continue working on my novel. My plans regarding PL were murky. I agreed with their call for revolution in the US, their support of the Cuban Revolution, and the insurgency in Vietnam and the People's Republic of China, but what appealed to me most was the party's militant, take-no-prisoners attitude, and despite the dogmatic nature of its publications, *PL Magazine* also published the radical poets who were based on the Lower East Side, including Victor Cruz, Danny Cassidy, and Amiri Baraka a.k.a. Leroi Jones, as well as the work of radical cultural icons like Bertolt Brecht, Pablo Neruda, and Peter Weiss (whose play, *Marat-Sade*, was then a Broadway sensation). Revolutionary politics and revolutionary art—I couldn't imagine a better combination. Unfortunately, art, except in its most Stalinist iteration, soon fell by the wayside. However, having no experience as an organizer of much of anything but myself— a definite work in progress, I had no idea of what I should do as a revolutionary. I saw it as a statement of belief accompanied, if the situation called for it, by some defiant revolutionary action. In short, I was ready to step up to the barricades, but I had no idea how to get there and what I would do in the meantime.

An answer presented itself a few weeks after I arrived in the Bay Area when HUAC issued subpoenas targeting antiwar activists around the country, many of whom were either in PL, M2M, or both, and included most of the PL student leadership in the Bay Area. I don't remember the details, but by default I was put in charge of organizing the Bay Area protest against the HUAC hearings. Somehow I put together a large mailing list to ask for donations to the legal defense fund and, with others, organized a mass assembly at a school auditorium in Berkeley inviting various Left and not-so-Left luminaries to speak out against the hearings. To my own and PL's surprise, donations poured in, the auditorium was packed, and first time out I became the revolutionary rainmaker and organizer of a successful coalition to defend PL against the ruling class. I was pleased, the party leadership was pleased, and when I enrolled for the fall semester at SF State, the all-male Bay Area PL leadership unceremoniously pushed aside Carolyn, the designated leader of the PL club at SF State and put me in charge. She rightly objected, but to no avail, and I arrived at SF State in the fall of 1966, with some ambivalence, as chairman of the PL club. SF State, in 1966, was a collection of squat mustard-colored cement buildings on the western edge of the city that on most days was enshrouded in a Pacific Ocean fog. It was formerly a teachers college that drew its student body largely from the San Francisco area or, more accurately, white San Francisco. The student population at SF State was 93 percent white while the city's public school population was 43 percent students of color. When I arrived on campus there were a number of community-based tutorial programs initiated by the Black Student Union (BSU) and others to address the obvious racial disparity, and demands were already being raised for a special admissions policy to address them.

That summer the PL National Committee had dissolved the May 2nd Movement and instructed its student cadre to join SDS chapters around the country, a move that was made possible when SDS's annual national convention removed the clause that banned communists from membership. PL's reasoning was straightforward enough: M2M was a small organization with a strong anti-imperialist position dominated by PL members, whereas SDS was a sprawling mass organization which, after its 1966 anti–Vietnam War demonstration in Washington, DC, became the go-to organization for students who supported civil rights and opposed the Vietnam War. PL was going where the masses were, and in 1966 on US campuses that was in SDS. There was internal opposition to the dissolution within M2M because it was done by fiat and without discussion or the consent of M2M members, many of whom were not PL members. The dissidents believed that M2M still had a valuable role to play as an anti-imperialist force in a largely reformist antiwar movement. I agreed with PL's political rational. The undemocratic way the decision was made didn't bother me at the time, although it should have.

At SF State my comrades and I joined a group of students of varied Left political perspectives and revived the campus chapter of SDS. The key issues were the war, the draft, and racism. PL's overriding strategy was to build a revolutionary worker-student alliance (WSA) that meant linking the antiwar movement wherever possible to workers' struggles, most prominently the grape boycott led by the United Farm Workers.

At SF State, SDS and PL were the left wing of the largely pacifist, single-issue antiwar movement that trumpeted the slogan "Negotiate Now." Under the banner of "Get Out Now!" we sought to convince other students that the war in Vietnam was not an ill-advised mistake by a gaggle of Cold Warriors who had captured LBJ's mind but an imperialist war of conquest. Given that all male students over eighteen faced the draft and subsequent service in Vietnam, we had an attentive and self-interested audience. Against the background of the black rebellions that were sweeping the country, we educated students through leaflets, forums, and actions on the role of racism in America, emphasizing its class basis. When the National Guard was sent into San Francisco that fall by Governor Reagan to suppress the rebellion that burst out in response to a police shooting of an unarmed African American in the Hunters Point ghetto, we put out leaflets supporting the right of self-defense and organized students to join a community picket line set up by PL, the Mission Tenants Union, and others at the Mission District Armory where the National Guard troops were bivouacked.

In the context of growing militancy and nationalism, we educated our fellow students on the systemic character of racism and urged them to support the Black Panther Party's right of armed self-defense. We exposed the racist nature of the Vietnam War, which was waged against people of color and used the poor of this country, who disproportionately came from communities of color, as cannon fodder. We issued a leaflet in support of Muhammad Ali when he refused induction into the army with the now iconic statement: "No Vietcong ever called me a nigger." We tried to move our fellow students from simply decrying racism as moral injustice to seeing it as an ideology used by the ruling class (the 1 percent) to divide the population along racial lines to maintain its hegemony. We held sit-ins at the administration building to demand that the administration not send class rankings to draft boards, which used them to select their draftees. We confronted a recruiter from Dow Chemical, supplier of the napalm that was being dropped by the ton on the citizens of Vietnam, and chased him off campus. We organized teach-ins and forums and brought students to picket lines at Safeway in support of the UFW grape boycott.

Along the way we recruited club members, shortly doubling the size of the PL club, and broadened it to include a number of students of color. At first, our organizing went smoothly. In response to our throwing the Dow recruiters off campus the liberal administration reached out and invited us to participate in a forum on free speech on campus. At the forum we argued that free speech did not include the right to recruit students to commit war crimes. The student body sentiment was strongly antiwar and, if not agreeing with SDS's more far-reaching analysis of imperialism and racism, students supported our activities and, with the draft threatening, saw them as being in their interest.

Within SDS, PL/WSA was the dominant force but by no means the only one. There was also a loose coalition of anarchists and independent socialists who called themselves the Joe Hill Caucus. Up until the SF State strike, the political differences between the two groups were secondary to our shared opposition to the war and racism. Members of the two caucuses were friends with each other, and there were also many SDS members who were not affiliated with either group and who gravitated to one or the other depending where they stood on a particular issue. Some of the differences were social in nature. Joe Hill members identified more with the counterculture and lived mostly in the Haight-Ashbury, while PL/WSA people were socially more conservative, identified more with the labor movement and community issues, and tended to live in the Mission District. Joe Hill people preferred pot; PL/WSA people mostly stuck to booze. But by the end of the school year SDS was an effective united front and an influential force on the San Francisco State campus.

By the beginning of the 1967 fall semester the weekly death toll of US troops in Vietnam averaged more than a hundred a week with no end in sight. On campuses in the Bay Area the future cannon fodder for "Amerika," as we spelled it then, were scared and angry. A group of radicals, who published *The Movement*, a newspaper loosely affiliated with SNCC and SDS, issued a call for a weeklong demonstration to shut down the Oakland Induction Center. I and two other members of SF State SDS joined the steering committee of what became known as "Stop the Draft Week." The epic week of resistance involved over 10,000 demonstrators who shut down the induction center for five days. It was the largest antidraft riot since World War I.

The politics around organizing the demonstration were complicated and intense. A strong faction of pacifists called for civil disobedience, whereas the majority of the steering committee called for militant self-defense. In the end, the pacifists withdrew from the coalition and conducted a separate demonstration where they submitted to arrest. The cops didn't see the difference. Many of the arrests and injuries that week were endured by the nonviolent demonstrators, who sat down in front of the induction center entrance to be arrested—which they were, after being clubbed and beaten by the cops. We supported the general plan for active self-defense but opposed a number of adventurist tactics that we felt would endanger the African American community that surrounded the induction center.

Despite these differences, we did indeed shut down the induction center and effectively upped the militancy of the struggle against the Vietnam War nationally from opposition to active resistance. SF State SDS organized hundreds of students to join and, as I recall, chartered buses to bring them as a group to the demonstrations. For many of us it was the first violent demonstration in which we had participated and it empowered us: yes, we could hold the streets and shut down government institutions, and yes, we could battle the cops toe to toe and take our knocks. The experience created a solid core of militants who became the backbone of the SDS chapter at SF State.

Less than a month later all hell broke loose on the SF State campus. A half-dozen students from the Black Student Union, incensed by a series of racist articles in *The Daily Gater*, the campus newspaper, by its sports editor, Jim Vaszko, and a blatantly racist cartoon ridiculing Muhammad Ali, barged into *The Gater*'s offices and demanded redress. Arguments erupted into fistfights; a typewriter was thrown through a window, and several students were injured, none seriously. The campus was shocked and many were outraged by the violence documented by the newspaper photographer, who shot photos during the fight that were subsequently published in *The Gater*. After a long debate in SDS between members who were shocked and frightened by the violence and PL/WSA members who argued that black students had a right to defend themselves against racist attacks, a divided SDS chapter issued a leaflet that defended the African American students, calling for due process and an open discussion of racism on campus. Despite the mildness of the SDS leaflet, they were often refused or shredded in front of us.

A few weeks later SF State's President John Summerskill, who had previously suspended the African American students and the sports editor, lifted the suspension of the sports editor but kept the suspension of the six black students in place. The BSU president demanded that the suspension of the black students be lifted by December 6 or there would be a mass convergence on the campus of their community supporters. PL/WSA pushed SDS to support the BSU's demand. After a contentious meeting, SDS voted to take action in support of the suspended BSU students, who not only faced possible suspension from the college but criminal charges as well.

On December 6, SDS and a few supporters, including a contingent of radical Iranian students and a couple of faculty members who were putting their jobs on the line, held a rally at the speakers platform located in the center of the campus. Most of the speeches were drowned out by boos and catcalls by a crowd of hostile students many times the size of the demonstration. Keeping with our plan, we marched to the administration building for a meeting with the President Summerskill to demand that he lift all the suspensions, but we found the doors locked. Before we had figured out what to do, one of the faculty members, John "Tito" Gerassi, the son of an anarchist Spanish civil war general, climbed through an open building window. Inspired by his action, some other students broke down the door and everyone stormed into the building and began a sit-in. Meanwhile, about three hundred Black students from other area colleges and high schools had arrived on campus in response to the BSU's call for support. Ignoring the BSU leadership, they roamed over the campus, getting into fights, breaking a few windows, and stealing food from the cafeteria before dispersing. Students on the campus were terrified. Instead of calling the cops, Summerskill, citing the need to avoid further violence, wisely closed the college for the day.

If we had felt isolated before, that was like being rock stars compared to our position after this. Violence was on everybody's minds, and all attempts to discuss the racism that had provoked it were met with stony stares or worse. The mood on campus was epitomized by a group of students self-identified as the "silent majority." They collected donations to repair the "breakage" we had caused and circulated a petition calling for our expulsion. Demoralization set in. PL/WSA members drifted away, retreating into their studies or into jugs of Red Mountain wine, while the Joe Hill caucus smoked a lot of pot and talked about moving out to rural communes (which some did).

For me it was the first setback, and it raised lingering self-doubts about my ability as a leader. My doubts were also fueled by PL's polemical attacks on Cuba for siding with the Soviet Union in the Sino–Soviet dispute and on Vietnam for being willing to negotiate with the United States for an end to the war. The fact that new positions were taken without any internal party debate or discussion beforehand was an issue for me, but frankly what loomed larger in my mind was the thought that if Cuba was going bad, and the Vietnamese leadership was selling out their people's war, what was left? Is it really possible to create a new socialist society, or do they all go bad?

The answer I came around to was the People's Republic of China. It would serve as an international beacon for world revolution, and I would rededicate myself to the immediate struggle against racism and imperialism at home. In our mass work we downplayed PL's criticisms of Vietnam and Cuba and emphasized that PL supported their right to self-determination and stood by the slogans "Hands off Cuba" and "US Get Out of Vietnam."

So what the hell: we regrouped and continued with our badly attended forums, our leaflets, and antiwar demonstrations. Then came the Marines. After we received word of their impending arrival, SDS made plans for a demonstration that would be loud but peaceful. Initially PL/WSA argued for a more militant confrontation, but when it became apparent that we had little support beyond our caucus, we backed off. The Marines landed in the shape of two recruiting sergeants, decked out in their dress blues with campaign ribbons and medals dripping from their tunics. They set up their booth on the campus quad where the speaker's platform was located and which was heretofore the unspoken territory of student protest movement. As agreed, SDS formed a loud but nonviolent picket line. But it turned out that it was not our choice to make. The demonstration had hardly begun when we were attacked by a phalanx of students allegedly organized out of the fraternities and athletic department. Punches were thrown, noses bloodied, and recruiting ended for the day.

Then the administration fumbled. Instead, as it did with the fight between the newspaper staff and black students, taking action against the "perpetrators" whose identities were clearly documented by photographs, they dismissed the attack on the demonstrators as a "campus brawl." We drove the point home, in speeches, leaflets, and discussions. We rushed out a broadside titled: White = Brawl: Black=Riot:

> The reason these two incidents were labeled with different terms is not because of the differences in the acts of violence but in the differences in those participating in these incidents. Last Friday those who were involved in the violence were ones whose main manner of behavior lies within the rigid confines of this society and whose position supports the society. Thus, violence which touched this society's own interest is excused as a college brawl.

Across campus the lights came on. What we had been saying for months about the racism on campus, exemplified by the lack of due process for students of color and lily-white admissions policies now made absolute sense to a wide range of students. That May, inspired in part by the rebellion in Paris and the student strike at Columbia, students led by the newly formed coalition of minority student organizations, the Third World Liberation Front (TWLF) and SDS occupied the administration building to demand that the university waive the usual requirements and admit 300 students of color, hire eleven faculty to provide the infrastructure to ensure the students' success, rehire Professor Juan Martinez to head up the program, and end the campus ROTC.

Not only was support strong on campus, but also in the community at large as many of the students involved had family roots in San Francisco. Community groups, trade union militants, and churches brought carloads of supporters to the demonstrations. We were no longer isolated on campus or from the community. A number of parents who had children in the sit-in came with trays of food. I remember one father who brought a large platter heaped with lumpia because it was the first time I had eaten Filipino food.

Just when the demonstration was losing steam, the San Francisco Police Tactical Squad, unprovoked, waded into the crowd of supporters outside the administration building with their batons flailing. A dozen students, and our volunteer lawyer and future San Francisco district attorney, Terrence "Kayo" Hallinan, were beaten and arrested. All of this was documented and broadcast on the local evening news. The uproar both on campus and in the community was deafening. After receiving delegations from the community, faculty, and elected city officials, President Summerskill, a staunch liberal, granted our demand for the special admission of 300 students, scheduled a campuswide referendum on the fate of the ROTC, and then resigned in time to catch a plane to Ethiopia, where a job awaited him as provost of Haile Selassie University courtesy of the Ford Foundation.

The triumvirate that replaced Summerskill quickly reversed the decision for a referendum on ROTC, but the special admissions of 300 students stood. Although we had won only one of the demands, we argued, along with others, that the semester was at an end and it would be next to impossible to maintain the fight over the summer.

What I felt equally important was that a broad alliance and an atmo-sphere of trust between the mostly white student antiwar movement and Third World student activists had been established.

The results would bear fruit the following fall when SF State's new president, Glenn Smith, reneged on the promise to provide an infrastructure and funds for the influx of Third World students. In response, the TWLF in alliance with the BSU drew up a list of fif-teen demands, the cornerstone of which was the establishment of a fully funded and staffed School of Ethnic Studies and open admission for students of color. They called for a campuswide strike unless the demands were granted, and on November 6, 1968, the longest student strike in the history of the United States began. As singular as the SF State strike was, it was not divorced from the earth-shaking events of 1968: the student/worker rebellion in Paris, the NLF's Tet offensive in Vietnam, and the assassinations of Martin Luther King and Robert Kennedy all reinforced the belief that fundamental change in America could not be accomplished through peaceful means. Suddenly every-one was a revolutionary!

As the strike deadline approached a debate developed in SDS between the PL/WSA caucus and members of the Joe Hill Caucus, who argued that SDS should have its own demands in return for our support of the TWLF/BSU strike—in particular, they said SDS should demand that the administration live up to Summerskill's pledge to hold a referendum on the continued presence of ROTC from campus. PL/WSA argued that as radicals and revolutionaries, ending racism and inequality on campus was our demand as well and that to characterize the TWLF/BSU demands as just demands of "the other" was incor-rect. The fifteen demands belonged to all of us. The discussion was heated, but at the end of the day SDS did not insist on its own demands and spearheaded the formation of the Strike Support Committee, con-ceived as a broad united front in which those who supported the strike could participate at whatever level their "comfort zone" allowed.

PL/WSA's role in the strike was multifaceted. PL cadres were lead-ers in the Strike Support Committee, whose nightly meetings drew up to a thousand students. PL members were also active in the TWLF and BSU, where they had a small but effective caucus. Off campus, PL trade union caucuses, community groups, and clubs on other Bay Area campuses organized support for the strike. They held forums, raised bail money, and brought their base to the picket lines that circled the campus.

Although there was mass support on the campus for the strike there was also general uneasiness. Many students were scared and put off by the militancy of the TWLF and BSU students, some of whom would address off-campus meetings of the Strike Support Committee wearing sidearms and proclaim their allegiance to a bloody revolution in fiery nationalistic rhetoric that made no differentiation between their white allies and white racists. We downplayed the most provocative statements, arguing that they didn't represent the nationalism of the majority of the TWLF/BSU, which was not against white students but against white racism.

After a rocky beginning, unity and trust was forged in daily demonstrations and on the picket lines, where a rainbow of students battled hundreds of police, including platoons of California Highway Patrol officers from as far away as Eureka who were mobilized by Ronald Reagan (who infamously declared SF State "a domestic Vietnam"). PL/WSA comrades in the TWLF and the Strike Support Committee argued for continued militancy and led by example in the daily battles with the police. We closed down buildings together, marched, chanted, and stood toe to toe against the armed might of the State of California. When the cops tried to arrest us, we freed each other, and when we failed at that we rode to jail in the same paddy wagons and to SF General Hospital's emergency room in the same ambulances. It was unity forged in blood. We fought as one and kept the campus closed. For me these were my proudest moments as a revolutionary communist.

As we had done the previous spring, we reached out to the larger community for support. SDS had active chapters on dozens of campuses on the West Coast. Contingents of supporters came to SF State in car pools and buses to join our lines and held rallies on their own campus to collect bail money and build support. At the more distance locales we sent representatives from our speakers' bureau to talk about the strike and raise bail money—we lined the pockets of many a bondsman that fall and winter.

We addressed unions and community groups around the Bay Area talking about the strike and asking for resolutions of support. Evening strike meetings began with a reading of telegrams that poured in from student groups, unions, and community organizations throughout the US. PL clubs in the Bay Area mobilized in support of the strike, bringing their comrades from union caucuses and community groups to the picket lines and demonstrations. And there were individuals who showed up on their own and asked what they could do to help. Some offered advice: I remember a grizzled labor organizer, probably the same age as I am now. "You know what you do with scabs," he said. "Grab a couple of 'em in an alley, take the clothes off of 'em and turn 'em loose on the street—they never come back."

We gave it some thought and adopted our own persuasive tactics. Special squads led mostly by women provided many incentives to students and faculty who didn't realize classes were closed for the duration. And through all the twists and turns, we won. Today San Francisco State University has the only school of ethnic studies in the country with its own faculty and staff. The campus student body now is 43 percent students of color—a sea change from 7 percent before the strike. It was an honor to be part of the strike at San Francisco State. For many of us who participated, it is the touchstone that to a great degree has guided our lives since. It was also the beginning of the end of my life in PL.

My estrangement from PL began in the middle of the strike at the national winter meeting of SDS in Ann Arbor. We arrived directly from the picket lines and police battles that for the previous months had been regular feature on national TV news. We were the heroes of the moment and deference was paid. Taking advantage of our moment in the sun, we wrote a resolution that supported the fifteen demands of the SF State strike, condemned racism on college campuses, and endorsed the strategy of building a worker- student alliance. It seemed simple enough, but when I introduced the resolution at a PL leadership caucus before the plenum session, Jared Israel, leader of Harvard PL, and Jeff Gordon, national leader of the PL student section, told me that the resolution was fine as far as it went but that it needed to take a stand that all nationalism is reactionary.

Gob-smacked doesn't begin to describe it. Stunned, I said that that wasn't the party's position. We are against reactionary nationalism but support revolutionary nationalism, which is in the interest of the working class. No longer, I was told. After a thorough and comprehensive discussion and analysis by the party leadership it had been decided that there is no such thing as revolutionary nationalism. I objected that there had been no discussion within the party as a whole or even at a National Committee meeting. So far as I was concerned, support for revolutionary nationalism was still the party's position.

There will be a discussion, was the reply but as of now the party position is that all nationalism is reactionary. I blustered a bit more and we reached a compromise. I would put a line in the resolution condemning nationalism as reactionary but leave in the resolution that SDS supports the SF State strike's fifteen demands. I dutifully introduced the resolution at the plenum session and amazingly it passed, not because most of the attendees supported the PL leadership's new diktat on nationalism but because I coated the resolution in a hefty dose of demagogy and framed it in such a way that it was seen as a vote to support the struggle at SF State, not as a vote against black nationalism. This was pure opportunism, and I knew it.

Returning home we faced multiple attacks. In SDS the Joe Hill Caucus scalded us for the position on nationalism, and in the TWLF PL members were attacked as well. Although a number of our allies distanced themselves from us, particularly in the TWLF, PL retained its influence in the strike, mostly because of the respect people had for our leadership and militancy but also because we opportunistically explained PL's position in such a way that allowed us to maintain our support for the strike demands. ("We all have philosophical differences but the issue before us was winning the fifteen demands of the strike, so let's go back on the line and fight and not continue this ideological squabble.")

"Less talk, more action!" became our slogan of choice, and it led to some dangerous adventurism from which we luckily emerged mostly unscathed, and a bad tactical decision to turn the trials in the aftermath of the strike into political theater. The militant core of the PL/WSA insisted on jury trials rather than take a plea deal in which we would get probation and no jail time. We acted as our defense attorneys and attacked capitalism, the war in Vietnam, and racism, and called for revolution. But few people other than fellow strikers and family attended the trial. We were preaching to the choir, and it was not a nice feeling. About three dozen of us were convicted and sentenced to anywhere from three months to eighteen months in the San Francisco County Jail. A couple of months after my first daughter, Jennifer, was born, I started a six-month sentence.

One positive about being locked in an eight-foot-by-four-foot cell for several months was that it gave me time to think and reflect. What I chewed on was this: If the party was correct that all nationalism is reactionary and counterrevolutionary, I, as a PL leader, was responsible for getting people beaten, jailed, and expelled from school for no good reason. I was not a leader but a misleader. On the other hand, if PL was wrong and its position on nationalism was reactionary and counterrevolutionary, what the hell was I was doing in PL? I also questioned the validity of democratic centralism as a way to govern a revolutionary organization (and still do), but I kept my doubts to myself. I had been in PL all of my adult life. The idea of striking out on my own was a frightening prospect.

Once out of jail, I soldiered on as a PL member. It took me three wasted years to leave PL. Wasted because I no longer believed PL, with its corrupted organizational structure and denunciations of every other revolutionary movement with which the party was ever allied. (By this time China too had joined the PL's pantheon of failed revolutionary movements.) So I drifted along as a party functionary assigned to various projects that I accomplished or not in desultory fashion, and when the regional PL leader grew exasperated by my performance and suggested I get a job, I became a switchman for Ma Bell. I spent another year or so as a semi-mute party backbencher until I summoned up the courage to resign and apply myself once again to my dream of becoming a writer.

I've been asked what advice I might have for the new generation of revolutionaries in the age of Trump. I've been out of the advice business for close to a half-century, but I would hope that the new revolutionary generation might draw some insight from the experiences detailed in my account and others in this book. There is one thing about which I want to be explicit. In my opinion, the Marxist-Leninist concept of democratic centralism and a vanguard party has failed. It failed in the Soviet Union, it failed in China, and it has failed in every country where a Marxist-Leninist party has seized power. In PL, the structure concentrated too much influence and organizational power in a leadership, which, despite its many talents and strengths, became entrenched and corrupted ideologically so that every new idea or difference was judged not on its merits but whether it threatened the hegemony of the leadership. New revolutionary organizational structures need to be created. I draw hope from the Zapatista movement in the liberated zone of Chiapas, who govern through a collective, rotating leadership, and I'm sure there are others aborning. But for certain, the vanguard party and democratic centralism should be consigned to the dustbin of history.

Fifty years later I have a few regrets, but also pride, in having been part of the momentous movement against the war in Vietnam and the fight for racial justice. PL, despite its profound failings, was an important force in standing up to the US government and its policies. The trips to Cuba in the early 1960s, the organizing of the first mass demonstrations against the was in Vietnam on May 2, 1964, our introduction of the worker-student alliance as a strategy for the student movement, and militant support of African American rebellions in

Harlem, Watts, and across the country should all be acknowledged—
and I am proud to have been a part of it.

John Levin lives in San Francisco Mission District with Paula Braveman and Moe. A book of his plays, Three Plays by John F. Levin, *was published by Black Apollo Press in 2015. johnflevin@gmail.com*

7

A New World Opens

Margaret Leahy
(San Francisco State University)

The Worker-Student Alliance was not an organization. It was not a party or something you joined. Rather, in my experience at San Francisco State, the WSA was the name given to a group of people who tended to view issues in similar ways and vote the same way in meetings. Most times they voted with the members of the Progressive Labor Party. My understanding of the issues, how they came about and were related, as well as my political alliances developed as a result of my participation in actions at SF State beginning in 1967.

In 1967 I was not particularly political. I did care about civil rights and the war in Vietnam, but I didn't really understand the causes of segregation and the war nor did I see any relationship between the two. More important, I didn't really have experiences in my life that made these issues personal. This began to change in September 1967 when I enrolled in my first International Relations (IR) class taught by Professor John "Tito" Gerassi. I don't remember the title of the course, but my experience in it changed my life forever.

I had no idea who the professor was, but everyone else in the class seemed to know his work and was familiar with his political beliefs. His book *The Great Fear in Latin America* had recently come out and seemed to be a reference for others in the class. When I read the book I was astonished at my own ignorance of the long history of US exploitation of the nations of Latin America. Feeling completely out of my element but fascinated with the discussions in class, I sat back, listened, and learned. Pretty soon all the pieces that were sitting atomized in my brain began to come together and what was happening in the world around me began to make sense. All of this might have remained academic had not a particular event occurred on campus.

In November, an editor of the alternative paper on campus was suspended for writing an alleged pornographic poem about the football coach. Soon after a group of African American students was suspended for allegedly beating up the editor of the official school paper, *The Daily Gater*. The black students went to the paper to protest a racist cartoon the paper had run concerning Muhammad Ali. A fight ensued and the black students were blamed for starting it. In each instance the students were suspended without a hearing. A group organized as the Movement Against Political Suspensions (MAPS), and a student meeting was called to discuss the situation and develop a student response. Believing that everyone was innocent until proven guilty, I readily went to the meeting. I felt comfortable going because the organizers of the meeting were students I had in my IR class, students whose viewpoints I had learned to respect over the course of the term.

Two students in particular were key in my action, Gordon De Marco and John Levin. Gordon befriended me in Gerassi's class, had me to dinner with him and his girlfriend, Debbie, and always answered my questions without making me feel as if I should have known the answers already. Although I didn't know John personally at the time, I had grown to respect his analysis of the issues as well as his demeanor. While he might disagree greatly with someone else's analysis, he always spoke to the issue and never demeaned the person with whom he differed. I felt that I could trust him.

MAPS demanded that the president of the university, John Summerskill, reinstate the students until a hearing was held on each case. The president agreed to reinstate the newspaper editor, who was white, but not the African American students, because, he said, their act was "violent." In my opinion this was prejudging the students before any academic hearing had been held, as well as being clearly racist. MAPS once again demanded the students' reinstatement and threatened a sit-in if reinstatement hadn't occurred by noon, December 6.

Summerskill didn't reinstate the students and following a noon rally students marched to the administration building where some would sit in as threatened. When students arrived the front doors were padlocked together, but the doors were glass and soon someone kicked them in. About the same time Professor Gerassi and some students, including "K," a leader of the Iranian students, climbed through a window into the president's office. As I moved up the stairs to the front of the administration building I saw the broken doors and students moving through them into the building. At the top of the stairs I had to make a decision: Was I going to take a stand, act against what I believed to be wrong, and join my fellow students—or would I just stand there safely and observe? I went in, and I guess I never turned back.

The action that day was isolated and did not get support from most students. In the meetings that followed, people discussed why they thought it had unfolded that way. The conclusion was twofold. First, we hadn't done enough organizing among the student body so that they understood the issues. Second, as a result, we allowed the administration to characterize what occurred as simply a violent act that included people who were not students. Again, certain people's analysis made the most sense. I learned they were mostly members of something called the Progressive Labor Party, whatever that was. Over the next year I learned the various groups involved in an umbrella organization called Students for a Democratic Society and which individuals from which groups made the most sense to me. Again, individuals from PL and what became known as the WSA usually made the most sense. This was really solidified in November 1968, when the Black Student Union and the Third World Liberation Front called a student strike demanding the creation of a College of Third World Studies.

SDS was asked to join in the strike in support of a set of demands put forth by the BSU and TWLF. I remember very clearly an SDS meeting called to discuss participation where a major difference emerged. Some wanted SDS to make its participation contingent on an additional demand being included—ending the war in Vietnam. Others, myself included, strongly disagreed. We argued that the strike had been called by the BSU and TWLF with specific demands articulated and with the BSU and TWLF in the leadership position. SDS was asked to join in support of those demands and respect for that leadership. Those demands were something that could be accomplished at the college level. The college couldn't stop the war. Perhaps most important, some of those wanting to add a demand on the war seemed to feel uncomfortable with the primarily white SDS taking a secondary role. The strong role played by individuals in PL and what had become known as the WSA in articulating this second position stands out as a moment when I knew with whom I stood. That's not to say that I didn't have friends who weren't associated with any group or that I respected all those in PL and WSA. I listened to everyone and stood with those whose arguments made most sense to me at the time.

As I got to know people associated with PL on a personal level and became friends with them I found we had many ideas in common, although I didn't agree with everything. Progressive Labor looked to an alliance between workers and students to effect change. Other students and groups were more oriented to what I would call "student power" and the culture issues of the 1960s. Having started to work at fifteen out of economic necessity, I understood the needs of those who worked with their hands. I also had the opportunity to go to college and there I was exposed to new ideas and had the time to analyze those ideas. While I believed that students had the right to demand relevant education, I didn't believe that overall societal change could come out of academia. I had learned how the political, economic, and social systems were connected and that these interconnections were organized to benefit those who controlled the overall system. Based on this view of things, I associated with what became known as the Worker-Student Alliance.

The SF State strike lasted over four months, the longest student strike in the United States. During that time individuals in the BSU, TWLF, SDS, and many, many unaffiliated students as well as community supporters participated. Every morning people met on the picket line set up on 19th Avenue and Holloway, the entrance to the university. Rain or shine we marched from 8 in the morning till the noon rally. Occasionally the police would attempt to grab one of the people they were most interested in getting. Attempts at individual arrests happened on the campus, as well. Certain people were obviously targeted, such as any one who was on the BSU or TWLF Central Committees, members of the Progressive Labor leadership such as Bridges Randall and Hari Dillon, Gordon De Marco of WSA, and "K," the leader of the Iranian student group.

While people fought to protect each individual the police tried to arrest, most of us knew that "K" was the most vulnerable if arrested. He was quite vocal and active in the anti-Shah movement in the Bay Area, and his arrest could lead to immediate deportation back to Iran and certain torture and death at the hands of the SAVAK, the Shah's secret police. I remember that the one time he was arrested he had to be bailed out immediately and driven out of the country. I put up the house I had inherited from my parents as collateral. Our bail bondsman, Jerry Barrish, knew the circumstances and didn't attempt to get his $7,000 back by taking my house. He said that he had made enough money from us.

I knew Jerry quite well by that time, as I somehow became the person running the bail fund. If I remember correctly, this all started on one of the first days of the strike when the first arrest occurred. People were "passing the hat," sometimes literally, to get bail money. Someone with a car near campus was needed to go to Barrish Bail Bonds and get the person out. Barrish Bonds was known as the place that bailed out those arrested during various sit-ins in San Francisco. (Their slogan was "Don't perish in jail. Call Barrish for bail.") We certainly took them up on their offer, with over six hundred people being bailed out, some more than once. Going to the bail office after a day of walking the picket line and running from the cops soon became the norm for me. I kept a change of clothes in my car in case I needed to appear before a judge in chambers after court hours and ask for a bail reduction. I had only plead my case before a judge one time before I became known—and I always got the reductions.

The need for all of us to be able to count on everyone else to cover our backs during this time drew people together. Acquaintances became friends, sometimes lifelong friends. For example, Tito Gerassi became such a close friend that he stood up with me at my wedding and I was with his daughter at his bedside when he died. John Levin and I still see each other and have lunch three or four times a year and talk on the phone or by email quite often. I really relied upon him to help me in holding a memorial for Tito. Gordon De Marco and I remained as close as siblings until his death; my children called him Uncle Gordie. I haven't been able to remain in contact with "K" for obvious reasons, but when I recently learned that he was still alive, I cried tears of happiness. Even now, almost fifty years later, people will run into another SF State striker on the street and act as if they had seen each other just yesterday, even if their hair is now grayer.

When I recount my experiences during the strike to others I am often asked why I never attempted to join the PL, since I was politically close to members of Progressive Labor. The fact that it was a "party" was at the core of my decision. As a party, members were expected to act in accordance with decisions made through a process of democratic centralism. As such, even if you disagreed with a particular decision to do or not do something, if word came down to do or not to do it, you followed that order. I was, and am, too independent to be bound by such discipline, although I understand the reasoning behind it. I need to personally reason something out by myself—perhaps with input of others—and make my own decision at the end. Maybe this is because I'm "shanty Irish," or maybe because I'm just fiercely independent and stubborn. I don't know.

Margaret Leahy is a retired professor of international relations who lives in San Francisco, where she was born and raised. She is currently trying to write a history of her parents and grandparents so that her grandchildren know their roots.

8

Toward Revolutionary Art

Ernie Brill
(San Francisco State University)

I grew up in a socialistic Jewish family in a Brooklyn project built for World War II vets. When the project integrated in the mid fifties, the New York Housing Authority placed all the black families in one building. When my sister walked home from school in fourth grade with a black kid, my parents found out.

"We think it is a better idea if you don't walk home with Larry Daniels."

"Why?" my sister asked. "He's nice; he's funny."

My mother hesitated, then blurted, "Do you want to have polka-dotted kids?"

In 1958 we moved to Long Island. The all-white town of Baldwin still had KKK members. The town's anti-Semitism shocked me, since Brooklyn had a huge Jewish population, and my mother's family had lost many people in the Holocaust. One night my mother said, "Finish your homework by seven. There's a show about the concentration camps." I replied, "I'm sick and tired of hearing about Hitler." For a second I thought she'd smack me. She glared, "Know your problem?" She didn't wait for an answer. "Your problem is you haven't heard *enough* about Hitler."

In eleventh grade, my first date with my current wife was at the Statue of Liberty, an all-night vigil for beleaguered Freedom Riders in the Southern civil rights movement. I entered Antioch College in the summer of 1963 and attended meetings of the Congress of Racial Equality (CORE), a civil rights group protesting a local barber's refusal to serve African Americans. I joined a sit-in, defying a court injunction forbidding more than two picketers. Authorities jailed one hundred of us for two days and nights before dropping all charges.

I dropped out of Antioch and headed to California, not understanding that doing so would lose me my student draft status. My draft board called me for duty—and due to my Antioch arrest, I had to see the Morals (!) Officer, a lieutenant, who asked me if I was a hippie since I had longish hair. I told him I had preferred long hair since I was six years old, and that I hated short hair, especially crew cuts. Then he asked me why I wouldn't fight for my country. I said if it were World War II, I would volunteer immediately. But I had no argument with the Vietnamese fighting for the same liberty we'd battled for against the British. A ferocious argument ensued. When he hotly declared, "The United States has never been involved in a war that didn't help thousands of people," I replied, "Oh no? Let's start with the Indians and work our way up." I had no idea what my new classification of 1-Y meant, so I visited the newly formed Draft Counseling Services at San Francisco State College. The head counselor chuckled: "That means you only get called when the Chinese junks invade LA harbor."

I lived with artists and writers, working odd jobs, then in 1966 transferred to San Francisco State, a bustling, rambunctious campus with older students, including Vietnam veterans, and many international students from Palestine to Peru. I audited classes at the newly formed Experimental College, a college within a college, which offered daring courses, including Revolution, Midwifery, Surrealist Poetry, Alternative Magazines, and the History of Zen Buddhism. I concentrated on my own fiction and poetry while dutifully taking classes. I avoided organizations like CORE or SDS that seemed strident, rhetoric-ridden. But I seethed restlessly. Most classes had no literature by black, Latino, Asian, Native American, or white working-class writers. These abysmal oversights pushed me toward activism.

In the spring of 1968, shocked and infuriated by the assassination of Martin Luther King, I attended an SDS emergency meeting. The only people possessing a clue about a response were the Worker-Student Alliance "They call themselves the WSA caucus, but they are actually PL—Progressive Labor Party, Maoist communists who want to control SDS and use this campus to make a revolution." I looked around at the gray buildings, some beautiful trees, the dull Student Center. I didn't see anything particularly useful in making a revolution.

"How would they do that?"

"Push their propaganda. Recruit people to the cause."

"What cause?"

"You know. Stop war. Smash racism. Smash imperialism. Use protests like student fee hikes and cafeteria workers' situations to stir shit up and manipulate people to join them."

There were many protests and fervent activity at SF State. Having not had a raise in years and laboring under harsh conditions, cafeteria workers were organizing a union. Many students supported the United Farm Workers' union drive and the nationwide grape and lettuce boycott. The Black Students Union was developing courses at the Experimental College for a Black Studies Department for which they'd lobbied for years to provide courses more relevant to the black community. The student government ran a highly successful tutorial program in the African American and Latino neighborhoods of San Francisco, but each year they had to wade through miles of red tape just to renew the bare-bones funding.

The campus turmoil culminated in a sit-in in the spring of 1968 that presented three main demands: the rehiring of Professor Juan Martinez and Dr. Nathan Hare (who had been hired in the first place to create a Black Studies Department!); the removal of the ROTC program; and open admissions for all Third World students.

The WSA people impressed me. In moments of tension and confusion, fleeing from the SFPD tactical squad with shoving and pushing, the WSAers stayed calm and led others. Jointly acting with the Third World Liberation Front, we sat in day and night in the main administration building, planning and voting as democratically as possible to stay or leave, with people arguing and proposing action. The WSA offered ideas, tactics, and strategies.

John, the leader of PL student work, and I became friends. I often wound up at the place he shared with his girlfriend. I admired their dedication and sense of humor in the midst of chaos. In their kitchen hung a huge Maoist poster: Harvest of the Ducklings. In a bright blue-white sunny sky a red-orange Mao Zedong beamed over hills whose meadows were full of plump grinning ducks tended by happy peasants, all of whom were over six feet tall and sturdy as a truck. We also hit it off because we were Jews from New York, English majors, and aspiring writers.

That summer I worked with PL folks on a citywide rent-control campaign. We were like family. Colorful Mission District PL leader John Ross, who later was heavily involved in movements in Mexico and wrote a powerful book about his experiences there, let six-year-old kids sign petitions.

"You wanna sign too? Why the hell not?"

When we presented the petitions at City Hall, one registrar frowned. "Some of these look like kid signatures!"

"That's right," John replied. "Even six-year-olds know what's good. *Everyone wants rent control!*"

I happily noticed that at PL events—marches, parties, picnics, forums, and movie screenings—there was a healthy mix of white, black, Chicano, and Asian families, who all seemed to get along together very well.

Sharpened apprehension and a barely subdued fury permeated the SF State campus that fall; one sensed a giant impending snap. The BSU announced a teach-in on campus to discuss ten demands they were making. Some of the key demands of the BSU were the creation of a fully funded Black Studies Department with twenty full-time teaching positions; that Dr. Hare receive a full professorship with comparable salary according to his qualifications; and that all black students wishing to do so be admitted for the fall 1968 semester. Soon the BSU joined with other campus groups of color to form the Third World Liberation Front. This new group included, along with the BSU, La Raza (the Latino students' organization), the Chinese Students Association, the Filipino Student Union, the Japan Society, and the Native American Association. The TWLF made five new demands, including the creation of a School of Ethnic Studies with students in each ethnic group having control over the hiring and retention of any faculty member, and that all applications from students of color be accepted for the fall 1969 semester.

Many white students balked.

"Why their own department? That's segregation in itself."

"They're not learning about themselves or their history or culture."

"Hey, I'm Jewish. I don't see Jewish studies classes."

"Or Irish. What about Gaelic studies?"

"Yeah, but at least they talk about Hitler in World History and sometimes in American Lit there's a Saul Bellow novel. Hell, I'm Armenian; there's nothing."

"The Chicanos say that, too. Nothing about them in the curriculum."

"And the Asians."

"What about Confucius?"

The campus buzzed like a giant aural kaleidoscope with myriad conversations on all sides of the issues. Some were tinged with resentment that "these people" should want ANYTHING.

"They should be happy just to be in college."

"But it's true about the courses. History, English, Sociology—zero, zilch.

"No place, no face."

On November 7, 1969, the SF State student strike began. Black students entered classrooms declaring the campus on strike, announcing the demands. They had planned for a three-day strike followed by a massive teach-in. But suddenly a typewriter crashed through a window of the business building. No one determined who threw it, but suddenly police tactical squads rushed onto campus, roughing up people and arresting, for no logical reason, a BSU leader who had been elsewhere. When students tried to free him, police drew and pointed guns. Later that afternoon, both the TWLF and BSU called for all-out strike.

PL leaders in WSA called for the creation of a mass umbrella group, the Strike Support Committee, which consisted mainly of white students. An emergency meeting was set for that evening at a church in San Francisco's Fillmore District; over three hundred students attended. Jan Solganick, a WSA leader, organized creation of a broadside to expose the college trustees and their corporate connections—for example, Dudley Swim, head of Del Monte Corp. Would the boss of thousands of fruit pickers want any of his kids to go to a college that might deprive him of his labor force? The flier flew down the list: why were leaders of corporations making decisions about college education?

We handed them out next day. Even students against the strike grabbed them; everyone hungered for information, including the initial ten BSU and five subsequent TWLF demands.

That same afternoon, George Murray, Black Panther Party Minister of Education and an instructor at SF State, spoke at an emergency rally about a racist attack in a dormitory at Fresno State College where some white students, armed with baseball bats and lead pipes, had assaulted a group of black students, hospitalizing some. Murray called for students to exercise their Second Amendment right of arming themselves. Three hours later the California State College Trustees fired Murray for "incendiary remarks having no business in the field of education." Students, faculty, and community members were outraged by the trustees' decision.

The strike mushroomed. White students, side by side with BSU and TWLF members, picketed from 6 a.m. to 4 p.m., marching through the campus chanting "On Strike! Shut It Down!" When the tactical squads attacked them, they retreated across campus, hurling back at the cops whatever came to hand.

A core of twenty SDS and Student Strike Committee members

worked with thirty TWLF students to do "classroom education." We would enter a class, introduce ourselves, politely request time to explain the strike, and answer questions. I went with Patsy, a fellow SDSer, and Tim, a BSU student, to an American literature class studying William Faulkner's novel *Light in August*. I'd read the same edition of the same book. The teacher agreed to ten minutes. I jumped in.

"So, you're reading *Light in August*."

They nodded, curious.

"I guess it's a no-brainer since we're striking about racism and you're reading about it. But—"

"No," said a heavyset student. "This is more about how everything in the South is so twisted that nobody wins."

"Maybe, but can you see the racism?"

"No."

"Not even a little?"

"No. In fact I think everyone overall is pretty damn nice to Joe Christmas."

"Turn to page 305."

The teacher did a double take.

"He's involved with Ellie Burden. Check it out—middle of the page: 'panting panting in the nigger night.'"

"That isn't racist."

"No?"

"It's their cultural milieu. Everybody there talks like that."

"How do you *know* that?" Tim said angrily.

"I saw that movie, *To Kill a Mockingbird*."

"That's Hollywood's crap." I said. "Worse than the book."

"Have *you* read the book?"

"I've read *Light in August* twice," I replied. "And fine, let's say it's their milieu, but is it not racist, the whole shebang 'the dark liquid primitive night that has always been there would always be there now and tomorrow and still unrepentantly remembered from yesterday.' Check the word choice: 'unrepentantly remembered'; I mean, unrepentant—I'm not turning away, I'm not turning back, and I don't give a damn how you feel about it cause I'll do what I damn well please. Like in Little Rock, like George Wallace in Alabama."

Some students scowled. Some folded their arms tighter.

A woman's voice in the back whispered, "Shit, he's right."

"This stuff's throughout the book. You think they have any kind of substantial relationship?"

One guy said, "Maybe Joe and her are just getting to know each other."

"Go through the book. List every time someone pants or gasps. And check this out, Faulkner and James Baldwin argued about civil rights. Faulkner said, 'You need to go slower.' Baldwin replied, 'We've been going slow for over two hundred years.'"

In the essay "Faulkner and Desegregation" in Baldwin's *Nobody Knows My Name*, Faulkner said in an interview printed in the *Reporter* newspaper that he would fight for Mississippi, "even if it meant going out into the streets and shooting Negroes."

The teacher reddened. "I think your time's up."

Patsy stepped in briskly.

"Any last minute questions about the demands?"

The students blinked. I realized that I had hogged the whole ten minutes, but I couldn't care less. Tim, the BSU student, was staring at me; I had no idea what he was thinking. Patsy was looking half-surprised and half-pissed.

"Thank you," the professor said. "This has been, um, different."

Later, three or four students from the class wanted to talk about Faulkner and racism, convincing me that we were on the right track. Instead of badgering students with dogmatic speeches at campus rallies, calling them "good Germans" if they did not immediately flock to us, we had to hit them where they lived. If colleges are knowledge factories manufacturing certain ideas and belief systems, then, to use Marxist terms, the point of production was *in* classrooms, where many insidious ideas—such as the justification of foreign land theft and the contingent support of dictatorships like South Vietnam's—flourished. It was fruitless to discuss racism as merely a bad attitude or ignorance without examining history's largest mass kidnapping and the billions of dollars in sales of African flesh.

Several afternoons later I met John at the Ecumenical House near the campus. "How would you like to go sniping tonight?"

I lost my breath and almost started choking. I wasn't ready to shoot anybody. I had never held a real gun in my life except at Coney Island, where I shot chalk pellets at moving cardboard ducks. I'd never touched a gun and he said it so nonchalantly, as if he had been doing it his entire life. I did feel complimented and honored that he would consider me for such an important, daring action. I felt bad that I was going to disappoint him.

"I don't think I'm ready for that, John. I mean, I appreciate you asking me, but I've never even touched a gun. I might be more of a liability than a help."

He stared at me, then laughed heartily.

"It's not what you think. Not at all. It's just a term for putting up posters."

"*Posters!*"

"Yeah. We go around, find good spots where lots of people will see them, then slap them on with a mixture of flour and evaporated Pet milk. It's amazing how they stick to telephone poles, mailboxes, windows, factory doors."

I almost blurted, "Isn't that kind of against the law?" But I was so overjoyed I wouldn't have to kill anyone that I grinned, "When do we start?"

The next night John and I "sniped" over two hundred posters all over the Mission District, Noe Valley, and Bernal Heights. We worked from 8:30 until 1 a.m., celebrating afterwards with tacos at an all-night mom-and-pop place in the Mission. The few fellow diners regarded us as painters or plasterers coming off a shift.

That night firmed up a friendship that continues to this day. Recently, Hollywood released a film about the Iraq wars entitled *American Sniper*. When I saw the title, for a second, I felt that misty San Francisco night driving in John's funky VW with brushes, fifty cans of evaporated milk, three bags of flour, and two hundred posters about the California State College Trustees entitled WANTED FOR RAC-ISM: DO NOT TRY TO APPREHEND BY YOURSELF. I still smile about that night, one of many incidents during our life-changing protest and ultimate victory at San Francisco State that helped set the pace for the nation.

Yes, we won the strike. But not before the national PL leadership unilaterally changed the party's line. PL attacked the TWLF, claiming that revolutionary nationalism was "reactionary" because it did not focus on the primacy of the revolutionary black working class. Genuine revolutionaries must fight for the leadership of the working class, particularly the minority working class, the most oppressed. PL also criticized the revolutionary nationalism of the Vietnamese liberation movement, and various Cuban and African liberation movements. Within PL, nationalism became almost a slur.

Many people at SF State in and around PL and WSA were furious. For over five months we had fought police from all over Northern California, side by side with our Third World sisters and brothers, gone to jail, risked suspension, expulsion, and possible ruination of any chance for academic careers, only for some Red couch potatoes to tell us our struggle had been in vain even though we had won. Not only was the first Black Studies Department in the US established, but an entire School of Ethnic Studies. Within PL and within the WSA, there were many bitter feelings and differences that were never really resolved. Some members voted with their feet and quit the struggle or went elsewhere, either to other groups or other pursuits.

After the strike, I obtained an MA in English with a dissertation on the controversial African American novelist Chester Himes. I also served thirty-five days in the county jail in San Bruno for disturbing the peace. I was one of four hundred people arrested at a campus rally known as The Great Mass Bust. Most of the eight hundred arrests at SF State were overturned in California State Appellate Court as violations of our First and Fourth Amendment rights. Ironically, many of us had served sentences ranging from thirty days to one year.

Until 1976 I stayed in PL, doing trade-union organizing at hospitals. I helped create The Red Theatre, PL's guerrilla street theater group, which performed at high schools, unemployment offices, and workplaces. I also wrote poems and book reviews for PL's newspaper *Challenge/Desafío*.

Two events constituted the last straw. The biggest was over a crucial struggle at Camp Pendleton in Oceanside (near San Diego), where racist white Marines attacked black Marines who fought back militantly. Northern California PL came to the defense of the black Marines, who were arrested and court-martialed. The PL national leadership and their supporters seemed more intent on attacking the black Marines' "nationalism" than demanding a thorough exposé of Klan activity and membership at Camp Pendleton.

California PL split in two. One half sided with the New York PL National Office while the Bay Area PL leadership and most of its members sided with the rank-and-file black Marines and accused the national leadership of racism. Years of friendships with comrades who had fought side by side dissolved in vitriolic accusations.

I'd seen some of the writing on the wall. An essential part of any Marxist-Leninist party is the crucial concept of democratic centralism. Every member in the party democratically discusses a new position, idea, or program. Everyone gets to have their say. Every rambunctious idea or offbeat suggestion is considered. Once the decision is made, however, every comrade carries it out, no matter if he or she has individual doubts or scruples. This is absolutely necessary for any movement forward.

PL began with democratic centralism. However, as with other ML parties, the PL leadership was often leery about the democratic part. It didn't want debates to become too unmanageable. And, often, the leadership of ML parties consisted of one main man, in our case Milt Rosen. This has been true in many radical American groups (the vaguely socialist groups *never* call themselves a party). After a while, the line becomes more important than people, no matter how ludicrous.

In 1975, after years of struggling with PL people to take a broader view of culture and literature and not be so dogmatic (they idealized socialist-realist art) I became the editor of *Challenge*'s cultural page). PL wanted art where workers won EVERY strike and were all seven feet tall with muscles like bowling balls. Soon after, Luis, the main editor of *Challenge*, called me on the phone.

"We got a problem. There's a really fascist movie out. Can you go see it, write a review, and get it to me for Monday?"

It was Friday. It would be no problem.

"What's the movie?"

"*The Producers*. It's this piece-of-crap fascist movie glorifying *Hitler*, man."

"What?"

I doubted that they were glorifying Hitler.

"It starts out with a big musical number 'Springtime for Hitler.'"

"Let me go see it and get back to you."

I went to see it, laughed my ass off, then called Luis back .

"It's a comedy, man. A satire."

"What do you mean? It's a piece of fascist drivel."

"First of all, the whole premise is absurd. These con artists want money. So they need a play to flop big-time. If it flops, they don't have to pay anybody back."

"It's a fascist movie. The main dance number is 'Springtime for Hitler' with all these dancing Nazis!"

"That's why it's so funny. You don't understand."

"What is there to understand" Luis snapped. "I don't think dancing Nazis are too hard to understand. They don't need understanding, comrade; they need killing."

"Historically, Americans go ape-shit for musicals. You can do any content as long you as you put it to music."

"I'm not getting you, man."

"You could do a musical about Stalin and the Gulag with dancing Cossack thugs crooning and as long as the music was catchy, they'd love it!"

A song was forming in my mind.

"Are you making fun of Stalin?"

"Joke, man. Joke."

In the complete silence, I tapped my foot and hummed softly. I had it:

Got problems with enemies
And don't know what to do
Well if you've got strong knees
Then I've got the dance for you:
YOU DO THE STALIN STOMP
(HEY! HEY! HEY!)
YOU DO THE STALIN STOMP

"Hello? Hello?"

"I think you've gone off the deep end, comrade."

"I just have a different take on it."

"If you feel that strongly we can get someone else to do the review. We just don't think this fascist trash should go unchallenged."

I wanted to congratulate him on his pun, but I restrained myself.

Before I went to sleep I typed up my resignation as *Challenge* Cultural Page editor, and from Progressive Labor. And the future seemed so much brighter even though I couldn't get the "Stalin Stomp" out of my head.

I remained a radical, joining the staff of TRA (*Towards Revolutionary Art* magazine) and becoming its poetry and fiction editor. With a new sense of aesthetic freedom, I started going to more poetry readings, and attending radical writers conferences, especially an intergenerational conference in Kansas City where I met the legendary writers Jack Conroy, Meridel Le Sueur, and Tom McGrath.

I wrote a book of short stories about hospital workers, *I Looked Over Jordan and Other Stories*, and moved back to New York City, publishing the book with the fledgling South End Press and becoming involved with writers in multicultural and labor arts movements. Through the creators of the Labor Theatre, Chuck Portz and Betty Craig, I met

Ruby Dee, who brilliantly performed my story "Crazy Hattie Enters the Ice Age" as part of a PBS series with her husband, Ossie Davis.

Throughout the eighties I worked with writers in New York around the Before Columbus Foundation, a multicultural publishing outfit started by Ishmael Reed, Steve Cannon, Bob Callahan, and others. I promoted various writers and presses, including Yardbird Press, West End Press, Sunbury Press, Curbstone Press, and Thunder's Mouth Press, getting together and reading with such writers as John A. Williams, Toni Cade Bambara, Alice Childress, Pedro Pietri, and Dan Georgakas. I was also a founding member of the National Writers Union and its first fiction writers group and published stories and poems in many small-press magazines in the US and Canada.

I worked as a high school English teacher for twenty years, creating curriculums around the Harlem Renaissance, gender projects in British lit, units on African, Latin American, and Middle East literature, and focusing on such world-class writers as Nikolai Gogol, Chinua Achebe, Isabel Allende, Pablo Neruda, Richard Wright, Cynthia Ozick, Bao Ninh, and Mahmoud Darwish. For me, there remains the monumental challenge W. E. B. Du Bois articulated at the turn of the twentieth century: the color line. Racism is the bedrock of America formed on oceans of blood, the foundation of our country's mighty fortune, and its most lethal pollutant.

PL in its heyday deserves credit. The party helped smash HUAC. They organized some of the earliest trips to Cuba and some of the supply caravans to beleaguered mining families of the Appalachian coal struggle. PL publicized the positive achievements of the Chinese Revolution. They led many antiracist struggles from Harlem to San Francisco. They tried to develop the political leadership of African American, Latino, and Asian American workers. PL brought a fighting communist perspective to unions and community groups. They brought a respect for working-class struggles into a basically white middle-class student movement, organizing students to support strikers and unions. We tried in so many ways in schools, neighborhoods, communities, factories, and offices to fight the beasts of racism.

At the same time, PL abandoned its credo of democratic central-ism: a nice idea, but hard to implement. There was too much control at the top. The "discussion" was often perfunctory, the decisions already made. Bay Area PL seemed an admirable exception. Discussions were substantial and occasionally fiery, with more freewheeling indepen-dent thinkers than found in the PL units in LA, Boston, and New York, where the membership seemed overwhelmed by the national leader-ship of ex–Communist Party members like Milt Rosen. But at least PL, unlike almost any other group, tried to seriously develop Third World leadership. They never seemed to go far enough, however, and allow African American, Latino, and Asian comrades to truly lead.

The strike at SF State remains my proudest, most life-changing time. My best friends are from the strike. My teaching "style" began there, questioning with humor, challenging racism, taking risks, pro-moting astonishing writers whose compassionate political artistry inspires and sustains people to engage for "a better world in birth."

Ernie Brill, from Northampton, Mass., via Brooklyn, is finishing a novel about the historic 1968 San Francisco State student strike against racism. His story "Crazy Hattie Enters the Ice Age" from his collection I Looked Over Jordan and Other Stories *(South End Press, 1980) was adapted and performed by Ruby Dee for public television. He's published stories and poems widely in the US and Canada.*

9

The Stakes Were Higher Than We Knew

Anatole Anton
(Stanford, San Francisco State University)

Introduction: My Background

I was a graduate student at Stanford University in the mid sixties, working toward a PhD in philosophy. I was in my twenties, torn between my desires to be a successful academic and a full-time activist. At that time I called myself an "independent Marxist," and I styled my politics along the lines of *Monthly Review* magazine. I tried to figure out what it would mean to be a *revolutionary* Marxist. In truth, I felt that being a Marxist was a long-term proposition, and I didn't know if I was really up to the task. Having been on the first Progressive Labor–organized trip to Cuba in 1963, however, and having tried to keep up with the literature on Marxism, I felt that I was at least on my way to getting a better grip on political issues than my careerist peers at Stanford. Very few of my fellow students were focused on opposing and exposing the war in Vietnam, which was becoming more of a priority for me, along with support for the civil rights movement.

I took a trip to New York in the summer of 1964. The Harlem rebellions had just taken place, friends in PL and the May 2nd Movement, along with others, were building a free university on 14th Street, and the antiwar movement was mushrooming. I returned to Stanford with renewed energy to oppose the war in Vietnam. The civil rights movement humbled me—I felt that it had tested both my courage to take a principled stand against racism and my commitment to become a real Marxist. Coming out of the McCarthy era, I wanted to make it clear that I was not a "communist," while nevertheless advocating Marxism. I didn't want to be ostracized, so I dodged the issue by verbal sleight of hand, sidestepping any specific questions about my connection with "communist" thought. Given the stigma attached to the word *communism* in that era, I shied away from it and was drawn more to socialist terminology (which tended to be reformist). By "independent" Marxism, I meant unaffiliated with either a communist party or Marxist orthodoxy. I thought that they were ultimately superficial in their analyses.

Predictably, there was turmoil in my personal life. Since these problems were mixed with my political activity, more and more challenges emerged. I wanted to be effective politically; I wanted to live my life by political criteria. At the same time, I wanted a bourgeois lifestyle, in contrast to my working-class/bohemian upbringing. Looking back now on becoming an academic professor and a political militant, I think I was trying to "square a circle," since it was impossible to achieve both at the same time. I didn't fit in at Stanford, while my working-class background had everything to do with my choice of a career: I was trying to move up in the world.

I was also dealing with my mother's sad existence—trapped in a bureaucratic civil-service job and married to my bohemian artist father. I wanted to please both my parents, but they were very different from each other. My mother was proud of me for getting a PhD; on the other hand, my father, Harold Anton, a friend of Franz Klein and other abstract-expressionist artists, was proud of my ability to think critically. The one thing he would never tire of repeating to me was, "Don't become a mediocrity, son."

The stakes were high for me. I wanted to build a revolutionary movement in the US, where ideas similar to the "mass line" (Maoist political, organizational, and leadership methodology) in China would be given voice. I owe a debt of gratitude to David and Nancy Milton,[1] who taught me about radical politics, including both the mass line and the deficiencies of the US Communist Party. The concept of the mass line appealed to me because at the time it signaled a connection to the great Chinese Revolution. I wanted to use my academic career to help build the Left in the US. Specifically, I wanted to see a more politically organized approach to the civil rights movement and the protests against the Vietnam War. I asked myself if it would be possible to create a revolutionary Left that was prepared to fight, take risks, and aggressively recruit students and workers.

An ideological fight was developing against corporate liberalism, and I joined that fight. The guiding idea for me was once again Mao's mass line: "From the masses to the masses!" This meant giving priority to bottom-up decision-making. An example of this was the Barefoot Doctors movement in China. They went to the workers and peasants and tried to learn their practices and grievances, and then tried to create theory out of these practices. The Barefoot Doctors, whose main emphasis was on getting medical care to the people of China, were influenced by both traditional Chinese medicine and Western medicine. It was a model for building a movement that went to the masses to discover what they wanted in their daily life. These discoveries could then be put into a more systematic, clearer theoretical expression for use as a guide to building further mass movements.

Cuba Trip

I learned about the Cuba trip from my friendship circle, most of whom were fellow travelers or members of PL. I quickly became aware that PL had organized this trip as an attack on the Cold War by exposing hundreds of students to the depth and excitement of what was happening in Cuba. Members of PL were ubiquitous throughout the trip. Thanks to them, I came to better understand the Cuban Revolution.

---

1 The Miltons subsequently published a book entitled *The Trees May Prefer the Calm But the Wind Will Not Subside*, which happens to be Mao Zedong's favorite Chinese adage.

In the early sixties there was a lot of political interest in Cuba. The Cuban Revolution was still new and books were coming out about it, including an influential one by Sartre (*Sartre on Cuba*), which featured an interview with Fidel Castro, and another by C. Wright Mills, *Listen Yankee*. There was an idea circulating that this revolution was a fresh start for socialism because of its flair and style. I had been to meetings with a group called Fair Play for Cuba, supported by people such as Arthur Miller. From my perspective, Cuba seemed exciting: I had never traveled outside the US and the opportunity to visit Cuba seemed like a perfect place to start. We had expected to be gone for no more than a month, but the State Department made it difficult for us to get back home and we wound up staying an extra month.

At first my parents didn't know about the trip. I had told them that I had been accepted into a PhD program for the fall and that I was going to study near Woodstock, but they learned about my real intentions when the FBI showed up on their doorstep, fishing for information and trying to use their concern to dissuade me from going. Even without the FBI, my parents disapproved of the trip. My father told me not to be a "schmuck." He thought it was a stupid thing to do because it would cause me a lot of trouble and probably threaten my plans for grad school at Stanford. But I was determined to go regardless of the consequences.

So I signed up for the Cuba trip, despite the fact that it was illegal to travel there. My friends and I were attracted to Cuba by the culture and we were fascinated by Fidel Castro and Che Guevara. Most important, we felt we had a *right* to go to Cuba and see the revolution with our own eyes, regardless of what we were told by the US State Department. We believed that the First Amendment protection of freedom of speech included a freedom to travel as well. We did this as an act of civil disobedience, and there was never any doubt in my mind that I, as a US citizen, had (and still have) a right to travel where I want.

We were thus challenging the reasons the State Department had for not allowing us to go to Cuba. I felt that the burden was on them to prove to me that I *didn't* have the right to travel wherever I desired;

that if they wanted to strip me of my rights they had to have a good reason to do so, and I did not feel that the reasons the government gave were sufficient. I was consciously supporting Justice Douglas's interpretation of the First Amendment, which was that the burden of proof is always on the one who wants to shut free speech down.

The eighty-three people who went with me could be divided into three groups: friends from New York, friends from the SF Bay Area, and people I didn't know. The latter seemed like they wouldn't normally even think of going to a country where a successful revolution had just occurred, let alone one in such open opposition to the US. I was drawn to these people, since they all seemed trustworthy (apart from the few who turned out to be agents). In a sense, the Cuba trip was not just a matter of traveling; it meant meeting people with different political views from my own. For instance, there was José Lima from Puerto Rico, who was a mathematician and a surrealist poet studying at UC Berkeley—I hadn't met anyone like him before. And meeting Cuban people was a real revelation. I immediately sensed the huge cultural, political, and social differences between the two countries, especially the way everything in Cuba was politicized.

The Cubans were tremendously hospitable. I saw a country in its early stages of liberation. It was a very vibrant society; you could feel a pulse everywhere—in the music, in the stories people had to tell, in their small shops, in the streets, and in their ever-present knowledge of recent Cuban history. I remember an inspirational trek that our group took to a spot that had been a revolutionary center for Fidel Castro and his July 26th Movement, called Minas del Frío, which was revered as a monument to the revolution. Young students would come to Minas del Frío to make themselves aware of the dangers the revolution had held for its founders. It certainly lived up to its name, since it was both cold and high in the mountains.

I distinctly remember being out of breath as I ascended the mountain. A friend of mine, Richie Valez, was encouraging me up the mountain as I was gasping for air. To the Cubans, going to that place was a way of keeping the memory of the Cuban Revolution alive. Besides this physically challenging site, I also remember the scenic beauty of Cuba, such as Varadero Beach, and was impressed by the Cuban people's attitude toward public places. Varadero had it all: beautiful beaches and vistas as well as a strong nightclub life. The Cuban Revolution had taken this spot, which was once reserved for tourists and the wealthy, and had given it to the Cuban workers as place to vacation.

The most memorable moments of our trip were our meetings with Fidel and Che. Che was a particularly good and witty commentator. He went around the room meeting the members of our student group and asking what their majors were. One young woman answered "political science"; Che took the opportunity to inform us that, in his opinion, "Politics is an art, my dear." When asked about revolution, Che said that it comes into being by putting pressure on the facts, and that it is not made sitting down. Fidel engaged the group by challenging many of us to ping-pong games, most of which he won. In these games, one could feel what it would be like to have easy, friendly relations between the US and Cuba. After all these years, my clearest impression is that they presented themselves as ordinary human beings; they made no effort to venerate themselves.

When I returned to the US, the House Un-American Activities Committee (HUAC), managed by a diminutive congressman, Joe Pool, immediately subpoenaed me. The recent legal rulings on the First Amendment were favorable toward us; we neither were nor pretended to be intimidated by Pool and his gang of politicians. One of our members, Arthur Kinoy, a lawyer who had helped develop our defense, was actually kicked out of the hearing room, with Pool and his associates citing him for contempt of Congress. Kinoy asked what the rules of evidence were, since we were on uncharted legal waters, and HUAC refused to answer.

Spearheaded by PL and other radical groups, there were demonstrations in New York and Washington in response to the HUAC hearings on the Cuba trip, which lasted a couple of days. This was the end of the McCarthy era, but HUAC still believed that communism was taking over the country and that they were the ones to stop it. Obviously, traveling to Cuba was in their eyes a crime and they were going to make an example out of us.

Nothing of real substance came of the hearings, nor was there an official ruling on our right to travel to Cuba. A case similar to ours, however, involving the journalist William Worthy, resulted in a ruling that HUAC was acting in unconstitutionally in restricting travel to communist countries. These hearings were instrumental in closing down HUAC for good.

SDS and the Struggles of the Sixties

Personal friendship drew me to PL, specifically my friendship with Levi Laub, whom I first met at summer camp in early adolescence. Levi was a revolutionary organizer. I was greatly impressed by his deep understanding of the politics of the US Left as well as both international and national politics. I also admired him for his ability to become friends and form political bonds with working-class people while still retaining his intellectual integrity. He introduced me to his group of comrades within PL, who impressed me by their experience in class struggle and their willingness to go beyond liberalism in resolving conflicts.

PL was an organization that seemed to have a clear political line and was aiming to create a united front. What attracted me most was their militancy and strong critiques of other organizations, such as the Communist Party. However, I took pains to avoid becoming a member of PL. In truth, I didn't join PL because I had academic ambitions. I wanted to be a professor of philosophy, and I thought that being an active member of PL would undermine my chances of success. Their dogmatism was also an obstacle. I didn't trust their level of political understanding; though essentially good people, they seemed simplistic in their thinking and I was afraid of being associated with their simplistic analyses. But more than just this complaint deterred me from joining—at bottom, I believed they weren't open to new influences.

For example, when I dared to criticize a small passage of the *Communist Manifesto*, or even talked about why Red must also be Green (communism joining the environmental movement), they wouldn't take me seriously and displayed their inherent conservatism. They criticized the innovative work of new Marxist authors such as James O'Connor, whom I greatly admired. In short, they weren't open to discussing Marxist errors. I was passionate about getting Marxist theory right and they essentially weren't open to discussion. I was equally afraid of becoming a party hack, those people who become caricatures of themselves in old age. I did, however, respect those in PL who had artistic aspirations, people such as Roger Taus, Chris Raisner, and Levi Laub. At a later point I became critical of PL because of their criticisms of the NLF's position at the Paris peace negotiations. As I saw it, PL was essentially telling the NLF what they should or shouldn't do, and I didn't think it was PL's role to tell those directly engaged in the war how to fight it. I found PL's position to be rigid and dogmatic, and I looked for more flexible ways of thinking.

I never formally joined PL, but I was on the fringes. I was protesting the Vietnam War with PL, marching in demonstrations with them, and participating in other events. I was drawn to PL because of their organization of the Cuba trip, which I was grateful to be a part of and which subsequently had a formative influence on my political development. Another aspect that appealed to me was that it was one of the very few organizations emphasizing opposition to US imperialism, of which the Vietnam war was emblematic.

The May 2nd Movement—which grew out of a need within PL for an affiliate that dealt with issues in education and culture—was, at the time of its creation, the de facto student wing of PL. The M2M came out of a meeting at Yale in 1964 where PL's chairman called for national demonstrations against the "imperialist" war in Vietnam. I wasn't there for that conference, but I ended up joining M2M some time in the summer of that year. In those early days there were some special virtues of M2M that appealed to students and academics such as myself. The most important for me was that M2M treated the Vietnam War as an imperialist, rather than a civil, war. One of the essential points that set M2M apart from SDS was that SDS defined the conflict as a civil war, one in which the US should stay out. The M2M, on the contrary, clearly identified it as an imperialist war in which the US was supporting its South Vietnamese collaborators with armaments and advisors. M2M had the courage of their convictions in a way that other organizations (such as SDS) didn't. At the height of M2M's influence, some prominent academic scholars, for example, Harvard philosopher Hilary Putnam, expressed interest in what we were doing. I thought we were taking up worthy issues, such as the connection between racism and various academic measures, such as IQ testing and the grading system. These devices were hierarchical and didn't reflect the real intelligence of the students being measured. There was no discussion, for instance, of the learning that peopled gained on urban ghetto streets. The elitism in prestigious universities, such as Harvard, Yale, Princeton, Berkeley, and Stanford, was taken for granted and never challenged.

In the beginning, M2M had established a cordial relationship with SDS. Like SDS, it wanted to extend the struggles happening in society at large into the academic realm. Inspired by the writings of C. Wright Mills, M2M also explored the meaning of white-collar work. This was an implicit extension of a Marxist analysis, updating it to meet the historical conditions of the mid twentieth century. They had a clear anti-imperialist line and at their best, in the writings of Shino'ya Ono,[2] they had a potentially radical view of bringing about revolutionary change. The way they initiated their projects, such as community organizing against civil rights problems like police brutality, healthcare, drug use, and housing, suited my temperament and beliefs. They had an intellectual approach to things we should have been studying in the classroom. They emphasized issues of democracy and democratic pluralism, as well as race and gender. However, my experience with M2M led me to see that the organization became nothing more than an extension of PL, when it was supposed to be an autonomous student group.

---

2 Graduate student in political science at Columbia University, whose articles and essays were published in the radical leftwing magazine *Leviathan*.

When examining SDS, one should begin by explicating its theoretical political underpinnings. SDS's main focus was the democratic critique of what Carl Oglesby identified as "corporate liberalism." Corporate liberalism, a concept espoused by Teddy Roosevelt and Woodrow Wilson, transfers the ideals of freedom from individuals to artificial entities like corporations and foundations. The resulting primary agency given over to these entities was in line with the decisions of the Supreme Court in the late nineteenth century.

Under this system, workers are nothing more than competitive individuals whose political power is ceded to capitalist entities. The line between individuals and corporations then becomes blurred, as does the line between fascism and liberalism (which we are seeing today). Democracy is no longer about individuals but rather groups (such as labor unions, government agencies, and industrial corporations) in which most individuals will have no power. This view came out of the work of William Appleman Williams, a historian who wrote *Contours of American History* and *The Tragedy of American Diplomacy*. At that time, prior to writing *The Great Evasion*, he had not identified as a Marxist and this was a huge drawback for me.

SDS was supposed to achieve a kind of ideological unity, but it ultimately failed. One of the reasons was that it didn't have the theoretical resources to unify the various groups that made it up. What was needed was a well-structured organization possessed of such resources to bring together the antiwar, ecology, feminist, and antiracist movements, among others. By the late sixties SDS had chapters all over the nation, but these local chapters were often out of sync with one another and with the SDS National Office. In my opinion, the main responsibility of the SDS National Office was to assert that there was a unified message binding together all the different groups who at that time identified with SDS. However, what you really found were different groups that, under the name of SDS, were saying and doing radically different and even contradictory things about similar issues. At its best, SDS was a place where different groups could meet and argue with each other and take stands. That was healthy, but ultimately it went too far, and people began to lose respect for one another.

PL promoted building an alliance between workers and students and, with their allies, formed the Worker-Student Alliance Caucus in SDS. As a Marxist-Leninist organization, PL saw it as a theoretical necessity for the student movement to ally with labor. Intuitively, this seemed like the right thing to do. Although there were labor struggles on campuses, it was my experience that workers' opposition to the war in Vietnam was a mixed bag at best. I knew quite a few people who dropped out of school to migrate or return back to the working class in order to organize workers. My impression was that they were unsuccessful. Nonetheless, one of the things I liked about the WSA was their critique of academia, including their disdain for IQ testing and the grading system in general.

Even though I wasn't officially a member, I was willing to speak out in support of WSA/SDS. As a young professor participating in two of the many mobilizations against the war in Vietnam, I spoke on the group's behalf to members of Longshoreman's and Painter's unions, inviting them to join our protests. A lot of conversations took place on the picket lines we joined in support of striking workers. Although we had little success, at least issues like the Vietnam War and racism were raised. I went to quite a few demonstrations, talks, and meetings that WSA sponsored. I helped to organize some of the demonstrations by putting out fliers, and I helped WSA build alliances when and where I could, in an effort to help the group become part of some sort of "united front." To this end, I pushed the idea that professors should think of themselves as workers. There were times when I carried a lunch pail instead of a briefcase to symbolically make this statement.

When SDS finally broke up, some people went underground, some tried to work out relationships with the Black Panthers, and some tried to dig in for the long haul in modest organizing efforts. In general, though, all they accomplished was to put each other down, one trying to outdo the other with their attacks. At that point my hopes evaporated and I decided to leave SDS. I didn't formally leave; I just dropped out and decided to take up individual issues on their merits as they came up. Most of my energy was focused on employment and raising a child.

Looking back now, I think that WSA/SDS was ultimately based on a mistake. It was doomed by mixing Marxist-Leninist-Maoist theory with concrete-practical ideas that didn't really fit this theoretical paradigm. As we have learned from Paulo Freire, John Dewey, and many others, education itself resists being squeezed into the narrow constraints of Marxist theory. In Dewey's words, "intelligence in action" is what education is all about.

In a certain sense, we could say that the WSA's biggest flaw was thinking that a scattering of ideas could have been brought together as a whole. As a result, the organization had serious theoretical obstacles, problems that were left unsolved, and logical connections that were left unconsidered. They didn't spell out what would be necessary to develop an applicable theory to ameliorate the situation of students and teachers at SF State, where I taught. The theoretical underpinnings for this solution hadn't yet been fully developed at the time.

What We Learned

My involvement in all these connected movements, groups, and projects of the sixties gave me a broader view of the world—especially of the communist/socialist world—than I previously possessed. I met many people who had similar aspirations, who openly called themselves communists and/or socialists, and who would eventually become lifelong friends. It also affected my work as a philosopher, because I was in a situation where I could bring together Marxism and philosophy. As a teacher, it determined my attitude toward the classroom. I saw that the average teacher with a dialectical outlook had the advantage of engaging in dialogue and seeking answers through collective discussion. By adopting a Marxist approach to both philosophy and teaching, one gets a sense of how much is absent from the ordinary political curriculum. For example, the debate about moral incentives versus material incentives, an issue of global significance, had hardly any resonance in US philosophy departments at all.

At a more immediate level, the sixties movements created a new group of people familiar with organizing demonstrations and picket lines, who faced down police violence, and who were ideologically committed to opposing US imperialism. I blended into this group as a young professor. There were some definite gains and losses for me. Whether our failures outweighed our strengths is an open question, but I personally have many regrets. Looking back, I can now see that I behaved in shallow ways that weren't responsive to the whole sweep of the movement. Jerry Rubin made a comment that I tend to agree with: We don't pick up our wounded from the battlefields. As a result of the movement, a lot of human relationships were trampled on, marriages were destroyed, and families were put under great stress. Responsibility toward children often conflicted with the demands of the movement. Any strike or arrest meant that the people involved weren't receiving an adequate income, which made rent, food, childcare, and other life necessities problematic. People's expectations proved to be unrealistic in relation to the demands of the movement, which needed money, resources, and seemingly unlimited time and energy. This often conflicted with the demands of family and personal life.

There were also failures of solidarity; unresolved conflicts around race, ethnicity, and sexism only got worse as they remained unaddressed. Again and again, I witnessed the inability of the movement to overcome these cultural differences. The old communist slogan "black and white, unite and fight" didn't go very far. Cultural divisions, and the disparity between life experiences and plans, between these two groups were too deep. For example, at one demonstration an African American comrade challenged me by saying I had never been hungry for even just one day in my entire life. This was true and demonstrated that the reality of poverty was more prevalent in the black community. Of course, I knew this at a theoretical level—but I had never experienced so intensely a black person's resentment of white privilege. We were together until the march ended, then went our separate ways.

Then there was the issue of gender. Women were commonly sexually harassed and their influence was marginalized. Looking back now, I regretfully realize how I engaged in what would now be regarded as sexist behavior. In spite of systematic male chauvinism, the women's movement grew and their voices began to be heard more frequently. Male privilege, just like white privilege, was challenged on a regular basis, both in society and in the movement.

Perhaps where we failed most completely was addressing the intersection of everyday life and political activism. What I began to see was that we didn't have enough understanding of what a revolutionary movement required of us. We originally thought revolution was a simple thing. However, human relationships—marriages and friendships—are not simple. Bertolt Brecht, in an attempt to answer his own question, "How do you bring together human relationships at all levels with political activism?" said, "We who tried to lay the basis for human kindness could not ourselves be kind."

Revolutions require courage, violence, and betrayals of intimacy; we simply did not have the theoretical and strategic resources to deal with the demands of becoming part of a large movement that was itself constantly changing. If we learned anything from this experience that could be of any use to future generations, it is perhaps that we got a better understanding of the need for both political and social organization.

One of the biggest lessons I learned from my involvement in the movement was the necessity of learning from and building on our experiences, as well as the need to see our situation in the light of historical, political, and social realities. Like so many before us, we wanted to envision a superior socialist way of being. Perhaps we took a baby step along the right path in this direction. As the German philosopher Husserl said, "We remain perpetual beginners."

There is one more thing that I feel I need to say. In writing this autobiographical note, I realize now that many of our failures stemmed from our more fundamental failure to follow the best among us. For me, that was James O'Connor. He was thought by many to be the most imaginative and creative Marxist economist, one who tried to "put Marx back into Marxism." I felt that he was leading the way, but that only a few were following. His leadership tended toward a collective approach, and he was perpetually in search of gifted students who were interested in communism. He set standards for debate, for theory, and for relating theory to practice, particularly regarding the sixties student strikes that were happening at universities all over the country. He opened up the whole field of Marxist ecology, clarifying why Red had to be simultaneously Green.

In the process he and his comrades founded two important journals: *Kapitalistate,* which took on the task of developing a theory of the state that was Marxist through and through; and *Capitalism Nature Socialism,* which tried to set the foundation for a Marxist ecology movement. It was he more than anyone else who studied the nature of corporations and talked about the corporate form of organization.

Now that Jim has passed away, there is a gaping hole in what is left of the movements that came out of the sixties. Again and again, he sought a genuine Marxist solution to the problems that came up within our struggles; however, he was anything but orthodox when it came to his Marxism. He left plenty of room for imagination and courage in his vision of a socialist world and future revolutionary possibilities, especially in ecology. The contradiction between capital and nature, what he called the "second contradiction of capitalism" (the first being that between capital and labor), was one of his greatest conceptual innovations and is even more important now that we face an impending ecological catastrophe. He was the biggest intellectual influence of my life. He was my mentor, always pushing me for more rigor and depth in my writing. Together with people like David Harvey and Fredric Jameson, James O'Connor pioneered a reinvigorated Marxism for today. It is a pity that we haven't followed his lead more, and I have no doubt that his work will be of vital importance in the future.

Anatole Anton is a professor emeritus of philosophy at San Francisco State University. He edited Not for Sale *with Milton Fisk and* Toward a New Socialism *with Richard Schmitt. He was an active participant in the student/faculty/staff strike of 1968/69 that led to the founding of the College of Ethnic Studies at San Francisco State. He lives in San Francisco with his wife, Kathy Johnson. He extends his thanks to Josh Adams for his invaluable editorial help in preparing this memoir.*

10

I Might Have To Kill Vietnamese People

Michael Balter
(UCLA and the US Army)

I enrolled at UCLA in 1965. I was studying pretty hard the first couple of years, so I didn't do a lot in terms of political activism. I did have political awareness, and I was antiwar. Although I had been a Goldwater Republican as recently as 1964, I went over to the Left as soon as I got to the university, as happened to a lot of people.

I had a girlfriend who had a friend who was in SDS, and she recruited me into SDS, or at least she asked me to come to a meeting. The people who I remembered there were Jim and Arley Dann. I don't think at first that I realized they were members of this big bad communist organization. They were in SDS, and they were providing a lot of leadership, as was the case in all SDS chapters where PL had a presence.

The thing that happened first was that SDS and another organization at UCLA called the Vietnam Day Committee joined together and became SDS-VDC. The organization had a newsletter called the *Aardvark*. The previous editor had quit and I volunteered to be the editor. That, I guess, propelled me to a leadership role in the organization. What was amusing was that I was completely naïve politically. All I knew was that I was antiwar and that I was against racism. I used the *Aardvark* to publicize events that were being organized by SDS and other groups on the campus. Onc time I wrote quite a raw poem to my girlfriend and put it on the back page of the *Aardvark*. Somebody said, "You know, you really shouldn't be putting personal stuff in this. It's supposed to be political." They were very gentle with me, especially, Jim and Arley Dann, because they saw me, obviously, as a possible recruit to the party.

I really liked them. I especially liked Arley because she was a wonderful person and somebody I could talk to. Jim Dann was the Jim Dann that everybody knew, gruff and very doctrinaire. Jim and Arley set about subtly trying to recruit me—and it didn't take long. I remember Jim and Arley would say things like, so and so is a real internationalist. It impressed me that that was something you should be. I was beginning to learn that being patriotic was not necessarily a good thing during the Vietnam War and that there was a lot to criticize about the United States.

The one thing that people set me right about very quickly was Israel. I had never heard people really criticize Israel. The 1967 war had just happened. And being Jewish, I was a little shocked to hear people in SDS criticizing Israel just kind of matter-of-factly. I began to listen to what they were saying, and I soon understood what it was that they were talking about. Anyway, it didn't take long for Jim and Arley to recruit me to PL. I don't think I really knew exactly what I was getting myself into. We had a student club at UCLA that wasn't very large; Jim, Arley, myself, and one or two other people.

I was very naïve at first. I remember saying to Arley, "You know, I think I've actually always been a communist." To me, it really meant justice, equality, people being paid equal wages for equal work, and stuff like that, even though I really didn't know anything theoretically. It was just sort of the basic concept of equality.

Then what happened, and I think this was true of a lot of people who joined the party, you start out very naïve — then the next thing, you're reading Lenin's *State and Revolution*, and *What Is to Be Done*, the *Communist Manifesto*, and going to study groups.

The interesting thing that I remember about the study group was that the main thing we read was *PL Magazine*. We read things that were written especially by the East Coast intellectuals in the party, especially things Milt Rosen, the PL chairman, and other party heavies wrote.

Maybe occasionally we would read something by Marx or Lenin, but that was less often. We started selling *Challenge*, PL's weekly paper. I would sell *Challenge* on campus. Not very many people would buy it, as I recall. It was never fun selling *Challenge*. We were communists and that was still not a very popular thing to be, but I found that people were much more open to the idea of buying a communist newspaper or communist ideas than I ever expected. Nobody ever attacked me. Nobody ever really got on my case. As students, we would sometimes go to a factory and sell *Challenge* there. The reception would actually be better there than it was on campus, which is not a surprise when I look back on it.

There was a pamphlet PL put out called "Build a Base in the Working Class." I remember reading it online once not that long ago. Not the whole thing, but looking at it and thinking, "You know, there's a lot of wisdom there." It's one thing to talk about doing it. It's another thing to actually do it. It would be like today, if I had to sit face to face with a Trump voter and struggle with them over their ideology. It's just easier said than done. Selling *Challenge* was just a very direct way to do it with people you didn't know.

It was in late 1968 or early 1969, that the Black Panthers came onto campus to organize. We tried to make an alliance with them. We met John Huggins, but then John Huggins and Bunchy Carter were gunned down in the ethnic studies building. It got a huge amount of publicity at the time. John Harris, who was the leading black member of PL in Los Angeles, got ahold of the PL student club and asked them to pass out a leaflet on campus with the title, "Panthers Killed, Nationalism Guilty" the day after these guys were killed. Looking back on it, it was like, "Hey, John. Why don't you pass this thing out on campus?" Only a couple of us would do it.

Most people looked at the headline and wouldn't take it. People, both white and black, gave us very cold stares. Again, it's really sort of funny. Here was John, basically putting our lives in danger, without a second thought. Yet the politics of the leaflet were correct.

I went to all of the SDS national meetings through the split in SDS in the summer of 1969. The situation was that PL was in a lot of SDS chapters where they built and led a Worker-Student Alliance caucus. PL/WSA was making a lot of headway because they were the most disciplined, they had the most time, and they did the most work. It was easy for the PL/WSA people to begin to play a leading role, not only in the chapters, but also nationally in SDS. As I remember it, when PL joined SDS, both at a national and a local level most SDSers tended not to be communist. They were antiwar radicals, antiracist activists.

Because PL was so disciplined organizationally and persuasive with its analysis of the imperialist nature of the Vietnam War and its class analysis of racism, the party was really making ideological headway within SDS. In reaction to that, the other radicals in the organization in many cases moved to the left and eventually started calling themselves communists as well. That was definitely true of the SDSers who formed the Revolutionary Youth Movement.

At the national meetings the main events were the plenary sessions where officers were elected and ideological debates would take place around positions SDS should take. There were individual workshops, which I do not remember very well at all, and lots of literature on tables, but these were all secondary.

There was basically the RYM faction and there was the PL/WSA faction. Michael Klonsky or another RYM leader would put forward a resolution. Then those of us in PL/WSA would sit back and wait for either Jeff Gordon, Jared Israel, or John Levin, the heavyweights in the party, to get up out of their seats, stroll down the aisle, come up to the microphone, and with a great deal of confidence present the PL/WSA position. For those of us in the party, it was kind of electrifying because the leaders of the party had a keen ability to argue the politics. I remember that being very exciting. My perception was that PL wasn't trying to take over SDS. But ultimately, that's what ended up happening in practice because PL was so strong and disciplined within

SDS that nobody else could really compete. I think that was one of the reasons for the split. PL/WSA never wanted the split, but they wanted SDS to closely reflect their politics. But because of how strong PL was within SDS, that ended up becoming the case. Where I really fault PL was that it did not see that it was being sectarian and did not realize that the way that it was operating within SDS was diminishing the possibility of having a really broad-based organization. We were insisting on too much ideological purity. I don't think anybody saw it that way at the time, but that was, in essence, what was really going on. If you're going to have Students for a Democratic Society as a broad-based organization, PL would have had to have been able to tolerate a lot more liberalism or just kind of run-of-the-mill radicalism, or even anticommunism. Although it wasn't PL that split, but the RYM faction, I think that PL bears a lot of responsibility for creating the conditions that led to the split.

After the split in SDS, PL started recruiting members to go into the military and organize against the war. Denny Davis was the pioneer in this regard and was very successful. He wrote a lot of articles for *Challenge* and was the pride of the party. I was asked to enlist. I had a girlfriend at that time and I didn't really want to leave LA, but this is what the party wanted me to do. I remember that I agreed and then wanted to back out. I remember one very famous meeting, because this was an example of the insensitivity of the party that later would lead me leave PL. There was a meeting of several party leaders with me, and maybe a couple of regular cadre to talk about what I would do when I went into the army. The assumption was that I was probably eventually going to go to Vietnam.

I remember getting very upset and saying, "If I go to Vietnam, I might have to kill Vietnamese people." I said, "I can't do that." Levi Laub, who was one of the PL leaders in LA at that time, said, "What? Are you a pacifist?" which was just such a complete non-sequitur to what I was upset about. I was all teared up and everything. I was going, "I still don't understand really what that had to do with my killing the Vietnamese." Levi was very smart, manipulative, and charismatic. One time I was going some place with him. He said, "I need to stop and make a phone call." I'm wandering around and thinking, "Oh, he's using the phone here at the Santa Monica Airport." The next thing I know coming around a curve, and stopping in front of me, is a little two-seater Cessna aircraft. The door opens up and there's Levi, telling me to get in. Levi explains to me that he had learned to fly because the party felt that during the revolution it would be useful to have some pilots to do "various things." That was Levi.

I almost backed out of going into the army at the very last minute. I had a 2-S deferment, a student deferment, and I sent back my deferment to the local draft board. Within less than a month, they indulged me and sent me back a 1-A, meaning that I was draftbait, and I was drafted within a month or two.

I had this girlfriend who I was quite smitten with. I was obviously very aware that if I went into the army, I was going to lose her, which turned out to be the case. I went to Levi and said, "You know, I really don't want to do this." He said, "Look, you're worried about maybe losing your girlfriend. If you don't do this, you're going to lose respect in her eyes." Which struck home because I thought she loved me, in part, because of my militancy. I think she fell in love with me when I attacked a cop during a picket line at the *Herald Examiner*. That's as good a reason for falling in love with somebody as anything else, because I attacked him for good cause. The cop had attacked another comrade and I was coming to his defense.

Levi said, "Look, if you don't go in, your relationship's probably going to fall apart eventually because you won't have done something that you were committed to do. She'll know that. You'll know that. It'll be bad for your relationship." That was a persuasive argument to me. That convinced me, and I went in.

My father was a navy lifer and pretty conservative, but despite the fact that he really knew that I was going into the army to raise a ruckus, he showed up at the induction center. He worked downtown at that point for a savings and loan. I'm kissing my girlfriend goodbye and I'm walking up the steps. Suddenly, there's my dad coming out of nowhere. Literally, he just appears out of nowhere shaking my hand and wishing me good luck....

Off I go to Fort Ord. If you haven't been through basic training, let me just say it's not fun. What they do is they immediately, from the time you get off the bus, they start calling you names and yelling at you. It's part of the intimidation.

The racism against the Vietnamese people was explicit from day one. All of the drill sergeants called the Vietnamese "gooks." There was artwork, some on the podiums the sergeants used and the sides of buildings, of racist depictions of Vietnamese people. They didn't do very much to try to convince us that the war was right. They didn't seem to feel they had to because they were intimidating us into not questioning anything. The intimidation was daily, hourly.

Once you get out of basic training, that lessens. When I was in basic, because there was just no time to do anything, the only thing that I was able to do was, if somebody said something racist, I would argue with them. If someone said something in support of the war, I would argue with them. We only had one or two, at the most, orientation classes about the Vietnam War.

There was a sergeant who gave us a talk about the history of the Vietnam War. I knew my history of the Vietnam War pretty well and I questioned a lot of the things that he said. He was pretty cool about it. I wasn't thrown out of the room. He basically agreed with a couple of things that I said. Looking back on it, I think he handled it pretty well.

The GIs didn't know why they were there. They were drafted or they had enlisted to try to get out of going to Vietnam, because if you enlisted for three years instead of being drafted for two, you had a higher chance of doing something stateside and not going to Vietnam, or even having a job in Vietnam that wasn't so risky, like being a clerk. Everybody wanted to be a clerk.

It's kind of a joke, but they asked you what you wanted to do, and you filled out a thing, your military occupational specialty. I asked to be a cook in Alaska, because, despite Levi's admonitions, I did not want to go to Vietnam and kill Vietnamese. I asked to be a cook in the army because cook is a hard job and nobody wanted to go to Alaska. I thought, "Okay, I'm going to ask for two things that nobody wants to do." Sure enough, at the end of basic training, I was assigned to be a cook in Alaska. But my FBI file had followed me into the army. The army knew when I went in that I was a student radical, and G2, which is the security outfit in the military, put a hold on me so that I couldn't ship out.

I stayed at Fort Ord for a year and a half and became a cook. I also had two court-martials. One was for passing out leaflets on the base. That was a court-martial where you just meet with an officer. Unlike in civilian life, ignorance of the law is an excuse in the military because you're not expected to be able to know all the aspects of the military code. I was silent. The officer was an honest guy. He looked at the statues and he said, "Okay, for me to find you guilty, I have to be able to prove that you knew that it was not legal to pass out leaflets at the base." I was standing on my right to be silent.

Finally, he says, "You don't want to talk. That's your right. I don't have any evidence that you knew that it was illegal, so I have to find you innocent." He called me back, I guess an hour or two later, because he had forgotten to have me sign the thing where I'm agreeing to the sentence. He said, "I'm really getting crap from the brass for this, because you knew." I just kind of went, "Sorry." He was a nice guy. He was an honest man. There were a lot of honest people in the army, a lot of good people in the army.

The other court-martial where I was convicted was a special court martial. A general court-martial is the worst. You don't want that. There were three types. Mine was in the middle, so I think it was probably a special court-martial, where I went before a three-judge panel. This would have been 1970, after Nixon's invasion of Cambodia, when the antiwar movement exploded again. A lot of the peace groups up in the Bay Area planned a march in front of the gates of Fort Ord. It was called "Free the Ford Ord 30,000." The military claimed that they had uncovered secret documents that showed that the peace groups were planning to invade the fort, which was nonsense.

What really was the case was that by 1970 the GIs were very open to the antiwar movement. They were either antiwar or didn't want to get killed in Vietnam. I'm a witness to the fact that there was a deep and broad receptiveness to the antiwar message among the GIs who were mostly working class, white, black, and Hispanic. You would think that being a communist in the military is something you would want to hide, but it was really like a novelty to people. I was an excellent cook. If you're a good cook in the army, you can do no wrong because the next meal is all anybody has to look forward to. I talked to people all the time about politics. Being in the army was probably the most wonderful time in my life as a political person. This was the one time, the one experience that I had actually doing what I was supposed to be doing in PL, which was building that base in the working class, all that I had joined the party for. That was the one time that I was really doing it and it was really working.

We did a lot. We had a group. There were probably about three of us in PL and we had a group of about fifteen GIs who would come to the meetings, which were almost every week. Sometimes they would actually be on the base, and sometimes they would be at a house in Seaside, a working-class community where GIs who had permanent assignments lived. The officers lived on-base in officer housing.

What happened was that the brass told the GIs that they had these secret documents that proved that the demonstrators were going to invade the post. They canceled all leaves and everybody had to stay on the base. I'm pretty sure they were afraid that there were going to be hundreds of GIs out at the front gates of the fort with the demonstrators right along Highway 1, either out of conviction or curiosity. That wasn't going to look very good.

At the time I was cooking for an infantry training company. If you were going to go to Vietnam, which was true of almost everybody, you would go into an infantry training company after basic training, and you would train to do serious infantry. That was another eight weeks. I was a cook in that company. A couple of days before this demonstration was supposed to happen, they were drilling the company with rifles out on what's called the company street, which is the street across the front of the barracks. They were drilling them in repelling the antiwar people. I think I came down from the mess hall to use the bathroom or something like that. Half of the guys had flowers in their hair and were dressed like the hippies and half of them had rifles. They were doing formations and repelling these "hippies" who were supposedly attacking the front gate.

I just started mouthing off. I said something like, "This is ridiculous. They're not going to attack the fort. They don't want to attack you. It's 'Free the Ford Ord 30,000.' They're with you. They're sympathetic to you"—whatever came into my head. I just kept mouthing off, and the sergeant who was leading it said, "Balter, get back to the mess hall." I just kept talking. "Balter, you get back to the mess hall." I'm pretty sure he said it three times, "Balter, get back to the mess hall." I didn't move.

Then a lieutenant came up, a very nice guy actually, a college guy. He just came up to me, kind of shook his head, and said, "Balter, you better go back to the mess hall. You need to go back to work." Then I went. The reason I went, as I'm sure most people know, is that it's a much more serious offense to disobey a commissioned officer than a noncommissioned officer.

I was then brought up on charges. Art Carpenter, another PL GI, defended me. You have the right to have a peer to speak in your defense. I was facing several months in the stockade. Again, I remained mute. Art said a few indignant things. I was found guilty of disobeying a direct order and compromising good order, or something like that. I was busted down to the lowest private rank, which means I lost a huge amount of money. I was confined to the base for three months. I was supposed to go to the stockade.

They then took me to the stockade. I went right to the door of the stockade. I think I was given thirty days. Then a phone call came and someone said, "Balter is not going to the stockade," and they just took me back to my company. I was confined to the fort for three months. The funny thing about that was that nobody took it seriously.

I would go to the beach with the sergeants and everybody else from the company.

The last thing that happened that was our group organized an antiwar demonstration at Fisherman's Wharf in Monterrey. We had fifteen or twenty GIs on Fisherman's Wharf in Monterrey in our uniforms parading up and down with antiwar signs. I don't think anybody realized at the time that this kind of stuff was going on. Who could imagine it?

That was it as far as the army was concerned, and they really split us up. I think Art was kicked out, one guy was sent to Vietnam, and another really was sent to Alaska.

I was called into the captain's office. He said, "Balter, you're gone."

I said, "What do you mean?" I sort of pretended to protest, but to tell you the truth, after seventeen months of the army, even though things were really going well in terms of my political work there, I wasn't crushed to be kicked out—especially when I found out that I was being kicked out under Reg. 212, which says that they can discharge you for the good of the army and without explanation. But they have to give you an honorable discharge, which meant that I'd get GI Bill benefits, and I wanted to finish school. This happened within just an hour or two. It was literally, "Balter, pack up your stuff. You're out of the army." The captain was in a state of glee because I had caused so much trouble while I was there, and it all made him look bad.

He said, "Pack up your stuff and be at the front gate." I think they actually put me in a jeep and dumped me at the fucking front gate of Fort Ord. I went to a payphone and called some party person and said, "They're throwing me out. What do I do?" The decision was made very quickly that I would go down to San Jose because I knew some people there. I don't remember whether I got on a bus or somebody came and got me, but the next thing I knew I was in San Jose.

I wanted to go back to school. This was in 1971. At that point, when I got out of the army, the party was kind of my safety net. I went to San Jose State University, to finish up the biology degree that I had started at UCLA.

I had left the party by the time I started at San Jose State and that would have been the fall of 1972. The key issue was the lack of party democracy. The party line was always decided before we began to discuss it at the local level. The party leaders saw their task as struggling with us to accept it. If you disagreed you could either change your mind or leave the party.

The party leaders would pretend that this was really democratic, but it wasn't because we had no say over what party policy was going to be. It was a farce. Everybody I knew in the party was uncomfortable with that, but we felt that we shouldn't make a big deal out of it for the good of the party and the good of the revolution.

We also saw what happened to people who didn't go along. They basically became enemies. One of the things about the party was that it sort of became our lives. You married somebody who was in the party. All your friends were in the party. I lost or rejected almost all of the friends that I had before I was in PL. All my friends were in the party, extremely counterintuitive to how you make a revolution, but that's the way it was. That was part of the sectarianism.

If you were asked to leave the party or had to leave the party because you could no longer go along with the party line, that meant a major personal break with people who you had become very close to. There were even marriages that split up.

At that point, although I was still very much a leftist, I was a little bit more dubious about communist revolution. I was more dubious about whether we really needed to have a vanguard party. By then we were criticizing China, Cuba, even Albania. There was no example in the socialist world that was any good.

The other thing was that having spent a year and a half with the working class, I wasn't so sure that I just wanted to give them a bunch of guns and let them do their worst. I did feel that the working class had a lot of progressive elements in it and that workers certainly were open to leftwing ideas.

One event that actually had a big effect on my decision to leave PL happened at an antiwar march that was led by a local leftist leader in

San Jose. He was kind of a hippie and a first-class asshole. We were marching past the post office and somebody climbed up a flagpole and grabbed the American flag. A postal worker ran out and grabbed the flag, and the asshole at the head of the march and the postal worker were both tugging on the flag. After three blocks, it started to get kind of embarrassing. The postal worker wouldn't let go of the flag, and the asshole wouldn't let go of the flag. Finally, some of the other demonstrators started saying, "Let him have it." The asshole finally lets go of the flag and the postal worker says, "It doesn't mean anything to you anyway," and he bundles it all up and he walks back to the post office.

It had a huge impact on me. Recalling it, I actually get a little bit emotional, to tell you the truth. I felt that if we were in an antagonistic relationship with somebody like that, then all of the bullshit that we were putting out about the working class, and the masses, and all that—we were going nowhere if we couldn't somehow make a connection or understand what he was feeling about the fact that we walked off with the flag. I think that it reinforced a lot of the feelings that I was having about PL and about the approach that we were taking to making social change.

Michael Balter is a freelance journalist. After spending nearly thirty years based in Paris, he now lives in the New York area (MichaelBalter.com). His work focuses on anthropology, mental health, and sexual harassment in the sciences.

11

PL and Me

Ed Morman
(City College of New York, University of Washington)

I remember being out with my mother when I was five or six years old and a leafleter approached us. My mother grabbed me and hurried me away, but as we crossed the street, I heard him shout "Rosenberg!" I asked my mother why we were running so fast and who Rosenberg was; she told me that it did not concern us. What she did not tell me was that my father—a moderately prosperous, chronically depressed small businessman—had some time earlier lent money to his cousin, Morton Sobell, for legal defense. In the months before Ethel and Julius Rosenberg were killed (and for years afterwards), my parents—good Roosevelt liberals—did not want their children to attach themselves to things, or people, associated with communism. It was too close to home.

Nonetheless, I succumbed to the romance of American communism, both as emblematic of some of the best in US history—helping build the CIO, supporting the Scottsboro Boys, fighting for democracy in Spain—and as an element in contemporary movements. Whether it was a Pete Seeger concert, a Rosenberg memorial meeting, a civil rights rally, a march against nuclear weapons, or chanting "Hands Off Cuba!" as a high school kid, I felt that there was something big that encompassed all this and a lot more. Whatever it was, it conformed to a moral code that I must have absorbed from my parents: *Treat people*

177

fairly and care about the less fortunate. I had had a fantasy of going away to college and living outside my parents' constraints. But their budget was not unlimited and it soon became clear that I would attend a commuter college and live at home. I chose the City College of New York even though it was an hour's subway ride from our apartment in Queens because of its reputation as a radical hotbed, where, it was said, leftists in the 1930s used to huddle in cafeteria alcoves, debating fine points of Marxism and socialist theory.

On September 15, 1963, just as I was starting at CCNY, the Sixteenth Street Baptist Church in Birmingham was bombed and four black girls killed. I'm embarrassed to say that, as I remember, I was more energized by the opportunity to protest racist violence in Alabama than I was angered by this act of terror and the death of four innocents.

A couple of months later, John Kennedy was assassinated. I did not grieve for him, but I wanted his death to signify a shift from the seemingly placid world of my 1950s childhood. Whatever was going to be happening, I wanted to be part of it. But I didn't know how; in fact, during my first year in college, I felt that I was in a rut—bored and going nowhere. I remember that feeling very well.

The following summer, Congress passed the Tonkin Gulf Resolution and Harlem experienced what was called a riot. Soon the Free Speech Movement developed at UC Berkeley. I felt jealous of those activist students and wanted even more to get out of my rut by participating in leftist politics. In the meantime, Progressive Labor had placed several cadres at CCNY, and I was intrigued by these people who claimed to be more communist than the Communist Party.

The summer's events in Harlem became the subject of a grand jury investigation that soon targeted Bill Epton, the African American Vice-Chairman of PL, and other PLers. Several party members, including four City College cadres, were offered immunity in exchange for testimony about internal PL discussions. Ellie Goldstein was the first student to be called, the first to refuse to testify, and the first to be jailed for contempt. PL then circulated a petition to the college president,

Buell Gallagher, calling on him to speak out against the DA meddling in the political affairs of CCNY students. Gallagher refused and in mid February 1965, fifty students held a sit-in in his office. I was thrilled: Berkeley-type activism was coming to New York.

I understood the demands of the PL petition to be contrived, but the PL leaders knew what they were doing. That campaign drew me out of my rut and attracted several of my friends as well. Connecting with PL not only provided political activity; there were also parties on upper Broadway and on the Lower East Side, and there were women. And though I never smoked pot with people in PL, somehow access to weed seemed to come with leftwing activism.

It was almost like dual power. Whereas the college, the government, and my parents all had certain rules, I now had the opportunity to live by an alternative code and in an alternative structure.

That spring I visited Cathy Prensky, another CCNY student jailed for contempt, at the Woman's House of Detention. I felt proud and independent: I was in a jail, visiting a political prisoner. And shortly afterward, I joined the May 2nd Movement—both to make more of my life and because the people I met in M2M were militant and spoke loudly about the key issues of the day: black liberation and the war in Vietnam. Moreover, PL, which openly set the agenda for M2M, presented a clear strategic perspective unlike others that I heard elsewhere; namely, that the student movement had to engage with the working class.

I don't recall what I did as a member of the May 2nd Movement during the fall semester of 1965. In fact, I probably spent more time hanging out with my pot-smoking friends on the Lower East Side. On the other hand, I also went downtown to a study group at the apartment of Harvey Mason and Cathy Prensky. I was glad to have access to this radical education as a counterpoint to the bourgeois subjects I was studying at college.

In January 1966, Mike Quill led a strike of New York bus and subway workers. President of the Transit Workers Union, Quill was one of the few old CP-aligned CIO leaders who retained his leftist roots.

He supported racial equality and stood out as an opponent of the Vietnam War. His confrontation with John Lindsay, the newly elected liberal Republican mayor, is legendary. He was locked up for defying an antistrike injunction, and a heart attack killed him only days after the transit workers returned to work with a large wage increase. Quill's legacy would be important to us the following year.

In May, I participated in an antidraft sit-in at the City College administration building. We had a sizable turnout, as many as two hundred students, and earned ourselves a front-page story, with a picture, in the *New York Times*. PL did not have that big a base at CCNY, and I cannot remember what role it may have played in the demonstration. Around the same time, PL decided to dissolve M2M and concentrate its campus efforts in Students for a Democratic Society. I joined SDS the following fall, at the start of my senior year.

But summer 1966 came first and it was a wonderful time for me. I was working at a job I loved, as a part-time clerk at the central Harlem branch of the New York Public Library. I was also subletting an apartment on the Lower East Side, from those pot-smoking friends whose parties had, oddly enough, been occasions for the assembled to sing Spanish Civil War songs.

I could also be found, many evenings that summer, on the E train, heading back to Queens, for work with the Queens Committee for Independent Politics (QCIP), circulating petitions to get Leslie Silberman on the ballot as a candidate for Congress. Leslie and her husband, Don, were older, probably around thirty, and looked to me like a conventional young married couple. But they were either closeted PL members or, like me, in the party's inner periphery. For some time, I had been going to QCIP meetings at the Silbermans' house, where I mixed with CPers, SWPers, Spartacists, and the folk singer Dave Van Ronk.

For the Silberman campaign, we would gather at the 179th Street-Jamaica subway stop and get assignments to knock on doors in one or another neighborhood within the congressional district. I was always pleased to be dispatched to an African American area, where I figured I was more likely to meet with a friendly response. Harvey Mason, who also had been going to QCIP meetings since the previous spring, was PL's point man on this project. More than anyone else at City College, it was Harvey who had brought my friends and me into the PL orbit. He was charming and witty, a genuinely decent human being.

In September 1966, Rick Rhoads and Steve Fraser appeared at City College to make a political base out of the "personal base" for which Harvey was being criticized. Rick was a difficult person; Steve was serious and hardworking, and had a good sense of humor. At campus SDS meetings the PL coterie had intense (if ill-informed) arguments with people from the New York SDS regional office. The regional office types held that the new working class—white-collar workers—was supplanting the industrial working class as a key social force. If there was a moment when I felt closest to PL, it was at SDS meetings that year. I loved arguing for the crucial role of people whose labor power, applied to the means of production, produced the surplus value that the bourgeoisie appropriated.

I had my first direct contact with that industrial working class in November, when several of us drove up to Schenectady to show support for striking workers at GE. I remember riding in the rear-facing back seat of Rick's station wagon, eager to distribute coffee and donuts to the workers on the picket line.

But there was no picket line; it was Sunday and the plant was closed.

Rick, not at all discouraged, was ready with an apposite quotation from Chairman Mao: "Turn a bad thing into a good thing." And that Rick did. He had had some experience in that part of the world and was able to identify local people who could put us up that night. Meanwhile, at his direction, we fanned out to area colleges to recruit other students to join us at the picket line on Monday. Rick insisted that we be good guests in the homes where we spent Sunday night and express our gratitude for the generosity of our hosts. That's what communists do.

Back at City College, not long after Rick won a seat on the Student Council, there was another antidraft sit-in. The *Times* also covered this one, this time under the headline "Communist Students Charged With Role in CCNY Sit-in." Buell Gallagher was quoted as saying, "City College is the number-one target of the American Communist Party and has been since 1927"; Rick was described as "the first avowed Communist to be elected to the student council in about thirty years."

PL continued to choose the right battles, and its next one at City College was with the US Army Materiel Command, which was scheduled to recruit at the placement office in December. The USAMC was responsible for procurement of the napalm used in Vietnam, and Dow Chemical, its manufacturer, was already widely despised. We sat in and disrupted the recruitment process, and a couple dozen of us were suspended and barred from campus for a week. But I believe we succeeded in winning hearts and minds.

Through all this I was faithful to the PL line, but I never joined the party. I was not ready for the discipline, and frankly, I was afraid of jeopardizing my future. For all my understanding of class privilege and how it kept petit-bourgeois intellectuals from truly serving the working class, I wanted to be free to make use of that privilege. After being suspended for the USAMC sit-in, I petitioned for permission to come to the campus to take the Miller Analogies Test. Gallagher obliged and I took the test as scheduled. I had applied to six graduate schools, including two in Canada, and I didn't want to kill my chances by not taking the test. And continuing in school meant extending my draft deferment.

During my final semester at CCNY, spring 1967, PL remained active in SDS and continued its struggle against the regional office, while also creating a separate group: CCNY Students for a Worker-Student Alliance against the War in Vietnam. Steve Fraser took the lead in this group.

Living in Baltimore now, where the overwhelming majority of bus drivers are black, and probably most are women, it's somewhat surprising to remember that bus drivers in 1967 New York City were typical of the predominantly male, largely white, unionized blue-collar working class. Leafleting with the WSA Committee at the Tran-

sit Authority bus barn on upper Broadway provided my next encounter with the world of white workers.

I must admit to feeling awkward engaging the men who drove and
maintained the buses. I felt too different from them, and I wanted to
believe that they would come to the conclusion that the war in Vietnam
was bad for working people simply by being handed mimeographed
sheets trumpeting Mike Quill's opposition to the war. One day a transit
worker told me that he had earlier been handed a leaflet by a member
of the Communist Party. I knew there were no CPers among us and
told him so. When he insisted that one of us had described himself as
a communist, I realized that he was talking about Steve, who, like all
open PLers, told everyone, right off, that he was a Red. I remember,
also, that Steve was physically attacked a few days later.

In June I graduated from CCNY and traveled to Montreal to go
to Expo '67 and visit Walter, a friend who belonged to the Canadian
sister organization of the Socialist Workers Party. I've recently been in
touch with Walter and asked him if he remembered anything I used
to say in those days in support of PL, Mao, and People's China. His
wry response was to send me a link to a website with a complete run
of *Peking Review* from the 1960s. Much that Walter told me in 1967—
about Trotsky, his role in the Russian Revolution, and the theory of
permanent revolution—made sense. But what made more sense was
the work PL was doing: orienting student activists to the working
class and, as I liked to believe, to the black community and workers
of all races.

Back in New York, I drove around industrial areas with a couple of
friends, looking for blue-collar jobs for the summer 1967 SDS work-in.
I found work at Macy's warehouse and I generally enjoyed being
there. I appreciated the shop steward's willingness to keep me on for
an extra month without the expense of joining the union. I was also
glad that PL had instructed us not to feel obliged to discuss politics,
and I hardly ever did. One guy on my floor turned out to be suspicious
of me but another told me that I shouldn't worry about him, which
made me feel good. I wanted to believe that simply by spending two

months at the warehouse I was learning something from the workers and thereby advancing the revolution. No need to talk politics, thank goodness.

Many evenings after work that summer, though, I did talk politics on the streets of upper Manhattan, mainly to Latinos and African Americans. PL needed an activity that would keep us busy while educating the public and attracting new recruits. A petition campaign would work, but there was no congressional election and New York had no provision for initiatives or referendums. Therefore, in order to talk with people about the war, we circulated petitions to create a new public office, a coordinator of municipal antiwar activities. Another contrived campaign, but, nonetheless, one more that got me moving.

At the end of that summer, after helping Steve Fraser move to Philadelphia (where PL was sending him to build a new student base), I left New York City for Seattle. I had chosen to go to graduate school at the University of Washington because I was offered financial aid there. I had no expectation of finishing a degree in experimental psychology, but I did get an extra year of draft deferral, and I managed to get about as far from home as possible, and with an institutional connection that would be a ready source of contacts and potential friends.

I had been looking forward to working with the PL group in Seattle, but not long before I headed west I learned that the Seattle club had split from the party. Its leader, Clayton Van Lydegraf, was a man in his fifties who had been a West Coast CP hardliner for decades before joining PL. He had split from the party after it denounced the Vietnamese for accepting arms from the Soviet revisionists. I could see his point. Who else was going to arm the NVA and the NLF? PL?

I also got in touch with John Levin in San Francisco and visited him twice. John has been kind enough to supply me with photocopies of our correspondence from 1967–68. I'm impressed by my seriousness and willingness to work.

Seattle was home to a large Left, including the CP, the SWP/YSA, and a local sect called the Freedom Socialist Party (FSP). There were several New Left groups, but the UW SDS chapter didn't count for much. So, at the first SDS meeting of fall 1967, a group congealed that rebuilt the chapter as a center of militancy on campus. It was at that meeting that I met several people associated with the FSP, one of several grouplets had that peeled off from the SWP during the early sixties. The FSP was contemptuous of the SWP for tailing black nationalists, and it regarded the SWP line on Cuba as insufficiently critical of Castro. It was also among the first groups to put forth a program of women's liberation and socialist feminism. Perhaps most important for me, the FSP had a position very unusual among Trotsky-ists—an orientation toward China and Mao. I drifted toward the FSP because of its position on China, but also because it had real work-ers among its members, because I supported the developing women's movement, because I liked its position on black liberation, and because I had quickly become very friendly with young people in its periphery.

Soon after I arrived in town, though, the FSP itself split, with both factions claiming the name. One side was dedicated to building the women's movement. It continues to exist, as does its affiliate, Radical Women. The other was more bound to the notion that Trotskyism and Maoism were convergent. My friends in the FSP periphery were amused by the split. They called the former group the "FSP (Stalinist)" because of the dominant leadership role of its founder, Clara Fraser; the latter they called "FSP (Menshevik)." We were all well-schooled in Left history.

Around this time, some local activists proposed establishing a Washington state Peace and Freedom Party. I was on my own now, still corresponding with John Levin, but drawn more closely to the FSP (Menshevik) faction, which was interested in Maoism. I operated as an individual, but I continued to tell people that I had a connection to PL. I cannot remember what PL thought of Peace and Freedom, but I had no one close at hand to tell me that what I was doing was wrong or contrary to the party line. Participating in PFP was something that seemed right.

On campus, I helped SDS organize a boycott of the food service, which was serving scab grapes. We dispatched members to buy burgers at fast-food joints and we sold them in front of the student union building. Our pro–working class group within SDS sang IWW songs at our literature table. We had good relations with the Vietnam Committee and, increasingly, Vietnam Committee members who disagreed with the tactic of building a single-issue movement joined SDS. Off campus, I participated in the Peace and Freedom Party. By that time PL had created a regional labor committee in New York, to offset the influence of the SDS regional office. I followed the lead of New York and participated in the formation of a joint PFP/SDS labor committee in Seattle. I thought that this would be the best way to build a revolutionary movement in town.

One of the members of the FSP (Menshevik) worked at the Todd Shipyard. So we went there with some regularity, armed with leaflets bearing much the same message that, with PL, I had been bringing to transit workers in Manhattan a year earlier.

It was an exciting time, especially given what was happening in New York, where the student strike at Columbia seemed to be forging an alliance between antiwar students and African Americans in Harlem. Among the leaders of the Columbia strike were PLers whom I had come to know at meetings and in study groups. In Seattle, we printed posters saying "Two, Three, Many, Columbias," echoing Che Guevara's call for "Two, Three, Many, Vietnams." Between the heroic people of Vietnam and a bunch of middle-class college kids in the US, we were bound to defeat US imperialism, worldwide, right?

But everything was about to change for me.

Sometime in spring 1968, after the assassinations of Martin Luther King and Robert Kennedy, a friend in City College PL let me know that he was about to follow Steve Fraser (and other PL leaders in New York and Philadelphia) out of the party and into a new faction that had developed in the New York SDS regional labor committee. As it happened, one of the people PL thought it was recruiting at Columbia, had also been collaborating with a man called L. Marcus in the West (Greenwich) Village Committee for Independent Political Action. This potential recruit had instead succeeded in recruiting Tony Papert and several others out of PL, convincing them of the theoretical and strategic superiority of Marcus's thought.

I recalled having seen a pamphlet by this L. Marcus lying around Steve Fraser's apartment when I was there for a study group in early 1967. I'm not sure when L. Marcus's influence became strong enough to tear Steve, Tony, and others from PL. But when people I liked and respected—and people I knew as personal friends—told me about the brilliant mind of L. Marcus, I was ready to sever ties with PL.

I went to the 1968 SDS convention in East Lansing intent on understanding the thought of L. Marcus. After spending part of the summer in New York, attending Labor Committee meetings and study groups, I returned to Seattle ready to recruit people to what was becoming the National Caucus of Labor Committees. Sad to say, some of the people I recruited have spent their subsequent years attached to L. Marcus, a.k.a. Lyndon LaRouche.

I'm not proud of how much I mouthed off in those days, almost always about things that I didn't know or understand, or how much my attachment to PL was based on romantic notions of revolution and on personal ties to friends in the party. But I regret no political action I engaged in as a friend of PL.

What I do regret is recruiting some very decent people into the Labor Committees. Sad as PL has become over the decades, I feel better about the comrades who stuck with it than I do about the people who continue submitting themselves to the poisonous leadership of Lyndon LaRouche.

Ed Morman is retired librarian who lives in Baltimore with his wife, Julie Solomon, a psychiatric nurse-practitioner. He's currently (at least on paper) a member of Jewish Voice for Peace and of Democratic Socialists of America. emorman@gmail.com

12

PL, the Struggle at Columbia, and the Road to Irrelevance

Eddie Goldman
(Columbia University)

That the Progressive Labor Party still exists is a testament to the flexibility of American bourgeois democracy, even under Trump. Let the sects have their own tables at the back of the bar, each the members of the vanguard and future one-party dictatorship. All praise to Zeus and Kahless that I have had nothing to do with these types for decades, and neither have, of course, the working class and oppressed peoples.

But it wasn't always that way. My relatively brief journey with PL took place during the last years of its somewhat vibrant time, even as it had already been decaying into irrelevance before my detour into its bubble.

My association with PL was to an important degree the result of chance. I was born in 1949 in Brooklyn, meaning that I was a college freshman in that revolutionary year of 1968, and malleable, passionate, naive, restless, idealistic, tough, and justice-oriented, a child of the 1960s. I also was not a red diaper baby and found my way to socialism on my own, of course as part of that era's revolutionary wave.

My father had a law degree but didn't practice, and was part of a small- to medium-sized family business (yes, in a type of plastics). He was more or less a mainstream Democrat, and a follower of Conservative Judaism. That meant we celebrated the various Jewish holidays and sometimes ate kosher food, except when he liked nonkosher food like shrimp. My mother, though also a college graduate and with a good background in mathematics, was a post–World War II "housewife" who read and accumulated piles of the popular women's magazines of the time. They moved from Brooklyn to the 'burbs in 1953 when I was too young to resist.

I attended the public schools in Lynbrook, New York, in Nassau County in Long Island, although we first lived for a couple of years starting in 1953 in East Rockaway and then, starting I think in 1955, in Hewlett. The school district borders and those of these various towns and villages overlapped from the days when there were mainly farms there and had never been changed, again showing the idiocy of suburban life.

I had a bar mitzvah and was a true believer for a few years after that, but then began hearing about atheist and antireligious criticism. I read works like Joseph Lewis's *The Bible Unmasked* and Bertand Russell's "Why I Am Not a Christian." Ever the independent thinker and skeptic, when I asked about these types of criticisms of religion, eventually I was told just to accept faith. When I asked why, besides family origin, choose one faith over another, I was basically told to stifle myself. For me, also a good math student, that proved that I was right and they were wrong. So it was quite liberating in what I believe was my senior year in high school when I went to class during the Jewish holidays, although I could have easily stayed home with no questions asked.

But although the Lynbrook Public Schools provided a top-notch mainstream academic education and placed many graduates in elite colleges, this area was very conservative politically and culturally. (Lynbrook got its name by reversing the syllables of Brooklyn, as apt a commentary on that place as there could be.)

That had an effect on me, especially since I saw so many liberal hypocrites in my area, which had turned me off to them. But my views changed as the slaughter in Vietnam continued, and the US government was more and more exposed as a bunch of liars, something absolutely shocking to a teenager brought up to believe that we lived in the land of the free, and so on.

A key turning point was in my senior year in high school when I read *The Autobiography of Malcolm X*, which had only recently been published. That opened my eyes to the terror of white supremacy and racism, from which I was largely shielded in schools with almost no black or Latino students and none in my class, and only a few mainly middle-class Asian students.

As I noted, I was a very good student academically and got accepted into several elite colleges. I also passionately loved sports and wrestled from 9th to 12th grade, although I was not good at it despite starting on the varsity. At that time I was also a baseball fanatic, a boxing fan, interested in music and tried playing the piano, and loved urban life (and still am if to different degrees). A recollection from as far back as kindergarten was that I wanted to live in the big city, and that meant only one place: New York. That was one of the key deciding factors for me choosing Columbia over the wooded campuses of Cornell and Brandeis. I also had spent the summer after my high school junior year studying at Columbia, and while far from being a radical, was already exposed to the student antiwar movement and various leftists, including PL.

So it was at the height of my intellectual search for truth and yearning for justice, whatever that may be, that I entered the political cauldron of Columbia in the fall of 1967. As a freshman I already supported some vague type of socialism and disdained the anti-intellectual Ivy League traditions that were still unchanged for decades at that time by what was to come.

Fast forward to the great Columbia strike and uprising of the spring of 1968. The best account of this, which reflected my own firsthand view of what happened, was written by someone not even born then, Stefan M. Bradley, entitled *Harlem vs. Columbia University: Black Student Power in the Late 1960s*. This book is still in print and highlights the central role of the Harlem community and the black students struggling against Columbia's racist attempt at building a gym on public land in Morningside Park, which, like its campus, is in Harlem. Today we see that this move was an early assault in the gentrification war being waged by the real estate sharks and their politicians.

At the time of the critical mass demonstration of April 23, 1968, that led to the takeover of Hamilton Hall and eventually several other buildings and the strike, I was not a radical or activist, although I did support the demands being put forward by the activists and radicals. My perspective on what happened must be understood that way, since an activist would have reacted differently. Nevertheless, it was instructive.

After failing to get into Low Library, where the school's top suits had offices then, and Morningside Park, the demonstrators took to the lobby of Hamilton Hall, which was the center of undergraduate classes. I actually left the demo, which was not yet a full sit-in and the building had not been barricaded, to go upstairs for a class. To my surprise, when I returned a few hours later, they were still there. But I returned to my dorm and went about my schoolwork.

That night, I heard they were still there, so probably somewhere late around midnight I decided to see what all the fuss was about. I went in the building and walked up all the stairs and looked in a few now-occupied classrooms. What this idealistic, skeptical not-yet-activist saw was white students mainly making out and smoking pot. These were hardly the types of things to turn someone like me radical, and were yet more examples of hypocrisy. So I left, a bit disgusted at these revolutionary poseurs.

Of course, as you may already know, the black students, who knew full well what confronting Columbia University and aligning themselves with Harlem community activists meant, threw out the white students in the middle of the night. Some of the more committed white leftists then took over President Kirk's office in Low Library, then more buildings were taken over, and a full strike was called, which actually ended only because the school year ran out.

In between there had been the two major busts, which were basically two NYPD riots where many people were attacked, demonstrators and passersby and even students in their dorms alike. We did not need to read *State and Revolution* to understand the repressive nature of the capitalist state apparatus.

A key feature of this uprising was the active participation of people from the Harlem and surrounding communities. There seemed to be demonstrations and marches every night. I recall the wondrous site of local high school students and youth marching, chanting:

Beep, beep
Bang, bang,
Umgawa,
Black Power!

That's how I remember these events, and not the whitewashed versions, which place the alienated offspring of the white petit bourgeoisie and bourgeoisie who did not want to go fight in Vietnam but wanted to smoke pot and wear flowers in their hair at the center of these historical events.

Sometime in the summer of 1968, influenced also by the police riot at the Democratic Convention in Chicago, I decided enough with the equivocating and criticisms from the outside: It was time to join SDS.

But Columbia SDS as an organization in the fall of 1968 was already losing its mass character. Many of the strike leaders had left the school, voluntarily or involuntarily. The active members were mainly lining up with one Leninist faction or another. The largest became the Weathermen (correctly called the right-wing of SDS by PL), followed by PL and also the LaRouchite nut jobs, then known simply as the Labor Committee. There were a few active independents or representatives of other groups at the meetings or on the SDS committees, meetings I was then regularly attending, although I still was open-minded and independent of all the factions. (As for the Trotskyites, the biggest group was SWP/YSA, which stayed outside SDS and generally opposed actions like strikes and building takeovers in favor of their single-issue "Bring the boys home" rallies with bourgeois liberals and which refused even to raise any antiracist issues. The other Trotskyites, like the Spartacists, were already wacko sects and just irritants. And the CPUSA had a handful of people at Columbia, also not in SDS, who did semi-invisible work.)

An anecdote can illustrate why I drifted to PL, to which you can already see I was more intellectually inclined than the hippie-dippie types. One evening early in my sophomore year (fall 1968) the fire alarms went off in my dorm, Carman Hall. After many of us left our rooms to go into the hall to see what was going on, someone checked and said there was no fire. A lot of disgusted students said that it must have been SDS that pulled the alarms. The ever-skeptical me questioned how they could know that. So I went downstairs and outside, only to find a handful of gleeful SDSers celebrating their revolutionary act of pulling the fire alarms and congratulating themselves for being the "hard core." These were the Weatherman-to-be, and a bunch of elitist, self-important, embarrassing creeps, in my view.

But it was not just their conceited actions that drew me to PL. I was looking for something authentic and not hypocritical. I found out that PL was organizing directly in the working class, including in what was then New York's Garment Center.

Most impressively to me, they had an active branch in Harlem, then led by PL Vice-Chairman Bill Epton, who had famously been arrested for "criminal anarchy" following the struggle against a racist police murder of a black youth in 1964, which was major news in the New York area. To this nineteen-year-old kid, a year and a half out of living in a stupid suburb, this was something authentic. And PL appeared to be a genuinely multinational organization and not simply a bunch of predominantly white yakkers pretending to talk about racism.

Most people in the position I was then in join the group or faction they think has the best practice in immediate struggles. Doubts or questions about Lenin, Stalin, and Mao become easy to answer if you like the people and the day-to-day practice of that group. You fill in the blanks later, pragmatically, and looking to accept rather than question, giving in to naïveté in the name of the apparent exigencies of the immediate struggles.

I had also known a prominent Columbia PL member a bit in high school and even roomed with him one year in college. And even though the PL member I had met during my high school junior year summer school stay there had later ended up as a LaRouchite, I was impressed by him when he was in PL. The members of the other groups I mostly regarded as snot-nosed fakers. So after working with their caucus in SDS for a few months, by the spring of 1969, in my sophomore year, I formally joined PL.

Our experience at the fateful December 1969 SDS convention in Chicago also served to solidify opposition to the Weathermen types and their allies. Although the convention was dominated by three factions all claiming to be Leninist, the rules of SDS were a leftover from its ultrademocratic *Port Huron Statement* days. Thus, anyone physically at the convention, rather than elected chapter delegates, could vote. By bringing more people to the convention, PL out-organized both opposition factions, who already were moving more away from campus activity anyway.

Both the RYM (Revolutionary Youth Movement) 1 faction, later essentially the play-terrorist Weathermen, and the RYM 2 faction, whose leaders later formed the rival Maoist "vanguard" parties CP-ML and RCP, were then shamelessly tailing after the Black Panther Party. In essence, they argued that if you criticized the Panthers, about their line that the lumpenproletariat were the vanguard, or anything else, you were racist since the US government had so brutally attacked them.

At the same time the modern women's movement was bursting forth, with each faction putting forth proposals reflecting their "correct" lines. Representatives of the Panthers, who had a major presence in Chicago, were brought in to address this and other issues.

What happened next was the best thing that could have ever happened for PL. One after another Panther speaker promoted the line of "pussy power" and said the place of women in the revolution was "prone." After two lesser representatives repeated this, a top leader, Bobby Rush, now a Democratic member of the US Congress, was brought in to try to clean up the mess. But in his speech, which the supposed real fighters for women's liberation in RYM 1 and RYM 2 expected to expose and crush PL, Rush repeated the same "pussy power" stuff. The PL faction was deliriously happy with their foes' utter humiliation. And when RYM 1's Bernardine Dohrn soon after took to the podium to denounce PL for a laundry list of offenses, the PL faction broke out in laughter. The formal split in SDS was next.

Earlier in the convention, when PL leader Jeff Gordon spoke, tensions were high and the threat of some violent confrontation, either involving hot-headed true believers and/or agents provocateurs, was real. So I was drafted at the last moment to be part of a group of presumed tough guys standing in front of him while he spoke. Of course, like almost all these "vanguards," there had been exactly zero training in any forms of martial arts or combat sports to use as self-defense.

The Columbia PL chapter was also somewhat unique in that the later shift of PL to the Worker-Student Alliance strategy of that time was somewhat successful, and not merely with ex-students working at a college. Two prominent proletarian leaders at Columbia, one an African American custodian and the other an Irish American electrician, actively worked with the PL chapter, and their many followers did as well.

In the spring of 1970 when hundreds of colleges went on strike following the US bombing of Cambodia and the killings at Kent State and Jackson State, it was the workers at Columbia who led the campus strike there, including the people who were working directly with PL.

But PL was already headed down a road to irrelevance and sect status. They condemned the heroic people of Vietnam fighting against US imperialism for "selling out" by agreeing to hold negotiations to get the US out. We all know how that ended.

PL also condemned all nationalism, making no distinction between those who were programmatically fighting capitalism and those who were not. The folly of this undialectical nonsense has been well documented, so there is no need here to repeat all this.

The wheels were coming off at Columbia, too. In the spring 1970 strike, a mass student group called the Third World Coalition decided to occupy a building during the antiwar activities. A large rally took place outside Low Library, with many PL members and supporters there. People there were unsure about what to do next, so, since I had good relations with the Third World Coalition, I was chosen to go into the occupied building to speak with them to coordinate our actions.

As I got into the darkened building and started to sit down to map out some joint action, I heard a big commotion outside. Someone came in and said that PL had tried to take over Low Library on their own but had been repelled by campus cops. Again, I was incredulous, since no such plan had ever been discussed, and I was the party representative trying to coordinate our efforts.

This meeting broke down and I went back outside. Yup, I was wrong again, and a handful of PLers had decided to try a ridiculous frontal assault on the barricaded doors of Low Library, the cops' strongest point. I was pissed, but was told, well, we thought it would work. Sun Tzu would have spit on them.

I also don't remember the exact course of events, but at one time I was made student editor of *Challenge*, where I learned a lot about newspaper production, although most of those methods are archaic today. I was later removed with no explanation given, which was curious to me since I was still a true believer in PL.

By the summer of 1970 an internal struggle in PL had become irresolvable between Bill Epton and the Harlem chapter, and the Milt Rosen–led leadership. Bill opposed the coming split with the Communist Party of China and the sectarian, and objectively white supremacist, attitude to the Black Liberation Movement, including PL's new opposition to setting up separate groups for black workers.

For some reason, even though I was not the leader of the Columbia PL chapter, I was invited to the closed party leader meeting, at the *Challenge* office, to announce the split with Epton. Instead of a point-by-point rebuttal of him ideologically and politically, there was mainly a barrage of personal attacks. While the political differences were real, this type of mud-slinging seemed closer to what I expected from people like Nixon and Agnew, and not revolutionaries. And since

PL upheld the charade of "democratic centralism," this split was not preceded by an inner-party discussion and debate on the issues. As in all Leninist outfits, it was democracy for a handful of top leaders and centralism for everyone else.

At Columbia, the majority of PL supporters, including all the workers, and some PL members were siding with the Epton group. PL was recklessly on an irreversible course of objective opposition to the mass movements, especially national liberation movements. I officially left in December 1970. By the end of 1970, the people with whom I was working, including Epton, were to become more orthodox Maoists, and on a new journey, in what became known as the New Communist Movement. That collapse is part of another story for another time, but for most of us at that point, our perception was that PL had become yet another sect. PL has never recovered its importance, even all these years later.

Although PL did it crudely and by upholding traditional conservative values, I still think they were correct to oppose all drug use, including that of marijuana. That liberated us from the drug culture and helped build some mental toughness, something refreshing to a former wrestler like myself.

My next years were spent in Maoist and post-Maoist "party-building," all ventures which ended either in establishing a few more sects or, in many more cases, dissolution and disillusionment. But after I had left the last of the Leninist-Stalinist grouplets I had been in, even though many of them had some very committed activists, I had to examine why all these groups collapsed across the board.

Again to make a long story short, I studied how early on in the Russian Revolution, the Bolsheviks had usurped power from the workers in the soviets, made them essentially rubber-stamp bodies for the party leadership, and suppressed all opposition through its secret police apparatus, the Cheka. Privileges for party leaders, even during times of famine, were established in *Animal Farm*–like fashion— only it wasn't just under Napoleon/Stalin, but began under Snowball/Lenin and when Trotsky was still a Bolshevik leader. A detailed analysis of this can be found in books such as *The Soviets: The Russian Workers, Peasants, and Soldiers Councils, 1905–1921* by Oskar Anweiler, and *The Russian Revolution in Retreat, 1920–24: Soviet Workers and the New Communist Elite* by Simon Pirani.

You see, the root of all this crazy, illogical, and self-serving activity by all these would-be "vanguard" parties and groups is that they put their perceived organizational needs first, above that of the masses, like any other business does. We all presumably became activists to fight all sorts of injustice, oppression, exploitation, and misery, and not to replace the existing rulers with a new bunch of exploiters and oppressors headed by us.

As PL became increasingly isolated from the mass movements, which were already ebbing in 1970, their anti-intellectual, antitheoretical, and voluntaristic approach to rekindling revolutionary activity drove them into a dead end. It was not the specifics of their bad politics that necessitated this alone, but also their bureaucratic top-down organization, which stifled any creativity and independent approaches to problem-solving. Thus, all the "vanguards" died either a quick or slow death.

Would that back in the time I was at Columbia there had been some strong group with good practice that was closer to the views on party and state of Rosa Luxemburg. There were a few such souls who had such views, but to the naïve newbies to the revolutionary movement like myself, they were drowned out by the Leninists of various stripes. It was only through the experiences of the disappointment of group after group for many of these same reasons that we could grasp the incredible truth of her criticisms of Lenin, for advocating a party and regime with the "servile spirit of the night-watchman state" and establishing Bolshevik rule through "decree, dictatorial force of the factory overseer, draconian penalties, rule by terror." (See her writings such as *The Mass Strike, the Political Party and the Trade Unions*, *The Russian Revolution*, and many others, including her letters, although I would add that I am not in agreement with all she wrote, including the issue of the right of self-determination.)

The writings of Victor Serge in warning, from a revolutionary anticapitalist perspective, of the dangers of authoritarianism are also remarkably prescient and relevant in light of the history and eventual self-destruction of the international communist movement. Again, there were some pro-Serge voices at Columbia, but most of us were swept up in the struggles of the day.

This also highlights a weakness of political education in PL and other Leninist groups. We had study groups that introduced people, including me, to many basic works of Marx, Engels, Lenin, Stalin, and Mao. But the main discussion was about the party's latest crazy line. So when we read *State and Revolution*, much of the discussion was about why they opposed all community control efforts, which were largely based in black and Latino communities, as reformist and building illusions about the nature of the capitalist state. Of course, almost all economic battles of workers for higher wages, better working conditions, etc., were supported and not denounced as merely building illusions about the nature of wage labor and surplus value under capitalism. A white-tinted economism was passed off as revolutionary.

When we read these texts, both those I still agree with and those I don't, there was little attempt to place them in historical context, or to examine if the theory they espoused matched the reality of the events of their time. So we just accepted what was said in *State and Revolution* that the workers ran the soviets and the Soviet Union under Lenin and Stalin, without examining the actual class, social, and economic relations in the USSR. That dogmatic approach led me to years of trying to shoehorn the square pegs of theory into the round holes of reality, rather than starting first with reality and then developing theory. Some of this may have been inevitable in the heat of struggle, and remember in 1968 we didn't think America today would be headed by someone like Trump. But as methodology it was dangerously flawed, and soon led to failure after failure.

Should I have known better? Well, yes and no. I was not Karl Marx, and a thorough examination of these types of issues, assuming I was even aware of them at the time, would have in practice meant a rather lonely withdrawal from the battles of the day. Many of us also naïvely looked for international leadership to China and Mao. When Mao died and China openly veered rightwards, some of us tried to hold onto our beliefs by saying that Mao and/or his opponents had abandoned Leninism, in various combinations of attempted explanations.

Another problem was the weakness of the revolutionary but non- or anti-Leninists. A lot of us tried to persist by creating or supporting newer or better Marxist-Leninist groups, even as this movement was rapidly collapsing. A downside of being a fighter is that you don't always know when to give up and move on to the next fight. And it only was when this New Communist Movement had run its course that a lot of us could move on and take the time to re-examine what had happened.

Still, I would say that being a Leninist for all those key years was the biggest mistake I have made in my life, even if it was at least partially unavoidable and a function of the times.

I nevertheless met many a good and serious person in PL, and still keep in touch with some of them. That also means we are all aging now, some more easily than others. Hopefully the lessons we learned can help new generations avoid our mistakes, both those that were avoidable and those that were unavoidable.

Always question everything, demand proof for whatever is said or advocated, and stand strong on principle. But be ready to fight, by any means necessary, and train yourself both mentally and physically to be able do so. It is a long, protracted struggle, but it cannot be won by waiting for perfection. Just try to learn what you can from past mistakes and tragedies, but also honor and learn from the contributions of those previous generations.

Eddie Goldman is the host and producer of the No Holds Barred international podcast and publisher of the No Holds Barred blog (http://eddiegoldman. com). He has covered the combat sports since the early 1990s and in 2008 was presented a journalism lifetime achievement award and named "The Conscience of Combat Sports" by Gladiator Magazine.

Steve Cherkoss, left, PL organizer, Berkeley.

ley arrests at demonstration against the university
a course taught by Black Panther Eldridge Cleaver;
n and Joan Kramer, center.

PL anti-Nazi demonstration, 1967. Danny Cassidy, far right; Jay Frank,
center.

Photo: El Puente de Claudio

Oakland Stop the Draft Week, October 1967.

John Ross, PL Mission Tenant Union candidate for supervisor, 1968.

San Francisco Mission Tenants Union Slum Mobile
protesting evictions, 1967.

Bridges Randall, left, PL and TWLF
student leader, San Francisco State.

San Francisco State strike pamphlet, 1968.

Portion of an agitprop poster targeting the new
neoconservative president of San Francisco State,
Sam Hayakawa.

Margaret Leahy.

John Levin, San Francisco State strike, 1968.

Photo: Nacio Jan Brown

Third World Liberation Front sit-in at San Francisco State, spring 1968.

Photo: Jeffrey Blankfort

Third World Liberation Front sit-in, 1968. Prof. Juan Martinez, center, Hari Dillon and Howie Foreman, right.

Photo: Jeffrey Blankfort

Community and student demonstration, San Francisco State strike, 1968.

Photo: Nacio Jan Brown

On Strike! Shut It Down! Pickets on the San Francisco State campus, 1968.

Challenge's take on the San Francisco State strike, 1968.

University of Washington. A meeting to protest the suspension of five students who led a demonstration against United Fruit Company recruiters, who they chased off campus. Left to right: Ed Morman , Robbie Stern, Karen Daenzer, Bill Bernstein, Lenny Sokolow.

Photo: Steve Ludwig.

May 2nd Movement antidraft button.

WSA Caucus meeting, SDS National Committee meeting, 1968. Bob Schwartz, far right.

Princeton: Renaissance Theatre Group. "The play's the thing wherein we'll catch the conscience of the establishment." Jerry Hoffman, draped in the US flag, plays the wolf.

Photo: Steve Ludwig.

Vietnam Committee lit table, University of Washington.

Students at the University of Iowa block a Dow Chemical recruiter, November 1967.

Iowa WSA/SDS member Bruce Johnson calls on students to confront a GE recruiter during the 1970 General Electric strike.

13

The East Was Red

Susan Tarr
(City University of New York, San Francisco)

Looking back on my brief (circa 1967–68) membership in the Progressive Labor Party, I feel both pride and embarrassment. Pride, because I persisted in the political work in spite of being (and remaining) temperamentally ill-suited for cooperative work (and especially for the rigors of PL political work). The conviction at that time that a socialist revolution was, if not imminent, at least possible, roused me to action. There is also the larger pride of having been part of the national progressive wave of the 1960s, including the anti–Vietnam War movement.

Most of my embarrassment stems from now recognizing that I was deficient in historical knowledge and ill-equipped to engage in serious critical analysis. Much of my political commitment was driven by an overabundance of emotion, impulsivity, and youthful confusion and discontent. But back then, the "East was Red and the Wind was Rising"; while my current reassessment is colored by information I then didn't have or chose to ignore. I also must admit that I had a crush on more than one revolutionary comrade. Ardor is ardor and my romantic focus included a student leader who I never even met in person. Seeing him stride to a podium and deliver an eloquent address to a room full of rowdy avidly Marxist-Leninist youth was quite enough to stir my overactive imagination.

I was recruited at CCNY and I had very little doubt that, of the political organizations operating at the time, PL was the smartest, the toughest, and the most uncompromising. The party's positions on the issues and developments of the day seemed to be for the most part the correct ones. There were numerous organizations representing different approaches to political work, which ran the gamut from left-of-left leftists calling for immediate armed revolution (dismissively designated as "infantile" by PL) to mildly pacifist "Peaceniks."

PL's criticism of SDS, assorted Trotskyist groups, the Black Panthers, SNCC, the Weather Underground, and anarchists of all stripes, etc., was usually right on the nose. My personal penchant for provocation and rebellion precluded an interest in Women's Strike for Peace, Peace Now, and other moderate liberal organizations. The primacy of the class struggle as the fundamental basis of historical analysis and action was straightforward and appealing. I was aware that the party's "purity" of thought and association fostered isolation from less rigid political organizations. I didn't see this isolation as leading to sectarianism or irrelevance, however, but rather as a sign of PL's clear-headed strength.

I did have reservations about my participation and remained ambivalent about several of the party's positions: I wasn't able to muster much enthusiasm for support of Enver Hoxha's Albanian regime (repressive even then) or for "Communists" like Ceausescu, but there were numerous others whose life and work were inspirational. PL's stand against all forms of nationalism was the correct one and, I think, still is. I was unmoved by the party's suggestion that I move out of my crappy, but large, $58-a-month (it was 1967, remember rent control?) First Avenue apartment to a more expensive, smaller place on the "less bourgeois" West Side. But clearly the Chinese revolution was a necessary corrective to the errant Russian endeavor. We urged draftees not to evade the draft or burn their draft cards but rather to go to Vietnam and, from within, organize soldiers against the war. Naturally, safe from the draft and far from Vietnam, I was an enthusiastic supporter of this position. And what fool would quibble with the party's support for the numerous worldwide liberation struggles of the time. I was hurt and confused when we were cursed and physically attacked by a group of New York City bus drivers at their uptown bus barn. Our antiwar leaflets and attempts at dialogue had elicited an unexpected degree of rage. Obviously, the sensible and appealing idea of the Worker-Student Alliance didn't make sense or appeal to everyone. But revolutionary hope springs eternal, and there was the practice of *group criticism and self-criticism.* Analyzing a failure such as the unexpected and perplexing clash with the bus drivers would serve to illuminate mistakes in tactics and determine the necessary correctives. Utilizing this collective way of addressing individual and party behaviors, thoughts, tactics, etc., could turn even a failure into a victory.

So, many of my doubts and my ambivalences was mitigated by respect and admiration for so many individuals and my belief in the party's principles.

I was in California for the summer of 1967, due in part to PL's suggestion that some of us work on the West Coast for a few months. The other inducement was my Lord Byron of a boyfriend; troubadour, poet, loony infantile leftist, and musician Irish Dan Cassidy, who had earlier left New York for San Francisco. On a Sixth Avenue corner, at a stoplight, was a red convertible sports car inhabited by a smiling, dark-eyed, beckoning beauty. Cassidy, without hesitating, had jumped into her car and ended up, a week later, in San Francisco, alone and abandoned. Then calling (collect) for the first time since he had disappeared he suggested that I join him (and not forget to bring his guitar, notebooks of poems, and his several volumes of the heavy and heavily annotated *Collected Works* of Joseph Stalin). For me, the twin appeal of political work and romance was irresistible. The romance soon foundered but the political work continued.

One of our assignments called for us each to sell a weekly quota of PL's West Coast newspaper. I found this difficult and very embarrassing, not because of the content of the newspaper, but because of the requirement that I stand on busy San Francisco street corners yelling as loud as I could: "Buy *SPARK!* It's a communist paper!" The idea was that "One Spark Will Start a Prairie Fire," and while I was all for the conflagration, shouting on the street corner was way out of what is now called my "comfort zone."

My only success during that San Francisco summer came in addressing (knees quaking and voice shaking) a small crowd of unexpectedly responsive and enthusiastic longshoremen; members of ILWU who were refusing to load ships filled with armaments headed for Vietnam. "Long Live Harry Bridges!"

If my less-than-serious tone gives the impression that I look back on my membership in PL ruefully or with regret, that is not the case. I do now see that much of what was motivating me was a form of "self-medication"; PL membership as part of my desired aim of being a better person and being thought of as such. But certainly the events of that period, especially 1967–68, demanded serious united political opposition to a government and a system responsible for death, destruction, inequity, and exploitation in this country and abroad. I don't see things very differently today, but, sadly, now have less confidence, less hope that profound revolutionary change is possible.

Susan Tarr is a retired film-worker. She currently lives on a small ranch in the mountains north of LA. In spite of the current disheartening US/world political situation, numerous four and two-legged creatures, cacti and high desert mountains do brighten her days. She is currently working on a six-part limited series for television.

14

The (Broken) Promise of the Worker-Student Alliance: Building a Base in Iowa

Steven Hiatt
(University of Iowa)

Why were young SDS radicals attracted to PL's worker-student alliance strategy? What did WSA-led SDS chapters do? How much did they accomplish? A close look at the development of the SDS chapter at the University of Iowa reveals some of the appeal of a worker-student alliance, the work that strategy suggested to us, and its ultimate failure to achieve what it had seemed to promise.

I arrived at the University of Iowa in January 1968, having transferred there after three semesters at Drake University in Des Moines. Several of us had campaigned for an SDS chapter at Drake, but our posters and lit table hadn't attracted much interest on campus, and we had ended up working within a religious-based coalition on antiwar education and vigils and leafleting once a week downtown. Many of my friends were at the University of Iowa, and I decided to leave Drake to join what had become a much larger, more activist-oriented chapter in Iowa City, just as the old year gave way to what turned out to be a year of reckoning.

The University of Iowa SDS chapter had been formed in the fall of 1964, one of a second wave of chapters established after the *Port Huron Statement*. It's significant that it was formed by students with experience in Friends of SNCC and the Ban the Bomb campaign (later SDS chapters came more directly out of draft-driven antiwar sentiment and the explosion of the counterculture). For example, Iowa Friends of SNCC member Steve Smith, later a member of SDS, had volunteered to register black voters in the south during Freedom Summer 1964, and was arrested and beaten in Canton, Mississippi, during his work there. My cousin Paul Clark, who had been active in Friends of SNCC (the Student Non-Violent Coordinating Committee), recalls attending an SDS meeting in Chicago to discuss the group's orientation toward future work and deciding that it would be a good idea to form an SDS chapter in Iowa City out of the small circle of radicals there. The chapter then had about twenty members and its early activities included its own small ERAP (Economic Research and Action) project in Iowa City's Goat Hollow community to aid recent migrant workers to the area who could find housing only in some shacks near the river.

In Des Moines, high school students who were also inspired by the civil rights movement had joined a group called Youth for Freedom (YFF) and worked with an ERAP-affiliated organizing project in the near north side neighborhood. They included several who would join SDS at the University of Iowa: Bruce Clark, Joe Berry, and Ross Peterson. YFF was organized by Jim Dunn, an African American social worker, and was mostly made up of young black kids around the Wilkie Settlement House on the city's near north side. YFF actions included a voter registration drive in September 1964 and marching for a city open-housing law in the spring of 1965.

A related group, Ames Youth for Equality, worked on a city open-housing campaign and collected food and clothing for Mississippi organizers. The white students who joined YFF also had close connections with the Des Moines Congress of Racial Equality (CORE) chapter led by Edna Griffin, a longtime civil rights leader in the city (and former member of the Communist Party) going back to early lunch-counter desegregation campaigns in the 1940s. YFF members later worked with a community organizing project established by Jim Dunn in the city's Southeast Bottoms neighborhood, forming relationships with people in that community and on the north side that would later figure in the work of Iowa City SDS.

With the escalation of the Vietnam War radical students were rapidly pulled into protests against the war and organizing against the draft, local protests that had national significance. A small group of SDSers, along with several Iowa peace groups, participated in the first national series of protests against US intervention in Vietnam on December 19, 1964, and in the much larger International Days of Protest on April 17 and October 15, 1965.

Catholic pacifist David Miller burned his draft card at the October 15 protests in New York City, causing a national sensation, and a few days later Steve Smith publicly burned his draft card at a rally at the Iowa student union. FBI agents soon arrived in Iowa City to take Smith into custody, with SDSers helping him evade arrest until he could arrange to turn himself in peacefully. Though not then a member of SDS, Smith asked the SDS chapter to raise money for his defense and SDS leaders called a meeting to discuss the request.

The next night 300 students turned out for the meeting, far more than any previous SDS meeting at Iowa. The students voted unanimously to support Smith, with one student declaring, "We applaud the moral courage necessary to confront the massed power of the United States government." An Iowa grad student then burned his draft card, and the chapter found itself in the middle of protest against the war, defending two draft card burners, handling coverage by national media, and contacting the SDS national office (NO) for aid and advice. The NO sent Midwest regional traveler Jane Adams and photographer D. Gorton to Iowa, and Iowa City SDS began making connections with radical students on other campuses around the state, at Grinnell College, Drake University in Des Moines, and Iowa State University in Ames (where Greg Calvert, later SDS national secretary, was teaching at the time).

In December 1965, YFF members Bruce Clark and Ross Peterson organized high school students to wear black armbands to protest the loss of life in the Vietnam War. Bruce Clark, John Tinker, Mary Beth

Tinker, and several other students were suspended from Des Moines high schools as a result. Clark opted for early graduation in January 1966 and went to the University of Iowa to join its SDS chapter. The younger students involved in the black armband protest remained in the district and became the focus of what became the *Tinker v. Des Moines* case, in which the Supreme Court in 1969 ruled that students had a right to peacefully express an (unpopular) opinion.

During 1966 and much of 1967 SDS in Iowa remained linked to the church-based peace movement and to a left-liberal civil rights program. Teach-ins, vigils, and marches were typical activities; the Iowa Vietnam Day Committee pushed for teach-ins on March 25; at Drake in Des Moines and in Iowa City there were weekly vigils along downtown streets to provide passers-by with a gentle reminder to (re)consider the costs of and reasons for the war. A torchlight protest march of 200 in Iowa City on the night of March 24 was greeted by counter-protesters shouting "Traitors!" and "Beatniks!" With the demonstrators surrounded at a rally in front of the Old Capital building on campus, eggs were thrown and pushing and shoving threatened to degenerate into fistfights. Paul Clark, the final speaker, managed to quiet the crowd with an appeal to democratic values and an emphasis on the theme of the march, which had called for an end to the war while mourning the dead on both sides.

SDS at Iowa was then part of a milieu encompassing writers and artists around the Writers' Workshop and a growing counterculture scene, together with an approving sector of faculty that would later coalesce around New University Conference. This was a radicalism—but one heavily influenced by the radical individualism of the beats and the folk and rock music scene. And indeed, there were certainly radical implications in Prof. Bob Sayre's explanation of the New Left: "We want a society where everyone enjoys himself and stops hitting people."

A more consistent Left influence was the Iowa Socialist League (ISL), led by Marxist anthropologist Don Barnett, several of whose members were also active in SDS. Barnett, who later wrote *Mau-Mau from Within*, about Kenya's Mau-Mau rebellion against British rule in the 1950s, was a passionate anti-imperialist, but also argued that the US working class was bought off and that revolution could only come through the success of Third World movements. Faith Carney of ISL argued, for example, that SDS should raise money to send medical supplies to the Vietnamese National Liberation Front: "If our war is unjust, then the other side is the victim of American aggression and there is nothing wrong with supplying them."

Such a position was well to the left of liberalism or traditional pacifism, but it reflected a variety of influences pushing in a more militant direction—from the SNCC kids sitting in at segregated lunch counters in the South to Mario Savio telling the Free Speech Movement in Berkeley that "you've got to put your bodies upon the gears" to more international influences such as Che Guevara, images of young Red Guards in China, and the popular film *The Battle of Algiers*. Left academics added their encouragement, with, for example, Alan Spitzer, Christopher Lasch, and Barnett leading what they called Cold War Colloquia articulating a Left critique of US foreign policy.

As the war in Vietnam intensified and draft calls increased, draft resistance became the work linking the older peace movement with a New Left rapidly moving in new directions. In April 1967, Bruce Clark told a rally of 400 at Iowa's Spring Mobilization Against the War, "We support the boys in Vietnam and we want to bring them home now. The time has come to stand up and say, 'I won't go and fight in a genocidal war in Vietnam. Resist the draft!'" He and Ross Peterson became actively involved in draft counseling, with Clark sponsored by the American Friends Service Committee traveling the state reaching out to radical youth during the summer of 1967.

Over the course of the year individual moral witness began giving way to collective direct action and confrontation with state and corporate power structures. In Oakland, California, Stop the Draft Week in October 1967 began with nonviolent actions and ended with running battles of 10,000 through downtown streets as insurgent protesters fought the cops and avoided their tear gas.

Students also began taking a closer look at the university and found that its connections with the Cold War state and corporate America were more important than its contributions to the liberal arts, and that training students for roles in the corporate and scientific apparatus was their key function in the rapid postwar expansion of higher education. Revelations that the CIA had funded the National Student Association and that Michigan State had helped set up and run South Vietnam's secret police apparatus brought home this analysis for many activists. The antiwar movement began a boycott of Dow Chemical, the corporate producer of napalm for the US military but also the producer of many consumer products, in an attempt to link personal and corporate responsibility to the Vietnam War. While students were taking the streets in Oakland, students at the University of Wisconsin-Madison blocked job candidates attempting to interview with Dow Chemical recruiters. The police responded with tear gas and clubs, in the process confirming for many students—both participants and observers—that the antiwar movement was right to link the Vietnam War abroad with a whole range of oppressions at home.

University of Iowa SDS was part of this national wave of militant protest. On November 1, 1967, protesters attempted to stop students from talking to Marine Corps recruiters by shoving through a line of protecting police and blocking access to the Memorial Union interview room. Some 1,500 students crowded around the Union, with police eventually arresting 108. A month later, 18 were arrested when students chanting "Dow must go now!" tried to block a Dow Chemical recruiter, then clashed with police in what the Des Moines Register termed "flareups worthy of the guerrilla genius of Mao Tse-tung." As SDSers returned to Iowa City in January 1968, ten faced grand jury indictments, including five for conspiracy, which carried a possible fifteen-year prison sentence. The conspiracy, according to the Johnson County district attorney, consisted of coordinating two groups of demonstrators by using a walkie-talkie.

At this point, police and university overreaction in the service of the government's Vietnam policies had the effect of turning large numbers of students against the system in general. White middle-class students were now facing prison terms: didn't this show that the system had to go? Though the Iowa SDS chapter seemed to have proved its militancy in a just cause and had acquired considerable prestige on campus, SDSers were unclear about what their strategic direction should be. Activists seemed to be caught in a cycle of provoking the cops, then using the police overreaction to radicalize students and bring them into the movement. But then what? Chapter meetings reflected this concern, with, for example, Faith Carney calling on the chapter to increase its militancy and its planning "so that next time we can pull off a march with some balls!" However, what that might be wasn't clear. In March the chapter was stymied in a debate fixated on a false dichotomy between a focus on internal education and political development of the current membership or on expanding the chapter rapidly to gather in larger numbers of sympathetic students.

I had just arrived in Iowa City in January and was new to this level of engagement: what could we do to consolidate this radicalization? The student movement was only a small piece of the puzzle. Certainly, some Iowa City radicals found the counterculture/student syndicalism a sufficient framework and looked with a mixture of fear and contempt at "straights"—rank-and-file working people. SDSers had of course been happy to attack the university's in loco parentis rules and other restrictions on student rights and freedoms. But we were contemptuous of the position that students and the university radical milieu constituted a class-in-itself, as argued, for example, in Jerry Farber's "The Student as Nigger," which reflected an attitude that circulated far more widely than his actual pamphlet, and which we held to be racist and self-indulgent (at best).

Events beyond the campus began to point the way. On January 30, 1968, the North Vietnamese army and the NLF forces launched the Tet Offensive, challenging US military power directly over several weeks and shaking public confidence in the optimistic pronouncements that had been coming from the Pentagon and the Johnson administration. At the end of March Lyndon Johnson was forced to withdraw his bid for a second term in the face of Eugene McCarthy's primary challenge in New Hampshire, confirming growing antiwar sentiment. I was part of a group of SDSers living in a farmhouse near Iowa City watching the evening news who were surprised by LBJ's announcement—with our surprise giving way to gleeful celebration. (Several of Everett Frost's excellent home-brewed beers were opened on that occasion.)

For many student activists, this was a first taste of being part of a movement able to shake power structures—and they wanted more. Their euphoria was interrupted days later with the assassination of Martin Luther King, Jr., on April 4, marking, if anyone needed reminding, just how far the authorities and their rightwing supporters would go to defend themselves against determined challenge from the civil rights movement. The riots that followed in black neighborhoods across the country underscored the depth of the political crisis. On campus, the Afro-American Students Association and SDS called a rally to denounce King's murder. At the rally several hundred students signed a telegram of support for the Memphis sanitation strikers King had gone to Memphis to support and called on the authorities to "begin a program towards Black control of Black neighborhoods and schools."

The French May events delivered a further answer as student demonstrations and then student strikes and campus occupations set off a chain reaction of rebellious uprising across France, with 11 million workers going on strike, occupying factories and taking control of whole districts of Paris. By the end of May the French state was tottering, with workers and students demanding not just more relevant education and higher wages, but new forms of education and worker control of factories.

In the US students were turning toward revolutionary politics and reading radical history in search of a usable past, from the Wobblies of the World War I era, the CIO's Flint sit-down strikes, and the Communist Party's militancy in the struggle against racial oppression. Now in France, we saw workers, often under the banner of various communist groups, again taking the lead in shaking the foundations of the state. The Cold War liberals had been wrong: Marxists were correct to think that the working class was positioned to lead the way to a new society. More directly, it seemed to us that Progressive Labor had something to offer in its worker-student alliance strategy—an agenda linking a rapidly radicalizing but strategically uncertain student movement with core forces in society that could lead the way out of that impasse. Marxism-Leninism was now starting to displace the radical liberalism of New Left culture, with even early SDS leader Carl Oglesby acknowledging that there is "no other coherent, integrated, and explicit philosophy of revolution"; and revolution, it seemed, was on the agenda.

SDSers in other chapters moved toward Marxism through contact with a variety of Left organizations, like the Trotskyist Socialist Workers Party or various antirevisionists who had left the CP, but in December 1967, Bruce Clark met with PL organizer Earl Silbar, who led PL student work in the Midwest, at SDS's Bloomington National Council (NC) meeting. Progressive Labor and its allies were pushing a worker-student alliance as SDS's strategic direction, and as part of that approach, they proposed a summer work-in to put students into factories. The work-in proposal passed at the Bloomington NC meeting, and PL student leaders focused on working to recruit SDSers to come to industrial (and PL party) centers to make the project a success.

By June 1968, the summer work-in seemed like a natural next step for a number of Iowa SDSers. Barricades were still burning in France, Bobby Kennedy had just been assassinated, and forecasts were for a long, hot summer in inner cities across the country. Many needed summer jobs in any case (having been cut off by their parents), so the prospect of working in Chicago during the summer of 1968 and continuing their political work and education under the formal tutelage of a Marxist party was appealing.

Participants included Bruce Clark and Carmen Kraemer from Iowa and Joe Berry from Grinnell College, who lived in the Old Town neighborhood on the near North Side of Chicago and worked days in a Teamster-organized ice cream factory on the South Side. PL led study groups on its own materials, such as *Build a Base in the Working Class* and *Primer on Imperialism*, as well as discussions of workplace experiences. The work-in's goal was never to convert the working class (a strawman story that *Time* magazine journalists dearly loved and that *Doonesbury* used as fodder for satire) but rather to have mostly "middle class" students learn about the working class and their lives and ideas. In this the work-in was a great success and consolidated many of us around the idea that workers, collectively, were the potential main force for revolution or any radical change in the US and that the WSA strategy for SDS was correct. The attention of Chicago's Red Squad also had the effect of suggesting to worker/students that this was serious business and that their program was on the right track.

In late August 1968 the Democratic Party held its nominating convention in Chicago, with the National Mobilization Committee to End the War in Vietnam (Mobe) and the Yippies planning major protests. The calls for action were heated ("There's not going to be a Democratic convention!"), and the SDS National Office (NO) and other SDSers were initially wary of involvement because of the disorganization and danger, but most participated when it became clear that thousands of "McCarthy kids" and other radical youth would come anyway. PL had a reputation for strident rhetoric but was wary of "wild in the streets" provocations as alienating workers, and some PL students in Chicago stayed away.

This was a sectarian response, and in the event most PLers and WSA kids acted in solidarity with the street mobilization against the war, the Cold War liberals running the Democratic Party, and the multitudes of blue-helmeted Chicago cops looking to bash heads. Joe Berry, for example, was on the streets near Grant Park with fellow WSAer Rich Schneirov from Grinnell and PL student organizer Earl Silbar, who had to leave his house by the back door to evade Red Squad officers watching the front. Whether students saw the official violence up close and in person on the streets of Chicago, or in clips broadcast on TV, thousands drew the conclusion that the power structure was unreformable and that a revolution was necessary.

The work-in students returned to Iowa City in September consolidated in their support for PL and its worker-student alliance strategy, and quickly set about pushing that strategy in the University of Iowa SDS chapter through their Worker-Student Alliance caucus. Since that group included many of the most active SDS leaders at Iowa (though not all), it became the de facto leadership of the chapter.

That chapter grew enormously; students felt the sense of crisis in the country, and SDS was clearly the place to be if you wanted to confront it. Four hundred students filled an auditorium for the first chapter meeting, with more left outside. The Iowa City chapter meanwhile served as a base for SDS regional travelers Joe Berry and Carmen Kraemer, who helped set up chapters at colleges around the state— ten new ones that fall alone.

SDS continued its radical antiwar program, including a rally/ teach-in at the University on November 1, followed by a statewide demonstration protesting the Nixon/ Humphrey/Wallace election contest in Des Moines on November 3, election day. This demonstration was cosponsored with the Des Moines chapter of the Black Panther Party (BPP) and the Iowa Peace and Freedom Party (I and other SDSers had been part of its founding meeting earlier in the year), and the prospect of the demonstration caused panic in official quarters. Iowa authorities mobilized some National Guard units and canceled police leaves, while on the ideological front the Des Moines schools reportedly assigned students to study a *Readers Digest* article about SDS to discourage their participation. On election day, several hundred students from a dozen colleges marched through emptied streets, with security provided by the Des Moines Panthers. While official intimidation discouraged watching crowds, the main slogan of the march, "The Elections Are a Hoax," reflected widespread alienation from the system—but offered nothing as an effective alternative. This was in keeping with the tendency of PL and a number of other Left groups to deceive themselves in seeing cynicism and alienation as reflecting a revolutionary stance, rather than as markers of resignation or quietism.

In keeping with a broader WSA outlook, Iowa City SDS also came to the defense of Joeanna Cheatom of Des Moines, a National Welfare Rights Organization activist charged by the Polk County DA with arson in connection with a lumber yard fire. SDS connections with the Panthers and Joeanna Cheatom went back several years to the work Bruce Clark, Joe Berry and others had done in Des Moines' near northside ghetto, coming to know people in the community who would later join or support the BPP, including Archie Moore, Charlie Knox, Danny Hall, and Mike Harris. In support, SDSers showed up at court hearings in Des Moines and publicized the case on campus. Joeanna Cheatom was found not guilty at trial—but heavy police pressure on the Des Moines Panthers as well as the bombing of the Panther headquarters (linked by the Panthers to the police) later led to the disbandment of the Des Moines BPP chapter.

SDS also actively sold the *Black Panther* (and the *National Guardian*, as well as PL literature such as *Challenge*), a combination that Chicago PLers were not happy about. At this point PL was rapidly retreating from its previous strong support for the black liberation movement, reasoning that "revolutionary nationalism is still nationalism," and doubling down on its critique of revisionism. Officially, PL's line was still "critical support" of the Panthers, and we Iowa City WSAers took that phrase literally: the key point, we thought, was to support the Panthers, even though the BPP had some problems. Since no actual PL members were based in Iowa, local SDSers pursued this approach based on personal connections with the Des Moines BPP chapter (which in turn was close to the Fred Hampton group in Chicago), and when the Des Moines group came under attack, University of Iowa SDSers led several days of protests at the Des Moines courthouse.

This work, which of course caused more of a ruckus than really challenged power, drew the malevolent attention of the state, which in Iowa was quite unused to public challenge (to say the least). SDS's initial contact and member lists were stolen from its locker in the student union (a COINTELPRO operation?). SDS also exposed a police informer on campus, one who had been recruited by the police on the promise of leniency on a drug charge. Similarly, at a spring 1969 regional SDS conference at Grinnell, SDSers exposed an attempt to bust students at the conference by planting dope in dorm rooms—an experience that led a number of WSAers to decide to avoid pot and other drugs rather than risk prison time. This of course served to further distance the WSAers from more countercultural radical students in the chapter.

In March Bill Hinton, author of an influential study of the Chinese revolution, *Fanshen: A Documentary of Revolution in a Chinese Village*, spoke on campus under SDS sponsorship. PL had recently attacked the Chinese Cultural Revolution leadership and declared that all nationalism was reactionary, a position Hinton opposed. As a marker of our sectarianism, several of us spent precious time with Hinton arguing with him rather than trying to learn from him. For his part, he rightly tried to get us to see that we needed to pursue more of a united front approach in our work on and off campus—an approach that those who "knew they were right" had trouble accepting. Indeed, we WSA/ SDSers at this point were spending far too much time concerned with the national organizational infighting within SDS, with a number of us traveling to the March 1969 Austin National Council meeting to mobilize against feared maneuvers by the SDS National Office faction (which of course had no intention at this point of united front work with PL and its supporters).

The 1968/69 year ended with a strike against a proposed tuition increase, a strike that closed the university. The increase was in part intended by the state legislature as revenge for radical activism on state university campuses. Iowa SDS played a leading role in organizing a campuswide class boycott and put out a pamphlet laying out a program to lower tuition for make it affordable for working-class and poor students and raise the corporate income tax to pay for it. PL criticized us on this point, since the party was now saying that the Left should not encourage or make it easier for working-class black (or white) kids to go to college and get their minds "polluted with bourgeois nonsense." We should have realized then that PL was backing itself into a sectarian corner; clearly our contacts in the Black Athletes Union were not about to accept such a position, and we didn't try to argue this line on campus. We did argue back in a limited fashion with PL, and the party didn't push the issue hard with us.

PL and the national SDS/WSA caucus decided to organize another summer work-in campaign in 1969, and most of the Iowa City WSAers moved to Chicago that June, finding work in printing plants, a car wax factory, an electronics assembly shop. The program was much the same as the previous year: observe the situation on the shop floor (many of these workplaces were nonunion), learn from fellow workers, raise our ideas when appropriate, and study and discuss the lessons in weekly meetings led by PL cadre. Of course, the first focus was the SDS national convention, at which WSA and its allies had a slight majority of delegates. Their opponents in the National Office and the Revolutionary Youth Movement factions responded by reading PL/ WSA out of the organization and splitting SDS irrevocably. WSA continued the convention and elected a slate of national officers, and we headed back to campus in the fall determined to build a WSA-oriented SDS, whose national office was now located in Boston.

The first SDS meeting on campus that fall drew hundreds of students, and we had the difficult task of explaining the split in the organization, especially in terms that made any sense to students who had not been absorbed in the infighting between WSA and the various other factions. We put forward, of course, that we were part of the "real" SDS, since WSA had had a majority of the delegates at the convention. The WSA caucus continued to meet, with about fifteen members, and attempted to steer the chapter in the "correct" direction—a strategy that could only appear as heavy-handed no matter how much respect its members might have had for their past political work on campus.

A change in PL's campus strategy didn't help. The party was now pushing a narrower "campus worker-student alliance" strategy. Since a number of SDSers needed campus jobs anyway, the group naturally adopted this approach at the beginning of the school year, taking jobs in campus food service, the hospital laundry, the library and other services. One thing did become apparent to us, and that was the arrogance with which many students, including both frat boys and countercultural types, treated campus workers. We attempted on occasion to sell PL lit to maintenance and other workers and were met with mostly bemused tolerance. Unlike Harvard and Columbia workers, who were often African Americans from neighborhoods near the schools, University of Iowa workers were mostly whites from small towns and farms in the countryside. PL, based in New York, was completely unable to fathom the difference between a strategy that made sense in New York or Boston and conditions in Midwest university towns.

The worker-student alliance strategy had further impacts on our personal lives. While the university community resonated mostly to countercultural radicalism, we took seriously PL's argument that students should move "from personal to social rebellion." A number of us paired up, and the WSA caucus soon consisted of couples, several of them married—hardly Hollywood's picture of student radicalism. PL at the time was widely derided by other Left groups for trying to integrate into the working class by affecting older working-class fashions ("wearing 1950s reindeer sweaters!")—but all the Left groups coming out of SDS soon adopted the same strategy to reach working-class people. Deirdre Peglar and I (we married in the fall of 1969) remember, for example, radical former NFL player Dave Meggyesy, someone far outside the PL camp, urging us to settle down and integrate long-term into a working-class community.

By contrast, much of the male campus Left was taking, consciously or unconsciously, its model from Norman Mailer's figure of the "white negro," merging existentialist nonconformity with an exploitative approach to relationships with women (while retaining the homophobic contempt for gays and lesbians with which they had grown up). We instead took the model of comradeship between men and women drawn (sometimes inaccurately) from an older Left history. While not at this point an advanced approach, this was still a positive factor in our relationships with other students who were looking for a long-term radical strategy, and led us also to take seriously Iowa City's growing women's movement (something PL, we noticed, was slow in doing). Iowa City's radical movement was in fact notable in that it was not dominated, as some other campuses were, by alpha-male heavies of the Mark Rudd type. Bruce Clark, who could have played such a role based on the street cred from his political history, disagreed with this approach to organizing and personally would have found it repugnant. Indeed, in this regard our WSA chapter continued to be marked by a certain New Left reluctance to define and push leadership roles.

Events soon pointed our WSA chapter in other, broader, directions beyond the narrow campus worker-student alliance. The chapter took up support that October for striking Cedar Rapids sanitation workers in Teamster Local 238. Our first contacts were uncertain; Bruce Clark and several others went to speak at a union meeting in Cedar Rapids, and sat in the back of the hall as the meeting wound through its agenda. Uncertain after a while that the Teamsters were in a mood to welcome them, they got up to go. Someone in the hall noticed them moving toward the door and asked in a loud voice, "Where are the students going?" They were then asked to come to the front and talk to the meeting, which they did to an enthusiastic response, and we started walking picket lines in Cedar Rapids, in turn persuading striking workers to speak at an antiwar rally on campus. Despite criticisms from Revolutionary Youth Movement supporters that the student Left should look only to young workers on the streets and avoid getting caught up in "economistic" labor struggles, we found that these Teamsters were no more keen on the Vietnam War than we were.

That winter, the chapter supported the Iowa Beef Packers strike, establishing 7 am pickets to turn back trucks delivering meat to the local A&P store. (This supposedly "economistic" strike was marked by street brawls, bombings, and at least one shooting of a company spy.) The chapter also continued its support for the Des Moines Black Panther Party, then under siege from city and county authorities. In all these initiatives, the chapter moved beyond the narrow campus worker-student alliance focus advocated by the PL leadership. However, a key weakness was that we did not figure out how to make our case to a larger number of radical students—in too many cases we mobilized only ourselves and a small periphery to come to a picket line or demo.

Our WSA caucus's focus on broader alliances in fact met with some criticism on campus. Even though the chapter had proposed a campaign to abolish ROTC on campus and sent a busload of students to the November 1969 Mobilization in Washington, DC, other radicals charged that the worker-student alliance strategy had led SDS to neglect the struggle against the Vietnam War. This criticism stung, and the chapter sought to counter it while maintaining its WSA focus. One initiative was an anti-ROTC demonstration that disrupted a ROTC Governor's Day drill competition, when hundreds of students occupied a fieldhouse where the event was to take place. Nixon's Cambodia incursion and the National Guard killings at Kent State and Jackson State shortly thereafter led to a massive strike that shut the university, along with colleges and universities across the country. SDS responded to the crisis, was on the strike leadership committee, and was openly acknowledged as an important student leadership organization.

For a few months after the June 1969 SDS split the remaining WSA-led organization included significant numbers of other radicals—but to PL this breadth of views was not tolerable and by the end of the year most of the independent radicals had left SDS. In its centers, PL/SDS was isolating itself with its increasingly strident criticism of the Panthers, its position that all nationalism was reactionary and must be openly opposed (even that of the Vietnamese or Cubans), its opposition to affirmative action in education just as students fought for open admissions and ethnic studies, and public attacks on the Vietnamese leadership in the name of antirevisionism.

The Iowa SDS chapter, with its own base in the state from years of work, and geographic distance from PL in Chicago, had more latitude. Even so, we still found arguing for a number of PL-based positions hard going. Few students were attracted to the WSA core of the chapter, despite wide respect for the work of SDS/WSA leaders. In 1969/70 another action showed how separated the WSA leadership of the SDS Iowa chapter had become from its formerly large student base. PL had begun a support campaign for a massive national strike at General Electric, with Nixon's Department of Labor intervening on the side of management. When we found out that the Labor Department was coming to campus to recruit, we saw this as a chance to bring the national WSA strategy home to Iowa and planned an action. However, we planned it in just the fashion of the Weathermen we so criticized: in a small closed group with high "security" that came up with an adventurist plan to enter the interview rooms and try to physically throw the recruiter off campus. We made no real effort to organize mass support—and we had no way to get the man off campus if we did eject him. Not surprisingly, our plan failed and the core activists were threatened with expulsion and charged by the county with felony assault.

We soon returned to our senses and began to do what we should have done before: canvass much of the campus, now including defending the charges against us. We were amazingly well received—to such an extent that the campus judicial system refused to discipline us and the administration had to ignore its own procedures to impose multi-semester suspensions on us, but not expulsions. The court charges were lowered to misdemeanor disturbing the peace, to which we pleaded no contest in order to put the whole mess behind us—and became the occasion for some of us to leave Iowa City. By the fall of 1970, PL pulled SDS leaders like Bruce and Carmen Clark in to its centers to consolidate them as PL cadre.

The WSA-led SDS chapter at Iowa continued for another couple of years, focusing on a campaign against the racist ideology of Prof. Richard Herrnstein of Harvard and his supporters. This work included a regional antiracism conference and did incorporate some successful outreach to other antiracist activists, who made use of some effective PL-produced material in their own work. The chapter also continued to do strike support, including sending a carload of students to support the bitter General Motors strike in Detroit in October 1970. We also supported Maytag strikers in Newton, Iowa, and Latina activist Delores Carillo, who was trying to win a union job at the Oscar Meyer plant in Davenport. This work was useful, but it didn't build longer-term relationships because of PL's narrowness, which sometimes led to pushing *Challenge* sales as a main activity. The chapter at this point was not set up for or organized around a long-term strategy for linking student radicalism and labor or community struggles. The WSA strategy PL had pushed had been mainly an orientation to winning influence within the student Left—and not, as we hoped it would be, a strategy to build a broader radical Left encompassing students and working people, unless they accepted the direct leadership of Progressive Labor. By the end of the 1971/72 school year, SDS had been kicked off campus for blocking a Defense Intelligence Agency (DIA) recruiter and challenging a speech by Herrnstein; a number of the remaining WSAers moved to Chicago to work with Progressive Labor or drifted away from support for PL/WSA.

The promising turn in Iowa toward an alliance between student radicals and a radicalizing working-class/African American freedom movement had sputtered to an end. Nevertheless, the work of the University of Iowa SDS chapter showed the possibilities of a real worker-student alliance. The campus movement against the Vietnam War coincided with a strike upsurge, one that echoed across Iowa in bitter strikes and wildcats in a number of plants. The war was itself an important factor, with workers moving into opposition despite flag-waving by some rightwingers. To take but one example, in January 1971 three separate statewide demonstrations converged in Des Moines when Richard Nixon came to give a speech at the Iowa State Capitol: union construction workers, antiwar students, and farmers. Wiseacre journalists predicted that the longhair students would have their butts whipped—but instead we found the construction workers happily giving us tips on the best ways to fight the cops! The Des Moines Black Panthers for their part had welcomed working with serious, dedicated allies and supporters.

However, while Iowa City SDS/WSA was able to distance itself to some extent from PL's sectarian ultraleftism, those positions alienated the chapter from many serious radicals on campus and many activists in community organizations. Nor did PL have the ability to provide guidance on turning the worker-student alliance into a long-term strategy for building a Left base in Iowa (or elsewhere) out of the social crisis of the sixties. The SDS/WSA work did help develop several of us into socialist organizers, all of whom left PL's orbit; but with further experience and political development we can see how much more could have been done.

Fifty years later, with the crisis of neoliberalism, the aggression of an openly fascist movement, and the rise of new leftwing people's movements talking about socialism for the first time in decades, it's useful to recall lessons from previous Left upsurges—registering both their achievements and their mistakes. Progressive Labor thought of Left politics as drawing rigid lines of demarcation—and drawing those lines tighter and tighter, retreating from mass struggles to avoid lapsing into revisionism under pressure from a base in active, diverse people's movements. What we've learned: Revolutionary transformation is a learning process, one that we can succeed in only when we engage ourselves in the struggles of the working class in its millions—rather than retreat from them for fear of contamination. Our method must echo Brecht's "Try. Fail. Try again. Fail better"—*hasta la victoria siempre.*

Steven Hiatt became a community college English teacher, first in Des Moines and later in Omaha, where he was president of the local NEA chapter. He moved to the San Francisco Bay Area in 1977, where he was able to transfer his teaching skills to publishing. He has worked as a copyeditor and book producer since then. He continued his political work with the Bay Area Socialist Organizing Committee (BASOC) and North Star Network in the 1980s, and was an editor of CrossRoads *magazine in the 1990s. He edited the collection* A Game as Old as Empire: The World of Economic Hit Men and the Web of Global Corruption *with John Perkins (2007) and has edited and helped develop a number of other books and written for a variety of other political publications.*

Commentary

Bruce Clark
University of Iowa WSA/SDS and PL

This account of SDS and WSA at the University of Iowa has reminded me that I have never taken the time over the last fifty years to chronicle my activities or to keep a running account of how I viewed them. In those days the self-appointed or, more likely, media-appointed, "leaders" of the New Left viewed their personal roles as all important and went on to write accounts. Many of us were too focused on creating a movement to chronicle our own role or how we evaluated it as it developed.

In any case, I am perhaps less critical in some ways of the role of the Progressive Labor Party in those days. I see every day lessons and ideas from that time in my life that I still apply constantly and pass on to others. When I went to Iowa City in the spring of 1966, SDS was still very much a child of the League for Industrial Democracy in its thinking. Many were academics and artists who had an increasingly critical analysis of the US. I recall in particular that they held what they called Cold War Colloquia led by Professor Alan Spitzer and Christopher Lasch in the History Department; anthropologist Don Barnett also participated as well as other faculty. These were certainly stimulating sessions. I also gravitated quickly to learning from some in the Iowa Socialist League, although I never joined. All in all, Iowa City SDS was a grab bag of Left tendencies.

One significant influence that I think should be recognized was Professor Don Barnett, author of *Mau Mau from Within*. Barnett was a passionate supporter of Third World revolution against US imperialism.

Unfortunately, he also saw the US working class as totally bought off and argued that revolution would come only from the Third World, which would finally overwhelm and defeat the US. His was I suppose a far more sophisticated and nuanced version of some of the more infantile "belly of the beast" positions of the later 1960s. I did not know him well, and this may be a somewhat distorted view of his politics, but the lack of a revolutionary force within the US was very clear in his thinking.

It may indeed have been the SDS Bloomington National Council meeting where I first had any real conversations with Earl Silbar of PL, although I seem to remember meeting him once through Ross Peterson, who may in fact have been the one to meet him first. As I recall it was at that Bloomington conference that PL put forward the "Build a Base in the Working Class" proposal as a vision of moving forward in the student movement. By this time, SDS at the University of Iowa had become very activist and led a large movement on campus, but the limits of the power of a student-only movement were becoming clear. I remember being hit by how obviously correct that argument was—that students were never going to make change on their own. I had an increasing appreciation that all the things I opposed clearly resulted from capitalism and that only the working class had the power to bring capitalism down.

We always fought to have more workshops at National Council meetings, because it was in these discussions where the WSA faction always met real students and had discussions about class and always won over large numbers of attendees.

So for me, class consciousness is the key to everything, and it is that which only PL brought to the student movement. SDS leaders in the mid 1960s were still basically social democrats. With every SDS conference I attended, I recall the SDS leadership feeling increasingly threatened by PL's ideas, since they were deeply anti–working class in the way that always dominated American liberalism. In fact, it is the central consistent tenet of American liberalism. At that time, there was a strong anti–working class prejudice among the vast majority of the campus "Left." Many students accepted the liberal academic view that workers were bought off and sat in front of their TVs drinking beer and didn't care what was going on.

And as PL's ideas gained a following pretty quickly on many campuses and within many SDS chapters where they had a presence, the SDS leadership was pushed further to the left, at least as a pretense, to counter PL's influence. I watched this trend develop over a few short years—I was on the SDS National Interim Committee in 1968/69—and in the end the SDS leadership had become a zoo of leaders like Bernadine Dorhn and others, who really did "wave the Red Flag to defeat the Red Flag."

It is owing entirely to PL that I have led a life of fifty years of class-conscious struggle, where I still try every day to impart the central importance of class within the labor movement and with workers in general. Other left factions may have grown up and claimed those ideas to some extent, but it was always clear to me that most of these were essentially "incredibly pissed off and militant liberals," since their practice always showed no real faith in the working class.

Another lesson that came from the years of PL's student work was the fight against racism. I am sure there is much room to argue about the party's approach here, but PL made it clear that the fight against racism was the central fight and central contradiction for the US working class. It was PL that led the fight against academic racists like Richard Herrnstein.

In another direction—about our work on campus. I saw a note from Earl Silbar asking how we did the work with the fights over campus military recruiters, etc. This does bear some analysis. In the atmosphere of a college campus of 20,000 students we certainly did systematic leafleting, maintained literature tables in the student union, spoke at the "Soap Box Soundoff" at the Student Union, etc. One weakness, though, was that with 20,000 students there were always more converts to be had. If you screwed up and alienated some folks unnecessarily, you could tell yourself that you would find other people tomorrow, and we usually always did.

As was noted, too, we were always ready to form coalitions and to work with other groups whenever possible. In fact, Carmen, my wife at the time, and I were suspended in part because of our efforts to call a student strike in support of Leona Durham, who was set to become the editor of the *Daily Iowan* and who supported the strike. The university refused to allow her to assume the editorship because of that. In response, we united with the women's movement group and picked up all the *Daily Iowans* as they were dropped off around campus and hid them in a sister's garage until night, when we hauled them all to the Pentacrest and burned them in a huge pile as the dean danced around screaming that we were going to burn down Old Capitol. (Of course, ironically, that would almost happen decades later when the university used cheap scab labor to work on the dome and they set it on fire.)

We were seen grabbing the newspapers and were charged with theft, with Law Professor Burns Weston arguing successfully in court that the paper had no value and therefore our taking of the papers could not be considered theft. It was then that we were suspended for a year in the spring of 1969. We went to Chicago again for the summer work-in and then were convinced by PL to move to Kansas City, Missouri, to colonize the party there, although we were still not members. At that time, one was "invited" to join the party, and by fits and starts PL would say that no more student types could join until so many workers had been recruited. It was no doubt a real recognition that if PL wanted to become the party of the working class they could not do so in the absence of working-class members. Nonetheless, it did create this odd system where many of us reached the point of practically submitting to democratic centralism without the membership part of the equation.

Looking back on our work at Iowa, I wonder how it might have been if we had been systematic in our approach—for example, using more of a base-building perspective from the labor movement, like organizing dorms floor by floor, etc., rather than our more amorphous "shotgun" approach. Given what I know now, I suspect that we could have made a much bigger impact with a different approach.

I don't share the apparently accepted premise that PL's approach to nationalism was wrong. It may have been put forward in a sectarian fashion and sometimes with a bit of deaf ear as to how it was being heard, but I do believe that communists and socialists have to recognize that the idea that nationalism is reactionary and undercuts class solidarity. Certainly one must fight alongside all sorts of struggles that take a "national" form due to the oppression of a nation (be it a race or actual nation). But within those struggles there have always been the contradictions of class, and nationalist revolutions have always been captured by the bourgeoisie of those nations. I am not the historian here despite my major, or the Marxist theoretician in the crowd. I think we all know I have been above all the activist who tried to learn what he needs to stay in the fight and hope to win. But I see how ideas play out in struggle, and that is how I evaluate them. The Left must participate in and help build a broad range of struggles of workers, minorities, women, LGBT, etc., but within that shared struggle for reforms, the role of the Left is not to uncritically support the sometimes narrow focus of these struggles but to make clear how those struggles relate to the class struggle and the historic fight to free all humanity from capitalism.

I still recall vividly the advice of Earl Silbar at some Midwest SDS function where we were fighting over some structural issue. He handed me a small note that said "PPF." I looked quizzical, I am sure, and he said: "Put Politics First." That was a sharp reminder to be clear and not to put form over content and to see the underlying contradictions and sharpen them. I have carried that lesson since then, and have passed it on in one form or another to others.

Here's a fun fact you may have forgotten. In the grand jury indictment of the five of us for conspiracy in January 1968 there was testimony from a little fascist member of Young Americans for Freedom at the time: Terry Brandstad, who went to become Iowa's Republican governor for way-too-many years. You may also recall that the leader of the Iowa ACLU at the time, Louise Noun, sent word they would not help us in any way. Someone directed us to the Emergency Civil Liberties Committee in New York, which sent Michael Kennedy out to Iowa City to help defend us. When the contradictions over the antiwar movement sharpened, the good liberals of the ACLU were nowhere to be found.

The conditions today are clearly again ripe for working-class rebellion, with low-wage workers leading the "Fight For $15" and the struggles of immigrant workers, teachers, and other public-sector workers fighting back against vicious attacks. The Bernie Sanders campaign and his identification as some sort of socialist have led to widespread interest in the idea of socialism and what it involves. But for this to become a significant movement it must embrace and encourage explicit class-consciousness. It is ironic that a large group of young people have been attracted to the idea of socialism but that many don't seem to connect that with the working class in particular. If a mass Left of any sort is to arise again, I would assert that it is the spread of class-consciousness and antiracism that will determine its success.

Bruce Clark and his then wife Carmen moved to Kansas City, Missouri, in the summer of 1971, where he worked at a National Can Co. plant and was a steward in the USW local there. In 1978 they moved back to Iowa to the Dubuque area, where he started working at the US Postal Service, becoming active in the American Postal Workers Union, first as steward and then as local president, which he remained until 2017. He was elected APWU state president In 1988, a position he held until his retirement in 2018. He helped found Workers for One Postal Union in 1991, a national effort to unite the four postal unions. He also served on the Iowa AFL-CIO Executive Council for many years and was inducted into the Iowa Labor Hall of Fame in August of 2017. He now resides in Connecticut with his husband, Richard Alper.

15

Movement Learning:
The Good, the Bad, and the Ugly

Joe Berry
(University of Iowa, San Francisco State University)

This short piece is meant to be a personal supplement to the collective essay drafted originally by Steve Hiatt on the work of the Worker-Student Alliance (WSA)–led SDS chapter at the University of Iowa in the late 1960s. It takes a more personal view and attempts to suggest some of the impacts of these experiences on myself as part of the University of Iowa SDS (and Grinnell SDS before that) and later, in San Francisco, at San Francisco State University, in the early 1970s.

The easiest way for me to conceptualize what I learned from my experiences in the WSA wing of SDS and the student movement generally is to make lists. The first list is of those things that I look back on and say, "It was lucky—or at least good—that I was exposed to this and internalized it." The second list is the parallel opposite: those attitudes, practices, and opinions that, in retrospect, were not helpful, to me individually or to the movement as a whole.

I should also make clear that, unlike some who were active in the organized Left and the revolutionary Left, in particular the WSA and the Progressive Labor Party, I still adhere to the general goals that I saw us fighting for as well as most of the specific reforms that we struggled to attain. I still believe that some form of socialism is the only humane way to organize a society in which people are encouraged and given incentives to treat each other decently, rather than a capitalist society that rewards avarice and competition. However, I must say that I have experienced some feelings of betrayal that so many of my ex-comrades and colleagues have dropped out of active politics completely, or fundamentally changed their views, in some cases quite radically. I wonder sometimes how many of us were ever really communists or Marxists? How much did many people actually think it through? I know I did. I felt impelled and encouraged— in fact, coerced— to think through the ideas of Marxism, to refine those ideas and figure out how to apply them. I continue on that path with some changes of ideas, of course, and certainly a different terrain than we faced in the late 1960s and early 1970s. I am encouraged that the recent political developments (Black Lives Matter, the Bernie Sanders campaign, and the election of #45 as president) in the US have brought many old radicals out of the woodwork and into activity again.

I remain overwhelmingly grateful to the movement as a whole and the part of it that had its greatest impact on me. It made real the one-line admonition given to me by my father, a career teacher who was a Christian socialist, the son of an IWW sympathizer Iowa dirt farmer and livestock trader. With the doors closed and the blinds pulled and my stepmother out of the room he said, "Well, of course, you can't really be a Christian and be for capitalism." The movement gave me an opportunity to do something with that idea that my father was never able to realize. Having said that, here are my lists:

The Plusses

1. On the positive side, PL and WSA connected my earlier activism in the civil rights and antiwar movements as a high school student to a Marxist worldview that could reinforce the ideas and practices of the movement and provide a vehicle to sift the experiences I was having and would continue to have. The introduction to Marxism as a practice, and seeing people who openly called themselves Marxists and communists, who were not just academics but people actively trying to change the world in an organized manner, was life changing to me.

It probably saved my life literally. PL and the WSA introduced me to a different set of values from those that dominated the world in central Iowa where I grew up. Only later did I discover that not everybody around me actively and privately adhered to those values. But the movement demonstrated a different set of priorities and one that laid out a different future for a young student than what was the default when I was growing up. In the same way, the introduction to Marxism was the next step on that path that certainly was to prove sustaining to me for the rest of my life. The notion of unity of action and study, of theory and practice (praxis), if not always realized, was at least presented and grappled with in a way that I found transformative and satisfying as an ideal and a model, probably more than any other single intellectual precept of my life. And as Mao said, "Correct ideas do not drop from the sky." They come from the collective struggle of other human beings.

2. Another important insight that I gained was the idea that history is the story of movement and change and that the movement *for* change has a history itself to be studied and learned from. The guidance to read and what to read and to discuss and interrogate it, and to urge other people to do so, was extremely reassuring to a bookish, religious, and isolated young student. The study groups that I joined in this period were more useful than any single class I ever took, introducing the concepts of imperialism, profit, exploitation, racism, and oppression, and then interrogating those concepts. I have used these lessons repeatedly in the years since and have tried to make all the classes I teach in some small way resemble the formal and informal study groups from which I learned so much. My students (and some colleagues) seem to have appreciated it from time to time.

3. One of the best aspects of PL's and WSA's version of Marxism was an emphasis on the importance of antiracism and antiracist practice by the white majority in the US to realize a workers' revolution and socialism. The concept was that this was something in the interests of most workers, and therefore most people; not just a matter of moral solidarity with justice, even though PL and the WSA caucus often implemented this idea in the movement in a dogmatic and narrow way—especially organizationally. Our polemic with the authors of "White Blind Spot," Noel Ignatin (a.k.a. Noel Ingatiev) and Ted Allen, was carried on in a sectarian and uncomradely fashion and prevented us from learning what they had to teach. Nevertheless, the value of emphasizing the link between the class interests and the need to oppose all forms of racism was a key contribution of PL/WSA.

And finally, the idea that effective opposition to racism among working people was possible. Most white workers were not inevitable racists and most black workers were not blind nationalists. A united workers' struggle against racism and against exploitation was possible. That was not a concept that I had absorbed automatically from my experiences in the civil rights movement. It remains one of the most important ideas in my ideological lexicon. I remember being reintroduced to Allen's brief version in *Radical America* of his epic work *The Invention of the White Race,* in the early 1980s at City College of San Francisco, where I was teaching history at the time. It immediately became a lodestar in all my teaching since and when, years later, I got the chance to meet Allen and have dinner with him at a conference, I had enough sense to appreciate the opportunity.

4. PL and the WSA caucus also introduced me to ways people actually organize around ideas: an ideology translated into a political strategy. This actual application of praxis, the link between the life of the mind and the real world, was one of the most hopeful experiences of my life. It showed me that, however imperfectly, we can make progress based on collective will and organized activity. This also included demonstrating how to be a caucus or a grouping with certain ideas operating within a larger organizational context. This became the core of a strategy I have since helped to popularize in my work with adjunct, nontenure-track, temporary college faculty, who are now 70 percent of college teachers and number over 100,000 nationwide. This "inside/

outside strategy" conceives the way that a group can organize to op-pose its second-class status in an organization or society as a whole. The basic concept is that the subject group must organize and unify itself separately to speak for itself directly (the outside strategy) while at the same time working as good militant members inside the larger and more powerful organization or movement to leverage that greater power as well. I see this as having been the strategy of various caucuses in the labor movement and of many other groups. I have applied and promoted this idea so vigorously, especially among adjunct teachers in the faculty union movement that some have actually credited me with inventing it. I have corrected them when possible, but with great pride and pleasure as well.

The manner in which we implemented those ideas was often deeply flawed in SDS and elsewhere, marred by sectarianism and dogmatism, but the concept of organizing around ideas and not personalities or immediate self-interest was dizzying to me. It opened up a whole world of study, practice, and ideas that have dominated the rest of my life. It included the idea that a truly effective all-around organizer and educator is the most important thing in the world.

In fact, that is what I have striven to be in whatever I was doing, whether in paid work, volunteer work, or recreation. I thank the movement, and in particular WSA/SDS, for having members who were skilled practitioners and actually demonstrated that you could organize around ideas if you had an effective strategy. You could build a base and people would follow you and learn in the process of that struggle. There are many people, who are politically progressive and humane, including those who are somewhat active, who never manage to have their ideas linked to organizational behavior that can generate power. Many people never get that. I am so lucky that I was at the right place at the right time to get that education, and I was doubly privi-leged to be able to pass it on, sometimes even to getting paid to do so.

5. I also still value having been presented with the organizational framework of democratic centralism: the theorizing of the tension between democracy— the constant bubbling up of experiences, assessments, opinions from the base, on the one hand, and the need for united action in order to make a difference in the world, on the other. This tension between those two ideas, one requiring the greatest amount of democracy possible, the other requiring sometimes iron discipline and centralism under extreme conditions, exists in all organized attempts to change the world, from a neighborhood group fighting for a stop sign to a group of parents trying to improve their school, to a trade union trying to bargain their contract and create a credible strike threat, to a revolutionary party trying to create a vision and reality of an entirely new society. The theoretical framework of, and for, democratic centralism exists in all of those situations.

The particular application of it that we experienced in PL was deeply flawed. It was mechanically applied and lacking elemental democracy in many situations where it could have been possible. This had lots of negative consequences within the organization, its base, and the broader society it was trying to impact. But nevertheless, the idea and the ideal of that relation between centralism and democracy, and having that posed to me as the way you organize human beings to create social change was transformative. To have it framed in a way that I could understand and grapple with at a young age was the beginning of an intellectual and practical road that I have followed throughout my entire life, as a teacher and a political activist.

Questions around the organizational concept of democratic centralism have repeatedly arisen in my life. I drafted the first version of a paper on democratic centralism for the Bay Area Socialist Organizing Committee, which was published as a chapter in its booklet. As a unionist and labor educator I also thought a lot about these ideas, since it seemed to me that a proper version of these principles was behind the effective solidarity in action that binds together any good and effective union. Finally, these ideas have been much in my mind in the last few years while living and teaching part-time in Vietnam. I have realized that I really think democratic centralism, properly applied, is appropriate and necessary for voluntary action organizations like unions and political parties, but should not be applied to the governance of a state. Citizens are not there by choice and the requirements for united action with no dissent after full democratic discussion should not be imposed upon them, except perhaps in the most extreme emergencies, and those decided by democratic means.

6. Another key idea that I learned and have kept is that most people in the US and worldwide are workers, and that the relations of production shape us all. This is the core reality; it tells us which class controls the economy and determines who controls society; that's the essence of capitalist society. The relations of production and the people who do the work are central to any society— precapitalist and postcapitalist. That was a concept that PL injected into the student movement with great effect. Unfortunately, this contribution has not been properly remembered and acknowledged for a variety of reasons. Hopefully, this book will have some impact in correcting this omission of the role of class ideas in the student movement and SDS.

The ancillary concept, then, that what students should be doing is figuring out their relationship to workers in society; that's the fulcrum around which any student movement has to rotate. That was the core concept of the WSA caucus. It was right then, it is right now, and it will continue to be right as long as young people are in the position of being predominantly learners in a society and capitalism persists and produces a majority working class. And for all those young people who become workers in the "gig economy" of low-paid, part-time, short-term, no-benefits jobs (95 percent of all new jobs since 2008). I remember now with pride our actively supporting workplace and community struggles and in arguments in the student movement, explaining workers' capacity to lead the fight. That experience led me to a life in the labor movement, and I can hardly imagine another.

7. Finally, the idea of internationalism was greatly reinforced by my contact with PL and WSA, as well as a deep suspicion of anything that portrayed itself as patriotic. I was especially ready for the concept by having been raised by an antinationalist father who said he would never fly the American flag, only the UN flag, if he flew any flag, and who took his family to the Third World (Iran) to live for a year when I was eleven years old. There I discovered that in fact everything in the US wasn't "better" or "only" or even "good" at all in many cases, and that the accident of being born a US citizen did not make anybody more honorable or, in the language I would have used at that time, closer to God. So later, when I was presented with the idea that, as workers, we have no country, we have each other, worldwide—that was an idea that was very easy for me to absorb in the midst of the Vietnam War. To have an organization that put internationalism forward consistently and integrated it with all its other ideas for revolutionary change worldwide was important to me and many student activists. The fact that PL turned this correct principle into a sectarian dogma does not make it less correct.

The Minuses

1. On the negative side, near the top of the list must be PL's retrograde positions on the women's movement, feminism, sex, gender roles, and personal life. Like much of the Left at the time, PL was aggressively homophobic, aping what it saw as working-class opinion. It never really came to terms with the women's movement, and many in PL opposed abortion rights and reproductive rights in general, though it was never the party line. Ironically, without the leadership of many strong women, especially in secondary and local leadership roles, PL would never have achieved what it did. These positions cost PL many fine militants, especially gay and female. I think I am not the only one who struggled to overcome some of this heritage in later years. It was my good fortune that strong women cared enough to struggle with and partly transform me. As I owe the movement my life in many ways, I owe the women's movement for giving me an idea of a different way to be a man than the way of my father and grandfathers, deeply patriarchal all. PL and WSA were only marginally helpful in that regard. PL and WSA also often interfered in a nonconstructive way in members' personal lives, for instance pressuring people to get married ("regular-ize their relationships"), or break up with "lost causes," and in other ways imitate what seemed to PL to be working-class life. I might have avoided a very bad too-early first marriage myself if not for this social pressure.

2. Also near the top of the list of negative legacies is PL's progres-sion toward sectarianism and narcissism. This was partly a defensive reaction to the extreme redbaiting and anticommunism that PL/WSA received in SDS and the movement generally, but it was the wrong re-action. I remember two examples in particular. One was after the 1969 SDS convention where the split occurred. We went back to Iowa and tried to implement the very narrow strategy that PL urged upon us, to the exclusion of all else: the Campus Worker-Student Alliance. It was basically a retreat from the antiwar and black liberation movements as well as the women's liberation movement, which we had never really fully joined, and we instead totally focused on building an alliance with campus workers. The only thing that saved us from total irrelevance to other students was the huge reaction to the Cambodia Invasion in spring of 1970, which we had the sense to join and help lead.

The other example was about five years later when I left PL, along with most of the other members and leaders in Northern California. I remember suddenly realizing that I was now free to read anything that I wanted to read and to talk to anyone I wanted about anything and not feel I was breaking discipline in doing so. Since the Left was still quite vibrant in the Bay Area at that time, this was a great moment of redis-covery of a broader movement for me. It was also a realization of how ingrown and sectarian PL had become in retreating from it. The full history of PL's descent into sectarianism is elucidated in *Five Retreats*, a book written in the 1970s by two former Bay Area PL members, Jim Dann and Hari Dillon.

3. Along with organizational sectarianism, and a style of discussion and debate partly inherited from the worst aspects of Lenin and the

Leninist tradition generally, PL became enmeshed in a deeply dogmatic style of politics, hostile to nuance, criticism, and ultimately to democracy itself. Some of this was the heritage of the communist movement generally, especially under Stalin, and inherited from the CPUSA. Some of it was from the style of the Chinese Communist Party and from the manner in which that party's writings were translated into English; but some of it was PL itself. In any case, this sort of political rigidity, inability to admit error, and failure to foster healthy internal discussion much less carry on transparent and healthy debate with others outside of PL, left a legacy of political habits that I suspect I am not alone in grappling with in the years since I left the party. I still try to make it a point to disagree with ideas in debate and not denigrate and insult the people who hold them. I often fail, but I try. Thinking back, I believe I might have even made some political and personal connections with my father in his later years if my dogmatic style had not been so intense.

4. Connected with the above was one of the foundational concepts around which PL was formed, namely support for the Chinese criticism of the Soviet Union and their leadership under the flag of "antirevisionism." This was deeply unfortunate. Many of the legitimate and correct criticisms of the direction of the Soviet Union and CPSU were bundled under the essentially fundamentalist label of revisionism. This could not help but reinforce tendencies toward blind orthodoxies and scriptural readings of Marx and Lenin rather than a lively critical discussion of the problems of communists holding state power in a mostly capitalist world, a discussion that was desperately needed.

I have seen in the years since that antirevisionism did not lead the Chinese party toward deepening socialism, but rather the reverse. Ironically, the Vietnamese party, which ultimately chose the other, pro-Soviet side, ended up in a very similar place in present-day Vietnam. I can't help but think that had this legitimate debate been carried out differently, we might have much more of a mass sentiment for socialism today.

5. This also was connected to another error of classical Leninism, or at least the variety I learned—the idea of the perpetually unified single vanguard party. Only now, after having lived for six months in Vietnam in 2015, do I realize how the idea of a single party vanguard, especially in the context of holding state power, cannot over time be relied upon to continue to represent the interests of the working-class majority, no matter how illustrious and heroic its history. My short visits to Cuba, and Grenada under the New Jewel Movement, were not sufficient to show this to me, but living in Vietnam made it clear. No human institution should be seen as permanent and above criticism, competition, and even attack, nor can it be fully trusted into future generations. This is totally undialectical and has proved false in practice.

6. Further, and connected with the above, was the ideological and political problem that Max Elbaum elucidates very well in his book *Revolution in the Air*: namely that PL shared with others on the Left the serious political error that having the most correct line, the most accurate description of reality, was always more important than any other aspect of the organization's political practice. If having the correct line didn't seem to be paying off, PL's response was to lean on the cadre to push the line harder. The idea that the organization might not be in a position to have people actually listen to it and that this was a much bigger problem than that some nuances of the political line were in error, was just not on the radar. This was an error that came from an overreaction to the US Communist Party, which submerged all talk of socialism and Marxism except for praise for the USSR in their mass work and required that most members keep their party affiliation secret. Criticizing that and being public was one of the virtues of PL so that a young person of the 1960s could say, "I knew people who were communists and they did a lot of good stuff. " However, drawing the conclusion that the answer to the CP's errors was to push the maximum line in every situation up to and including making every article in PL's newspaper end with the need for socialism and revolution, whether anyone was reading it or not, whether it had any influence in the real world or not, was a terrible mistake. Luckily, the daily political practice of many members was much better than what showed up in print in the newspaper. But this concept had a terrible effect on the inner life of the organization.

7. This, in turn, led to a common error, referred to even then as an "employee mentality," where you just did your work and took orders. Having an "employee mentality" might be criticized rhetorically, but no one was ever disciplined for following orders. People were only disciplined for asking questions and refusing orders. Discipline, in such cases, might involve demotion from leadership, not getting appointed to do something, losing support in your mass work or in your position, rumor-mongering, ostracism, criticism of your personal life, or expulsion from the organization. In short, many of these sectarian, dogmatic, narrow antidemocratic practices, internally and toward the external world, gave PL and most of the parties in the New Communist Movement an aspect of cult-ness that was not healthy. It was certainly not healthy for growth and influence and the continued dialectical inflow of new people and ideas necessary to keep the organization relevant.

This is especially ironic because one of the few criticisms that PL made early on of China, while it was still a very China-friendly organization and had the "China franchise" in the United States, had to do with the cult of Mao. PL took measures purportedly intended to prevent a cult of personality from developing, like publishing articles without bylines or under pseudonyms. The effect of this was to make it impossible to interact and debate laterally about the ideas that people wrote about. This was especially a problem when you are talking about a movement of students, where the trying out of new ideas and ways of communicating them are central to their daily existence. It also which gave a superstatus to the party's chairman, Milt Rosen, who was the nearly only publicly identifiable figure in PL's publications—maybe not a cult of personality but close.

Conclusion

I still feel strongly in many ways about my experiences in PL and WSA. I feel mostly gratitude, some criticism, a little shame, and a lot of pride. I suspect I am not alone. But on balance, what I learned was much more good than bad. It pointed me in the direction that has carried me the whole rest of my life, as a teacher, an activist, a trade unionist, a labor educator, and a socialist. There are aspects of this experience that were negative, and that I have struggled to overcome.

Some of the tools (self-examination, criticism/self-criticism, and holding practice up to the light of theory) that I learned in those years have been useful in my attempt to improve myself and my work and correct some of the harmful legacies from PL and WSA—the very organizations that gave me these wonderful tools.

Joe Berry lives in Berkeley, where he is still involved in union and Left political politics. He is working on a book (his second) about organizing, and still thinks education and organizing are the best things for any socialist to be doing. He does this among contingent faculty in the US and also in Vietnam. Contact him at joeberry@igc.org.

Work-In 68

A number of Iowa SDS people were involved this summer in Chicago and Iowa City… Participants met weekly for work-in groups that discussed on more or less a theoretical level the work experiences that people had at their jobs… Apart from the constant contact we all had with working people everyday, education combined with activism at two significant times that were invaluable.

The first of these was a wildcat strike led by the Black Chicago Transit Authority drivers, which was supported by over 10% of the white drivers. The issue was primarily the fact that the present union is controlled by drivers who have no contact with present job problems but still are voting members of the union. This resulted in a racist white-controlled union that, by dividing the workers, made the white drivers a bit better off than the blacks, but kept both of them down…

In this initial strike, our only action was to go to a few of their meetings to rap and also to do some leafleting at factories and subway stations in their suppors… The other major action concerned a similar wildcat by drivers at the Railway Express Agency…. An injunction was issued against picketing, and work-in people picketed for the strikers and our lines were respected by over half of the incoming drivers who deliver goods to the REA depot. Many good contacts were made with the REA drivers and many of these were very receptive to a radical analysis of society…

Convention week was a fitting conclusion to our work … The CTA strike was on and many kids in for the week walked picket lines and got to know the drivers. National SDS was so unresponsive that they told the strikers "too busy" when called for help. Nonetheless, many SDSers were among the 2,000 who, joined by 300 strikers, marched to the bus barn at Clark and Diversey to show support … It was perhaps the only march of the whole week so militant that the chants were not "Peace Now" but "2-4-6-8—Organize to Smash the State!" … The streets may belong to the people, but it won't mean a damn til the factories and corporations also do and this is perhaps the single most important general lesson of the Work-In.

Joe Berry
Pterodactyl, September 9, 1968
[an underground newspaper based at Grinnell College]

16

A Life on the Left

Joan Kramer (1947–2017)
(UC Berkeley, WSA/SDS)

I was born in Washington, DC, and spent the first six years of my life on the East Coast. When the FBI and CIA had appeared to have abandoned their pursuit of my father, who had been accused of being a spy for the Russians by President Truman, we ended up in Hollywood, California. One family friend told me that my father was "the most blacklisted person she had ever known." I was a red diaper baby and The Weavers were my pop heroes, not the Beach Boys: I grew up knowing the words to "Freiheit," "Viva La Quince Brigada," "We Shall Overcome," "There Once Was a Union Maid."

In 1964 I graduated from Hollywood High with a ceremony at the famous Hollywood Bowl. None of my family was present at my high school graduation. My mother was in North Carolina taking care of her dying mother. My father, unfortunately by this time a functioning alcoholic, showed up after the ceremony was over. And my sister was in Cuba, where she was visiting with the second Progressive Labor group attempting to break the US travel ban. The organizers of the Cuba trip, whom I had met at a summer camp, had initially contacted me to see if I wanted to go, but my sister had taken the call. She was about twenty-one at the time and anxious to take off. That trip to Cuba had enormous effects on my sister's life (she met her future husband, Charles Johnson, there), and on mine as well.

247

Later that year I went to San Francisco State College, as it was then known. I immediately sought out leftist groups because, as a red diaper baby, I was almost literally an activist from birth. At that time, however, the Communist Party did not seem revolutionary at all to me. But there was a W.E.B. Du Bois Club on the campus and I attended a few meetings, which were mostly cultural in nature; James Dean was the subject of one of them. And there was the May 2nd Movement table and the SNCC table, where I sat daily with a friend named Alex Stein. I was only seventeen and very naive about people. Alex was encouraging, kind, and very knowledgeable—he kept us all informed. It was 1964 and the civil rights movement was reaching its greatest intensity. Had I been bolder, I would have gone south and registered voters and sat in at lunch counters. But here in San Francisco, I could at least let people know the truth.

The following year I transferred to UC Berkeley, where the majority of my closest friends had matriculated in 1964. It took a very short time for me to get involved in the SDS chapter and become one of its main worker bees to "man" the table daily in Sproul Plaza. SDS at Berkeley was divided between two factions—the anarchists and the Progressive Labor Party. Naively, I thought I could work with both. I was hugely attracted to the PL faction because of their discipline, the study groups they offered, and the camaraderie they afforded me as a fairly shy and insecure female. I began studying with Jim Cohen and Steve Hamilton. I also found that Progressive Labor gave me a way to define myself as different from and opposed to my parents, who were members of or at least associated with the Communist Party USA. The anarchist faction seemed full of arrogant married male graduate students who were out to have liaisons with single women. I wasn't interested in breaking up families.

I did a lot of work with SDS—I went to the induction center early many mornings to encourage people not to go into the army, while always being sympathetic to the recruits. I remember going down to support the heroic Ken Epstein, who went in saying he would organize fellow recruits to oppose the war. (He was rejected.) Another demonstration was for John Roemer, the son of a family friend from Los Angeles.

At some point I joined the Bay Area Radical Teachers Organizing Collective (BARTOC) and the Bay Area Progressive Musicians Association (BAPMA). BARTOC was a teachers' group (I was planning to go to graduate school to get my teaching credential), and the latter a music group that performed for many striking workers around the Bay Area and also at left-wing celebrations. BAPMA was composed of professional musicians with one exception—me! This was because I knew by heart all the solidarity songs of the labor movement, such as "The International," as well as some Chinese Communist Party, Spanish Civil War, multicultural, and civil rights songs of solidarity. I often carried a large drum and pounded on it. This was the highlight of my political life, since I found that music was a wonderful way to unite people. I also loved to sing and felt physically and mentally alive when I sang and played guitar.

At that time, in the late 1960s and early 1970s, there were many workers' strikes, and I remember going with BAPMA to march and sing labor songs in support. We also went to some parties at the homes of workers. In particular, I remember a Safeway workers strike celebration. When the workers finally got a check from their union to buy food, they went and spent it on a party for all their friends and supporters, including us. I distinctly recall one PL leader telling the workers not to smoke dope because it would make them less militant and, besides, that's what the ruling class wanted us to do—become dopers. At the time it seemed patently ridiculous to tell these militant workers to stop smoking dope, and now it seems even more so.

Perhaps the biggest event of my time at UC Berkeley was the demonstration at Moses Hall, when we stormed the building and took it over to demand that Eldridge Cleaver, a spokesperson for the Black Panther Party, be allowed to teach on campus. The UC administration position was that Cleaver couldn't teach there because he didn't have a college degree! Considering the fact that the rightwinger Eric Hoffer, who hadn't even gone to high school, taught at UC and even had an office, showed that the administration position was utter nonsense, and, we contended, racist. This was 1968—the Black Panther Party was very prominent in Oakland, and many of us supported what they were doing in the black community. We thought that Cleaver's anti-imperialist and antiracist understanding needed to be shared widely with other students.

The administration called in the cops and we were arrested, sentenced to ten days in jail, with a further ninety days suspended sentence, and a $300 fine. Most of us didn't have the $300, since we were working students. I was able to raise a bit among my parents' leftist friends, even though I don't think that the CP had probably approved. Nor did we have the support of most students at Berkeley, who also disapproved since they believed the administration's allegations that we had destroyed their records, which had been housed in Moses Hall. In fact, the only destruction committed that evening was committed by the police. I will also never forget that Tom Hayden, the high muckety-muck priest of SDS, the leader who wrote the *Port Huron Statement*, showed up and urged us to attack the police. We ignored him, fortunately, and he was nowhere in sight when the police showed up to arrest us.

A few months later, in September 1969, when I was still on probation from the Moses Hall incident, I went to a demonstration in San Francisco against the International Industrialists Conference. Most of us were outside shouting and demonstrating with signs. A few people were able to get inside, including Marian Cohen, who was tall and beautiful and looked every bit the Republican she once had been. I was arrested along with the wife of the leader of the Venceremos faction of SDS (H. Bruce Franklin) and another woman for "breaking windows," which were actually broken by a group of young men running ahead of us. Later I learned that some Weatherpeople—or a precursor to the Weather faction—had apparently encouraged this and that was why the demo had degenerated into breaking windows. I know I would never have gone there had I known that was going to happen: I was opposed to destruction for destruction's sake. Apparently the

Weathermen were there to riot. And, in the end, it was people such as myself who got arrested. Here's a comment on the IIC demonstration from a letter at the bottom of an article by Bill Ayers, who would be elected education secretary of the Weatherman faction when it took over at the SDS convention the following month: "In Sept. 1969 we did a 'Days of Rage' at the International Industrialists Conference in San Francisco in which I took a bust and a beatdown. I always saw we were a precursor to the rumble in Chi-town the following month." This "rumble" was the Weatherman-inspired "Days of Rage" in Chicago, October 8–11, 1969.

That summer I also participated in the Work-In, a project of PL's Worker-Student Alliance to get students into working-class jobs to bring them into contact with working people and learn what their lives were like. I applied to the telephone company but wasn't hired. That summer I met Audrey Bomse, who had been sent to Berkeley for the summer by the New York Progressive Labor Party. Audrey was the most magnificent person I had met in my short time on the planet. She was—and still is—a fighter, a defender, and a completely and utterly courageous woman. We both had trouble finding jobs, but Audrey knew a man who worked in a rural area of central California where we might be able to get jobs working in the fields. We did finally pick peaches for one day (it's very difficult to climb a rickety ladder and pick this fruit) and tomatoes for three days. I was so slow that the workers took pity on us and would share some of their pickings. The conditions were oppressive, to say the least. No bathrooms, no place to wash our hands, and of course nowhere to sit down. We ate the lunches we had brought with us with our hands covered in dangerous insecticides. We started at 6 a.m. and returned home at 3 p.m. I would collapse in a chair and immediately fall asleep: I never had trouble sleeping when I worked in the fields. But summer ended and Audrey returned to New York. I never saw her again but tried to keep track of her life and her courageous contributions to the struggle.

An account in Wikipedia on SDS and its split in 1969 reminds me that Progressive Labor was in the vanguard of the emerging women's liberation movement, though I am not sure it intended that to happen. In the early days of Berkeley SDS, I, Marion Cohen, and others formed a women's caucus. We met separately and also tried to raise issues in the regular meetings, but it was extremely difficult in those early days—many of the men laughed us out of the room. Betty Friedan's *The Feminist Mystique* had been out for a couple of years, and while I personally could not become completely involved in the feminist movement, feeling, at that point, that it was racist and classist, we at least had begun the formation of women's groups that would spread throughout the country. We made contact with women in other areas, and I distinctly remember getting a letter from Chicago praising us for raising this most important issue and forming a group. Wikipedia makes it sound as if women's issues were not raised until 1969—but that's not true.

At some point, PL began telling me not to hang out with some of my SDS friends—mainly my best friend, Laurie. We were roommates and did most things together—sitting at the SDS table in Sproul Plaza, going to the induction center to try to convince people not to enlist, organizing the Black Power Conference—though she was much more active than I was. PL thought I should move away from her, but I had nowhere to go—and in fact I had invited her to live with me, so technically it was my apartment. That began a period when I had to move eight times until I found a permanent place to live. I was miserable. If PL thought Laurie's influence on me was so great, they should have worked harder to win me over, not artificially separate me from my friends. In any case, it wasn't effective in the long run. If I separated from PL, it was for my own reasons and not because of Laurie. I felt that Progressive Labor interfered too much in peoples' personal lives and essentially used that interference as a way to hold on to people, rather than winning us over to their ideas. I never formally joined the party in any case.

Then there was the question of a boyfriend I met in SDS. He had been a Southern Student Organizing Committee (SSOC) organizer at the University of Virginia. Neither faction of SDS liked him, and this made him more attractive, since I didn't really agree with either faction in the long run. One issue he openly challenged PL people about was the fact that the party was telling young students of color to drop out of college and go to work in factories to organize. Meanwhile, most of the PL leaders already had their degrees, and some had become doctors or lawyers. I felt then it was racist to ask first-generation students to leave school when everything in their lives had positioned college as the way out of poverty. In any case, I never did tell anyone to drop out—I could not in good conscience.

Although I never joined the party, I went along with much of the work and attended study groups; however, I found in PL a rigidity in attitude, a sense of superiority, and a tendency to distance that artificially kept us from the people we wanted to win over, and I felt this was a sure way to lose. I found using Marxist terminology unhelpful; I felt ordinary words could explain the class struggle just fine. Ultimately, I was judged as "not revolutionary." I would find out about meetings that I had never been told about because someone would ask me why I wasn't there. Clearly, the tactic to throw me out was just to keep me uninformed. So I quietly withdrew without a fight.

I moved on. I went to graduate school at Berkeley and in 1971 I moved to Dar es Salaam, Tanzania, on the invitation of my sister's friend, Abdulrahman Mohammed Babu, whom I had met in New York on his annual visit to the UN. While in New York several people met with him, including the great Amiri Baraka, who called to ask if he wanted a security accompaniment. Babu simply politely refused and asked what did he have to be afraid of? I thought if I went to Tanzania I could teach in the government schools at the time. I largely went because my boyfriend wanted us to meet the Chinese, who were building a railroad from Zambia through Tanzania to the coast. We would ask them if we could teach English in China. We were big fans of Chairman Mao and wanted to be in his country, whatever that meant.

Tanzania's president in 1971, Julius Nyerere, was the most enlightened and least corrupt of African rulers. While he was not a revolutionary, he was progressive, wanting the best even for women, and welcomed African Americans to live there to escape US racism. In addition, all the revolutionary movements of Africa were located in Dar es Salaam, including the MPLA of Mozambique, Angola's UNITA, and the South African ANC. I know that is the main reason I was followed there and back; the CIA had a huge stake in knowing what was going on and I, although I didn't know it, was hanging out with the leading players.

Babu was by then the minister of economic planning. He lived in a large house with five children—three were his and two were the children of his sister, who had died of cancer. Babu's wife, Ashura, was an amazing woman, with total openness and generosity toward me, at a level I would never experience again. She welcomed me into her family, shared with me the rituals and experiences of daily life, allowed me to experience a wedding (five days long) and a funeral, the rituals of Ramadan, the camaraderie that women in Muslim society actually experience in their daily lives. Though I didn't understand Swahili, I was able to witness the remarkable people that surrounded this amazing family. Babu was just as generous as his wife, and his small salary (about $300 per month, enormous compared with the rest of the society) was shared with relatives who may have needed help or a place to stay.

One day in spring 1972 I had a reservation to fly to the island of Zanzibar—the Spice Island, as it was known—because I wanted to see the beautiful place where my friends had grown up. But we were told that all flights had been canceled because of unrest. The next thing I knew, Babu and many of the friends I had met at his house had been arrested, including the fisherman with whom I had fished on the Indian Ocean. At this point I admit I began to feel very worried. The police had entered Babu's home, and with guns drawn had arrested him in front of his children.

I moved back to Los Angeles and worked briefly with a Chinese American–based Maoist Marxist-Leninist Party (the Communist Workers Party) all of whose leaders are now mainstream politicians in Los Angeles and the Bay Area. I worked with the Sbicca shoe workers, mostly from Zacatecas, Mexico. They were fighting for their right to stay in the United States and to organize a union. The CWP did not have the ability to lead this monumental type of struggle, and the AFL-CIO was not interested in a fight by undocumented workers, so this workers struggle was defeated. By 1976 I felt that the movement had already died, and that we could forget ever forming a real proletarian party that would lead the masses in the US. When my active party affiliation attempts ended, so did my feeling of purpose. It was a kind of death for me from which I have not recovered.

Joan Kramer lived in Los Angeles with her husband, Brian Hudson. They attended every demonstration they could to protest the current regime. As a retired school librarian, Joan fought against the privatizers for the last ten years while in remission from two cancers. She succumbed this past year.

17

The Spread of Maoism: A Story

Bárbara Selfridge
(UC Berkeley)

Listen, ludicrous things happen to the young and Maoist. Believe me,
I was there myself, in right up to the nuts for over a semester. But just
because I describe some of that ludicrosity, it doesn't mean I want to
offend anybody. Especially not Ellen, and that's what I want to make
real clear, right off the bat, because even though she was the butt of
the whole thing in some ways, in other ways Timur and I were the
butts and the real point is that some scenes like the one at Dave's Diner
have just got to be told. They're classics.

Okay, a little background. After a while Nixon started parroting
LBJ's "light at the end of the tunnel," but back in the spring of '70 he
was bombing the shit out of Southeast Asia, and we were all going
a little nutso trying to stop him. I was at NYU, twenty, red-blooded,
extremely draftable, and suddenly it seemed inevitable for me to fly
out to Berkeley. Everybody was nutso in Berkeley.

I knew two people out there: Chris Mott, who used to page with
me at the New York Public Library, and Chris's friend Ellen. Chris and
Ellen were freshmen dorm-mates except not really because Chris spent
all her time over with Jimmy Kirk in this animal hole he had above
the *Berkeley Barb* offices. Jimmy, Chris, and Ellen were all fresh recruits
to the campus Maoists—also known as (AKA, as it says in the police
reports) PL, Progressive Labor, the assassins of SDS, the Stalinist ass-

257

holes, the closet Trots, etc. Jimmy Kirk's of no significance whatsoever, but Chris Mott and I at one time would have been lovers except that right at that moment her father practically walks in on us.

Chris and Ellen go way back, so I met Ellen the first time when she was visiting Chris over Christmas '68, and then again summer '69 in Europe. Imagine this scene, will you: I'm in my *penzione* room in Rome, alone with Ellen, and suddenly she pulls her dress off over her head and proceeds to wash it out in my sink. Even puffed up with Italian pasta, Ellen's body drives me berserk, and for about two hours she stands there scrubbing with her ass jiggling and her tits half out of her bra and pointing at me in the mirror.

"You don't mind, do you?" she asks, looking up about five minutes into the exhibition. No clue on what she expects of me, and basically I spend the entire next year pissed at her for it.

Then finally that spring I asked her about it, point blank: "Which was it: to make or not to make?"

Ellen just stares at me like I'm some kind of pervert.

"Hey, baby," I say, "don't look at me like that!" (Let me explain. I get away with the "baby" stuff because I said there was a Ellen in my second grade who made me really hate the name. It was just a line—no such person but Ellen's like that: a sucker for any line.)

But anyway, I tell Ellen, "You've got to admit that two hours is a fucking long time to wash one dress."

"Oh, Frank, no!" Ellen never cops to anything. "That dress was filthy! It started changing color—patch by patch—and I couldn't stop. Not till it was all done."

Ellen's a sweet kid, though, even if she is a goddamn cock-tease exhibitionist. She assumes automatically that I'll stay with her in the dorm room: and every night she uses Chris's meal card to bring me "sick trays" from the dining hall. So, of course, who was I to object to having to sneak showers in the all-female bathroom at the end of the hall? Anyway, by the time I got to Berkeley, Chris, Jimmy, and Ellen were already hard-core fanatics, scheduled up to their asses in meetings, demonstrations, leaflets, and other shit-work for PL. It was all right though, because the rest of the campus was all running around just as fanatic. That was the spring of the big anti-ROTC offensive, the Postal Workers' wildcat, Kent State, Jackson State, all that shit, and it got to the point where anytime Nixon lifted a finger or more likely a bomber—we hit the streets.

My job, I saw right away, was to provide a little comic relief for the troops. I went along when they rented the bullhorns, painted the banners, etc., and I'd sing songs, crack jokes, whatever it took to remind my fellow fanatics that the revolution isn't just for robots.

So like if I stayed up all night with Chris, running off ten thousand fliers for the next day's demo, I'd pick one up and pretend to read it:

With trembling fingers, Sid tore her dress. She bit his ear in a frenzy of passion. Take me, she screamed, her hot breath exciting him to new heights of want and desire.

Then I'd look up: "Say, are you sure you want the masses reading this stuff?"

Ellen's favorite bit was the song about the Red Squad, the three plain-clothed pigs named—no joke—Casey, Lacy, and Spacey, who were specifically assigned to hassle campus radicals. I said I'd heard them down in the Sproul Hall police station, singing their own version of *Funiculi, Funicula:*

Last night,
I stayed up late to masturbate.
It felt so good.
I knew it would.
Last night,
I stayed up late to masturbate.
It felt so nice.
I did it twice.
Swing it, fling it,
Up against the wall.

Mash it, bash it,
Do anything at all.
Some say to copulate is really grand,
But for all-around enjoyment,
There is nothing like a hand.

Ellen's so nuts. She doesn't have anybody, I don't have anybody, we're staying alone in the same fucking dorm room, and I, for one, am whacking off every fucking night, but you ask Ellen why she likes that song, and she says: "Because it's anti-pig."

Swear to god.

At that time Ellen had trouble just going two sentences without saying *struggle* or *build a base*. Build a base, I love that one. "Chris is on the phone building a base," Ellen says, no comprehension that she's not speaking English. She means recruitment: that Chris is talking to some poor slob, pushing Progressive Labor's line, trying to "win" his agreement.

Likewise this "winning" agreement is what Ellen means in the line she repeats all the time: *Dare to Struggle, Dare to Win.*

Luckily for me, Ellen gets the idea that I'm Chris's base and since it's wrong to *poach* on somebody else's base, she gives up struggling with me. Struggle is hard on Ellen anyway, because basically she's got ziltch in the theory department.

But see, this could look like I'm making fun of Ellen, which I'm not. In her own way Ellen was a wonderful little communist, running out there with her papers, smiling at every goddamn GM worker in Fremont and telling them to "Unite and Fight the Bosses!" Of course, they only buy the paper because she's wearing a miniskirt and smiling and if any workers bother to read it they find out instantly what self-important bullshit PL is, but that's not Ellen's fault.

Basically it's hard to imagine a worse torture than selling PL's illiterate rag. "*Challenge!* The communist paper! Only a dime for a paper that tells the truth about working people!" What a lie that was. It's embarrassing even now to admit that I actually sold it myself.

"Why did you?" my sociology prof asked when I got back to New York and copped a free dinner off him. My friends put it a little cruder: "Anything to get some left-wing pussy, eh, Frank?"

None of them would have accepted that I'd done it out of belief. Not after I'd spent the evening exercising my wit at the expense of PL. I answered "Boredom" to my prof; and "Damn straight" to my friends.

You won't believe this, but I was tempted to point out the male chauvinism in the pussy comments. I really was. How could I, though? Basically, they were true. I only sold the fucking *Challenge*s to get past Ellen's defenses, so what was I supposed to deny? It was already ludicrous enough that I was doing all that garbage and not getting any pussy.

Male chauvinism was one of those terms Chris couldn't stop using and Ellen couldn't stop misspelling, but neither one of them had any idea what it really meant.

Okay, but let's start the story here, enough background.

This is the chronology: I arrive in Berkeley on March 27. By April 9 the living-with-Ellen-but-not-fucking-her got too weird and I flew home. I get as far as Kennedy International, call my father for a loan, and fly back to Berkeley. Ellen's in her nightgown, washing her face, and I drop my suitcase in the doorway of the sixth floor bathroom.

"Hey, baby," I called, too scared to hold out my arms. "I came back."

Ellen stares at me a little too long and then finally she comes running over and throws her arms around my neck. "Oh, Frank!" she says. "You're so nuts." But it was nice.

I stayed that time till April 21, at which point things seemed really dead on the anti-ROTC/antiwar front. Then, naturally, the day after I split there's a big bust at an SDS disciplinary hearing. Chris and Jimmy are part of the group trapped inside by the pigs, and meanwhile Ellen's outside inciting a riot, chanting "Off the Pig!" with a bullhorn while a million pig-photographers take her picture. I felt guilty as shit.

Then in June, I'm working in the library when suddenly it hits me—Bam! like a simultaneous translation at the UN—that I want to go back to Berkeley. There wasn't jack-shit going on in New York. Ellen runs up my phone bill telling me how nuts it is to fly five times across the country, but I tell her she doesn't understand the yo-yo mentality and I come anyway.

By that point all the fish-brains in the party leadership have been kicked off campus and they get together and decide that we've been ignoring the working class all spring (!!). So to atone, they make all their recruits (a group I affectionately name The Whole Sick Crew—half of them are weird as shit) sell *Challenges* twenty hours a week. It's so stupid.

On top of that, one of the fish-brains—probably Melinda Mercer, the ideal choice if the mood ever struck you to make love to a frozen toothpick—Melinda Mercer or one of the other fish-brains decides to make Ellen the head of a *Challenge*-selling team. "She's enthusiastic," the party says. "Dare to Struggle, Dare to Win," Ellen says. Pure barf-dom.

Chris and Jimmy and the rest of the Whole Sick Crew are part of the big selling team, with all their unsold *Challenges* piling up in the back of Jimmy's Rambler till it's impossible to see out the rear window. Meanwhile there are only three people in Ellen's team: Ellen, somebody's girlfriend who rarely shows up to anything, and Timur Hagen.

_____The first time I saw Timur, he was talking to Ellen at the fountain and he looked like the ultimate spoof of a Marxist intellectual: long black coat, big black briefcase, hair stringing down past his collar, and a beard that curled down into two scraggly points. Plus he was much older—twenty-seven—and all the way across Sproul Plaza I'd watched his shoulders and hands dipping and diving around in some kind of fancy flight pattern.

"These findings," he was saying, "mark a real breakthrough for women. The end to dependence on men for sexual satisfaction."

"But the party's against homosexuals," Ellen answers, seeing me at the same moment. I try to wipe all the prurient interest off my face, but she throws me her "you pervert!" look anyway.

"Not against their civil rights." Timur recaptures Ellen's attention by leaning over, not toward her but over the fountain till he's about to fall in. "It's only for security reasons," he says, "because of the homo-sexual's fear of exposure, that the party doesn't want them actually in the party."

"But what if women want to have a vaginal orgasm?" Ellen says, still trying to ignore me. I was still trying to figure out who Timur was.

"But see," he pushes on, "Masters and Johnson haven't said that women can't achieve orgasm through penetration, only that it's exactly the same orgasm as the so-called clitoral orgasm."

I heard later, from Chris, that all Timur's feminist fervor came from his ex-wife who'd left him to become a lesbian Spart. Sparts are members of the Sparticist League, which is absolutely the most obnoxious of all the obnoxious Trotskyist sects in the US Left—they make PLers look like open-minded united-fronters. The idea of being married to a Spart is worse, believe it or not, than the idea of being married to a lesbian. Swear to God.

But anyway, that first time I didn't know what to make of Timur. I had to admire his ability to get Ellen into a discussion of orgasms, but it was pretty easy to guess his motives: if I could see plenty beneath Ellen's T-shirts, so could he. Teaching assistants at UC are notorious for that kind of shit anyway.

Ellen was in Timur's section of Econ 1A that summer, and all the time she started coming home with little things he'd said. Like—"Hey, Frank! You know what? We could have Zero Population Growth easy if we just had socialist health care. Timur says people have kids because that's the only old-age insurance they've got." Or "Hey, Frank, you know the demand for day-care centers? Timur says there were a million of them during World War II because that's when the bosses needed women workers."

It made me kind of sad, at first, because I knew Ellen's susceptibility to instant information like that, to capsulized socialism she could take right out and spread around. I was sure she had no idea what Timur's game was.

"Hey, Frank!" she says. "You know what keeps wages down?"

"What, baby?" With her face all lit up, Ellen looked incredibly young, incredibly cute, and I patted the dorm bed beside me. "Come tell your Uncle Frankie."

"It's the size of the pool of surplus labor! Timur showed us the curve."

That's not all the old fart would like to show you, I thought, but I kept quiet, just playing with Ellen's hair and letting her talk.

"See, when there's full employment, then workers aren't scared of losing their jobs and they can organize for higher wages. That's why workers have to organize together whites and blacks, men and women, US workers and the international proletariat. That way the bosses can't divide us and create new pools of surplus labor!"

The final straw is a labor statistic Ellen brings home about black men earning more money than white women. She asks me: "Does that mean male chauvinism is a bigger tool of the bosses than racism?"

Then I was pissed. What a letch, I thought, telling an innocent baby like Ellen that she's more exploited than a black male—just to soften her up. So the next time Ellen went to Timur's section, I went too.

"Inflation is a spiral," he was saying. "Wages go up, prices go up, and though it's never mentioned by the capitalist apologists, profits keep going up. Economists like Milton Friedman don't like to mention profits because they don't want anybody to get the idea that inflation could be stopped by a freeze on profits. But why shouldn't the spiral stop there?"

Timur looked like shit without his beard—the head creeps in the party had forced him to shave before he could sell their rotten rag—but he was still the mad gesturer, doing some kind of lateral dip that put him in two places at the same time. A human question mark.

Everybody laughs and he goes on: "Especially since the current inflation spiral started in the mid-sixties when Johnson paid for the Vietnam War by printing money the Treasury couldn't back up. All that money meant tremendous profits for the war industry, immediate price hikes everywhere else, and a tremendous drop in real wages for workers tied to three-year contracts."

Timur keeps talking and it's all Marxist stuff, but it's solid, you know what I mean? The kind of thing that makes you feel, for once, that the Left has a chance, that it isn't completely mindless. Watching Timur bob around was like watching a pelican try to swallow an elephant, but he managed to keep everybody awake and interested—no mean task in Econ IA.

So it was funny, I totally changed my view of Timur that day. I realized he was the best-informed Marxist anywhere around the party and that Melinda "Fish-Brain" Mercer must have hated his guts. The party's so fucking anti-intellectual anyway.

After class Ellen's babbling away with the other students, not exactly building a base, but close enough to make her happy. Then when they leave, she tries to make herself over into Timur's dare-to-struggle leadership. "If you have your notebook, Timur, then we can figure out your selling times."

Timur acts as if it's completely natural for him to take orders from an ignorant little pip-squeak, except that he won't meet my eye till the charade is over. I'm watching him like a hawk but he shows no more sexual interest in Ellen than he would in a new puppy.

But there was something about the way he looked at her, and suddenly I got a flash of Ellen as a lifelong revolutionary, someone who'd get to Timur's age and really have her shit together. Incredible.

I think it was about that time that I decided to teach Ellen self-defense. I mean, what's the good of an urban guerrilla who can't street-fight?

"Come on, baby, it'll be good for you." I even made Ellen set time aside on her schedule. "Just imagine some rapist is after you. Or some fascist right-winger. Come on, he's coming at you! What are you going to do?'

"Oh, Frank, I can't fight."

"Learn, baby. Just hit my hand. Look at it and pretend you're going to go right through it."

"I can't!"

"Baby, you're being submissive."

I teach her how to make a fist with the thumb on the outside, and after a lot of coaxing she finally throws a couple of punches into the palm of my hand.

"Just remember," I tell her, "the key places are the nose, the jaw, and—if he gets in close enough—give him a knee to the groin. Don't waste your time jabbing at the body."

The next time we work out, Ellen starts getting good at throwing those little fists into my palm. I should have left it right there. Instead I lay my arms down at my sides and tell her just to hit me one.

She says she can't.

"Don't worry," I say, "you can't hurt me. Just pretend I'm a rapist and hit me. Hey, big tits—show me some more!"

Ellen keeps saying she can't while I alternately cajole and bait her. Finally I give up: "Okay, baby, just hit my hand again."

That's when, out of nowhere, Ellen hauls off and socks me in the jaw. My hands fly up to see if it's dislocated and meanwhile Ellen moves in and knees me in the groin. I couldn't believe it.

"Baby!! Stop! !" Screaming, I crumple down to the floor.

"What the fuck are you trying to do?"

"Oh, Frank, I'm sorry! I didn't mean to!" Ellen kneels down, kissing my shoulders, elbows, back, any part of my body she thinks might still be friendly. It was nice, of course, and I pulled her down next to me, but that didn't stop the pain. "Shit, baby! What were you trying to do!?"

"But Frank, you told me to!"

I made Ellen go on apologizing and pampering me all weekend, but that ended the self-defense course. I figured I may as well stick around and fight off the fascists myself. Ellen was already pretty dependent on me anyway. How else do you explain the way she waits to say "Hi, Frank" till her face is only a couple inches from my shoulder? Naturally I'm going to say "Hey, baby, how you doing?" and pull her into an Uncle-Frankie style embrace.

Plus there was the night Ellen and I were leaning over the meat counter at the Mayfair supermarket on Telegraph because of some revolutionary dinner with all the recruits under orders to bring "two pounds of chicken and all your base."

"You know what, Frank?' Ellen asks, looking up from the packages of chicken pieces. "I love grocery shopping."

It's a funny confession, said as if she'd named some filthy piece of bourgeois decadence, but what I love is her obvious faith that the Secret is safe with me.

Before I can say anything—what would you say to that anyway?— Ellen turns back to the chicken. "Timur says the party used to be less sectarian," she says. "I think he means doing united front work, but Melinda always says the party is less sectarian now because we're building a base in the dorms. What is sectarianism, Frank?"

Proof that the PL pinheads have been feeding her nothing but double-talk, and at that moment I want to line them up and slaughter them with my bare hands.

"Sectarianism, baby," I say, "has to do with sects, or small groups, which form around any belief, not necessarily political beliefs. When a sect becomes self-defined, closed in its membership or thinking, then it's known as sectarian."

I know I sound incredibly stilted, but I can't afford to slip and say something overtly anti-PL. I could lose Ellen in a second.

"So it's like you spend all your time with your comrades and never any time with your base? Like that?"

"Yeah, maybe," I say, "but I think when Timur and I talk about sectarianism, it has more to do with ideas." I figure that Timur can't be too blind if he's talking to Ellen about sectarianism. "A sectarian group rejects all ideas that aren't its own."

Ellen doesn't get it though. "Like what Mao says about the party has to learn from the masses?"

"Oh, baby, the party can learn from anybody." I bend over and sniff her hair, which always has this great smell except for the day after she washes it. "Even the Sparts could have a good idea once in a while."

Bad example—Ellen laughs her head off—but I figured it was a start.

A dinner of revolutionary chicken sounds dismal, but it wasn't that bad. Ellen was depressed because none of her base showed up—after she'd spent two days straight calling every worker she'd ever met selling *Challenges*. "Don't worry," I told her, "I'll be your base," but she was barely willing to sit with me. "You're Chris's base," she said.

There was wine and beer though—the party has a totally asinine, two-faced line that prohibits pot while it plies the working class with booze—and after dinner Ellen started loosening up. They showed *Salt of the Earth*, which is this dynamite antiracist, antisexist commie movie that came out during the McCarthy era.

All PL's snot-nosed theoreticians are saying that it "smacks of CP revisionism" or some such bullshit, but you can tell Ellen really likes it, and I thought it was cute that she ran the projector, the only one there who knew how. The party snot-noses like to make sure they don't know how to do any shit-work.

The next weekend was the Mendocino trip, which I have to tell because it shows the whole competition/territorial thing between Chris and Ellen, which turns out to be crucial. The Mendo thing is a camping trip Chris and Jimmy are planning to take with a bunch of party hanger-oners who live in the Parker Street house (originally "Shangri-La;" renamed "Shangri-Lumpen" by yours truly). Naturally Chris invites Ellen, and I can't believe it when Ellen says she's not going.

"I can't go, Frank."

We were lying on the dorm bed in the half-hour that sometimes happened between *Challenge*-selling and dinner in the dining hall. Ellen's little notebook scheduled her to make phone calls to all her "contacts," but usually I could talk her into lying down "for a minute" instead. I lay there with my thigh across her butt, letting her talk while I played with her hair and rubbed her back. It always amazed me that Ellen never felt sexually compromised in those situations, but I wasn't about to suggest anything she didn't see herself.

"Why can't you go?" I asked.

"Because! It would be sectarian."

"Baby, that's not sectarian. That's giving yourself a well-deserved two-day vacation."

Ellen gives the party line: "It is sectarian. There's no base going."

Bullshit. I say "What am I—Melinda Mercer!? What are Barry and Lynn and Doug and Dopey and Slappie and Sneezie? We're all base!"

It turns out we're not Ellen's base, and if Ellen goes—simply as Chris's oldest friend—she'll be guilty of stopping Chris from struggling with Chris's base. It's all asshole dogma, but I play along: "You can struggle with them, too, baby. You're good at that."

A lie, I admit, but the real, unspoken truth was that I was hoping that outside Berkeley, in some kind of natural setting, Ellen might wake up to the naturalness of the two of us becoming lovers.

"No, Frank, that's poaching." Poaching takes the cake for PL bullshit.

"What about Chris and Jimmy?" I say. "Are they poaching on each other's base? Is it sectarian for them to go camping together? My god, they live together! How incredibly sectarian!"

"Oh, Frank! They're a couple. That's different."

That's different, all right, and when I ask Ellen if she isn't allowed anybody, she drops her voice and hands me this vomit: "You know how I feel about Mark Schafer."

Mark Schafer is another PL recruit, a probable faggot/obnoxious toothpick type from Southern California. Impossible to take seriously.

"Mark Schafer is a wimp," I say, limiting myself. And I ask her how she and old Schafer-face are supposed to find each other since the two of them hadn't exchanged more than fifty words at the Revolutionary Dinner.

"I don't know," Ellen says. "Maybe it would be okay for me to go to Mendocino if Mark Schafer were going."

I could have strangled her. Then on top of that, the party's head cretins come out with the same monkey turd.

The Mendo trip is "sectarian," they say, and they want it canceled. According to Melinda Mercer et al., the crew Chris calls her base are unwinnable: "not worth the struggle."

Chris cries to me over the phone: "Ellen's trying to make me look bad!" Apparently Ellen jumps on all Chris's weaknesses to prove to the leadership that she's more politically correct than Chris. Or this is what Chris says.

So I was pissed at Ellen, Chris was almost suspended for going camping anyway, and the long and the short of it is that I went up to Mendocino and slept with Lynn Bogardus.

I don't know what the fuck I was doing. I was thinking of Ellen—swear to God—when I slipped off my jeans to give Lynn Bogardus the best screw of her life. That I remember, but everything else is a sex-and-drug-induced haze.

Lynn Bogardus!

But at least Lynn is not truly weird. The award for truly weird has to go to Barry Shutes, a true Marquis de Weirdo. Barry talks exactly like a '45 record being played at 33 rpm, and on the Mendo trip he explains that the huge scar on his neck comes from being run over by a truck. Swear to God. All my life I've quoted the stock ending from the *Mad Magazine* Famous Writers' School: "Suddenly _____ (your main character) is run over by a truck. The End." And then here's Barry Shutes, a weirdo moron who's actually lived to tell about it—if anybody could stand to listen.

Lynn Bogardus wasn't anywhere near that bad. A little dodo-brained, maybe, but tall and big-assed, an ass she tends to throw into men's faces. More or less the gesture of a cat in heat, and I had to beat out one of the other slappies to get her, but that's not really any excuse.

I was going nuts on the trip back, just thinking about what Ellen would say. There was some chance she'd be jealous—and my mind was quite willing to dwell on that possibility—but the odds were better that she'd think I had lost my marbles. My fear was that she'd completely shut herself off from me, as if I were an "unwinnable" leper. She could do it.

I broke the news casual yet enthusiastic, as if Lynn Bogardus were just a short but interesting segment of the Mendo report. Then I'm blabbing away, squirm-city inside, and trying not to pay any attention to the fact that Ellen's gone catatonic. Finally I can't stand it.

"Earth to Ellen, come in! Hey, baby, it's your Uncle Frankie, remember? Hey, say something!"

"Oh!" she says. "I'm surprised, that's all. I thought you were still hung up on Chris." And then, spell broken, she goes into a little PL speech about struggle relationships. Calm as all get out.

I ignore the PL bullshit, of course, and I guess I was so relieved I ignored all the rest too. Only later I wondered why Ellen had never caught on that it was her, not Chris, who'd kept me in California. Shit, the stuff with Chris was long dead, dead even before the Rome disrobing. Ellen was nuts.

Then, for about half a week, I thought I was in California for Lynn Bogardus. We talked about getting a place together and a lot of party goofballs said how good that would be for both of us. Meanwhile Lynn has this little ritual where she purses her lips, fishlike, puts her forefinger on them, smacks, and then plants that slobbery finger on my face. By the sixth fuck I'd passed my limit.

At that point, and I mean this sincerely, Ellen was a complete saint, an angel. If it hadn't been for her, I would have probably yo-yo'ed back to New York pronto. Instead I went back to the dorm and held Ellen, smelling her dirty hair again for the first time in almost a week.

"Ba-, baby," I pleaded. "You have to help me."

Her little face was all serious, but Ellen didn't struggle with me, didn't dump any of the party's twisted morals on me. Ellen was just Ellen, hearing out all my lunacy, asking how many fucks were involved, and then inviting Lynn Bogardus to go swimming with us at Ellen's folks' house that same night.

I'll never forget that. Ellen was such a saint. "So," she says, turning to Lynn the minute we pull out of the Bay Bridge toll plaza, "how much struggle do you guys have in your relationship?" Typical Ellen.

I couldn't say a word myself, which I know was really shitty, and then in the pool I was even worse and actually started humping Lynn. I couldn't help it.

Ellen never quit, though. She kept up with her own sweet mouthing of the PL lines on female submissiveness and sexual objectification, and afterwards it was easy to tell Lynn goodbye. I told her our relationship was founded on a lot of male chauvinism and sexual objectification on my part, and I suggested she talk to Ellen. She did. Ellen is such a saint.

I don't how if it was after the Lynn Bogardus thing or after the time Ellen got sick and I had to nurse her all night with grapefruit and Nyquil that I gave up and started selling *Challenge* full time. The alarm clock goes off at 5 fucking a.m. and I ask Ellen, "Do you have to go?" Once she said no, which filled me all out of proportion with happiness, but if she says yes, then I get up and meet the dawn of workers' consciousness with her.

"*Challenge!*" I call out, holding them up. "Communist paper for a dime! The red flag of the working class!" And if a hippie comes by, or a good-looking secy, I add, "Absolutely nothing in here about Tricia Nixon!" or something else to get them to crack a smile.

But if Ellen and I are covering separate gates, then I take a fair share of cigarette and sit-down breaks and usually leave a half-dozen *Challenges* under some bush on my way back.

"How many did you sell?" Ellen always asks, marking it down in her notebook, but also I think, really wanting me to have sold a lot. Many sales equal lots of fun, to quote Mao.

"Twelve," I say, pretending to have to count backwards from twenty, to figure it out. "And you?"

"Only seven." Ellen says that and I want to run back to my bush and pull out five papers, which after all represent fifty cents of my own money.

"You probably got into more conversations," I say, offering the standard PL consolation. "Did you get any phone numbers?"

"Just one."

One! It was so impossible to get people to talk to you at all, let alone give you their phone number, but Ellen got them all the time. "We want to know what you think blah, blah, blah," she'd say, speaking way too fast but right into their eyes, "because we want to organize a core of workers blah, blah, blah.

It was PL's rap, but she was pretty and meant it and it worked. Of course half of them were wrong numbers—and Ellen never saw that as deliberate—but the other half really were bona fide contacts.

For a while I held off from going out selling when Timur went. I figured we were spelling each other, taking turns to keep Ellen from knowing how badly the party was using her, but then I decided what the hell, I might as well join them. What the fuck else was I doing with my summer anyway?

At one time Timur and Ellen sold on campus, the party's token concession to their old Campus Worker-Student Alliance campaign. Then Timur made the mistake of admitting, at some mass meeting of *Challenge*-sellers, that he encouraged students to buy the paper to "See how radical politics get translated for the working class!" (I loved that line, loved to rewrite it for Ellen: "See how Martian politics get translated for people outside this solar system!

Naturally the leadership freaked. Timur's attitude "feeds the petit-bourgeois arrogance of students," they say, and they drop campus selling altogether.

Actually the party was dead wrong about students. I met this prof in the Poli-Sci department who offered me the use of his office after I told him some sob story about being a leftwing journalist from New York and needing a place to write. I meant to write, too, but usually I'd just stretch out on the guy's desk and sleep. Like a baby. That desk was so fucking comfortable.

But anyway, the prof asks me to come talk to his class about Vietnam. I went and just talked off the top of my head, outlining some of the points in PL's "People's War vs Negotiations" pamphlet. I couldn't believe how expert I sounded, but the big shock was the student reaction. They ate it up.

I even threw in the danger of Soviet imperialism, the need to tie in the exploitation of Vietnamese and American working class, and they were all asking questions, hanging on my words, the whole deal.

After class a bunch of them asked me what they could do, and I was really caught.

Just try to stay aware," I told them, "and get involved wherever you can." That was chicken-shit, I know, but the last thing I wanted was to hand them over to PL and *Challenge*-selling.

Anyway, back to Timur. The great thing about Timur was the way he handled Ellen. One time we're in Timur's bug, driving back from the International Harvester plant in San Leandro, and Timur and I are joking about our millions if the party only paid I-LAW scale for *Challenge*-selling. Ellen's in the front seat and I'm massaging her shoulders and I can tell something's wrong.

Finally she says, "Yeah, so we just did $33 worth of work to sell $3.90 worth of papers? Where's the surplus value of labor in that?"

"But we're not selling a product!" Timur says, taking both hands off the wheel to gesture. "We're spreading Marxist-Leninist ideas, and that's your strength, Ellen—you don't limit yourself to selling the papers. I've always said that."

"But what happens," she asks, her voice going, "if they don't listen to the ideas? What if somebody just thinks you're a woman and ignores everything else?"

I brought my head up next to hers and asked what happened.

"Nothing," she says. Then it comes out that some asshole called her cute or something, and she tried to brush him off with the party's line on sexual objectification, but he ends up holding her fingers when she gives him his change.

It doesn't sound that bad, but Ellen's speaking into her shirt front and I want to go back and punch the jerk out.

Timur looks over at me and shrugs, a huge Timur Hagen shrug that says he takes full blame on himself.

Then he jumps right in: "What does Mao say? Mao says always overestimate your enemy tactically and underestimate him strategically. So tactically, in our day-to-day dealings with the masses, we have to assume they've all adopted male chauvinist ideology. Right?"

Right," Ellen says reluctantly. "Like when Marx says that the ideas of the dominant class in a society are the dominant ideas of that society."

"Right!" Timur loves quotes. "But since male superiority is a myth, we know that the proletariat, in the act of overthrowing the capitalist class, will see through that myth. Strategically, then, we underestimate the power of male chauvinism."

"Male chauvinism is a paper tiger?"

"Exactly!" Timur gives Ellen a smile so big it practically takes us off the freeway.

So Ellen's cute: she cheers up and suggests selling at the Singer plant. A horrible idea, bound to catch us in even more rush-hour traffic, but the Singer workers are mainly women, and Ellen's thinking tactically: the party needs women from the industrial working class. In a way she was right.

Timur and Ellen also sold three mornings a week at Oakland Tech. Selling to high school kids is okay because they don't know yet how to ignore you, but also a bitch because even summer school starts so goddamn early in the morning.

Then my second week of selling there, I happen to go across the street to buy some cigarettes at Dave's Diner. (Ah, yes, you remember: Dave's Diner!) So I look up and there's Timur, sitting at the counter. I couldn't believe It—here Ellen and I are hawking the party's rag to school kids and meanwhile Timur's over at Dave's Diner, eating his fucking breakfast and reading the *Wall Street Journal*.

It was so audacious and for a whole minute I stood there with my mouth hanging open, but then I slid onto the stool next to him. I can't tell you how right it felt. Timur nodded at me, not embarrassed but not talking either, and I read the menu, ordered, and then reached over to pick up a *San Francisco Chronicle*.

We sat there, eating and reading, till the school bell rang. Then Timur downed, all at once, a big glass of buttermilk and smacked his lips. "A milkshake in every glass!" he said. That was all.

We met Ellen just after the tardy bell. I threw a handful of *Challenges* into the trash on the way, but Timur pretended not to notice.

That became our routine. Except for Timur's "Milkshake in every glass!" which always cracked me up—we never talked. I knew how he felt, though. We both knew Ellen was crazy, driven, and that she'd see any attempt to sell less as contempt for her "leadership." We didn't talk because we didn't want to violate any more of Ellen's confidences than we had to.

Even without talk, though, I felt close to Timur. I had this idea that someday he and I and Ellen would do something to change PL and re-invent communism. I figured out, after the time in the Poli-Sci class, that people really want theory, the same way they want to know what's going on. What they don't want is a bunch of sectarian assholes cramming the theory into jargon and then cramming it down your throat. That was my idea, and I always thought I'd get around to telling it to Timur, but I never did.

I kept it up for a couple weeks after that, half-doing what I half-believed in, waiting for Ellen to stop over-doing what she over-believed in and wondering which of us was the bigger fool. Then one day I'm over at the Shangri-Lumpen and Chris tells me that Melinda Mercer's called me "unwinnable."

At first I thought that Melinda was onto me—that she'd seen me planting *Challenges* under some bush—but then I knew it wasn't that at all. The bitch was just protecting her ice-cube dictatorship—she wanted me to slobber all over her and beg to come to meetings and get brow-beaten by all the high-ranking assholes.

What really burned me up was that Melinda Mercer had seen me a million times with either Ellen or Chris but she never gave me the time of day except for that half-week I was hooked up with Lynn Bogardus. Then suddenly I was getting big smiles—"Hi, Frank! How are you?" and once even a short stupid lecture on the importance of interpersonal commitment within overall revolutionary commitment, blah, blah, blah. So I knew I could reverse the unwinnable charge just by getting back together with Lynn or some other clit around the party.

Obviously though, the party doesn't count that I live with Ellen, that I get up at 5 fucking a.m. to sell their fucking papers with her, and that I go along and probably save her from being raped when she's at some worker's house talking dictatorship of the fucking proletariat. The party only counts relationships it can walk in on and control, the way they do with Chris and Jimmy. The party is sick.

Anyway, if the Mercer bitch is calling me unwinnable, it's the kiss of death and Chris and I both know it. I ask her if Ellen's heard. Chris says she doesn't think so.

I told Ellen myself the next afternoon. We'd just pulled into a cheapo gas station on our way home from selling. "Listen, baby," I say, "you know the party and I don't see eye-to-eye on a lot of things. Sooner or later you're going to end up in the middle and you have to decide, baby. What are you going to do if the party calls me unwinnable?"

"Oh, Frank! You're not unwinnable. Don't say that."

"Baby, I'm not saying it. Melinda Mercer's saying it."

"But Frank, she can't! You sell *Challenge*s and you talk to workers …"

"Ellen! Stop it and listen!" Ellen's eyes went twice their size and I tried to lighten up. "Just listen, baby. What are you going to do if Melinda tells you I'm unwinnable?"

"I don't know, Frank. What am I supposed to do?"

I don't know why I got so mad. I don't usually get that mad at Ellen, but it was a hot day and the cheapo station was selling gas at 29 cents a gallon and completely packed. Across the street there was a deserted Chevron station selling full-serve gas at 38 cents a gallon. Just once, I thought, I'd like to be rich enough to zip over there and sit in the car, in the shade, while some other jerk-off fills my tank.

"Open your eyes, Ellen," I said. "You can't just sit back and let the party destroy all your friendships."

I pulled the car up to the pump and we both got out. I started filling the tank and Ellen just stood there, watching the figures spin in the pump. I was really pissed.

"I don't know what I'd do," she said. "I try to spend time with my base—I really do—but I can't seem to make friends with anybody."

"That's not your fault, baby. That's PL. You can go ahead and do all their shit if you want to, if you believe in it, but you've got to do something for yourself, too. You need somebody who'll be there for you, not for the party or the working class, but just for you."

"I know." Ellen wouldn't look at me, just kept her eyes on the gas pump. "Everybody says my biggest weakness is that I never make personal commitments, but what am I supposed to do? I never even see Mark Schafer."

"Jesus, Ellen! Don't give me any of that bullshit. I'm not talking about Mark Schafer and you know it. I'm talking about you and me and what you're going to do to protect our relationship from Melinda Mercer. You've already let the party come between you and Chris, and if you don't do something now you're going to lose the only friend you've got left!"

That was too much and I knew it. Even as I said it I knew it. Ellen didn't say anything, but she did something I've never seen anybody do either before or since. She walked over and sat down on that filthy disgusting cement island at the base of the gas pumps. She sat there staring at the asphalt between her legs. I could see the worn spot in the inner thigh of her cords and I wanted to shoot myself. I put the nozzle back in the gas pump and stood over her. "Come on, baby. You can't sit here. Come on, I'm sorry—just get up and go sit in the car."

Ellen didn't move. "I don't know what I'd do, Frank." She looked up at me, her face a dead white. "If Melinda tells me that I have to struggle with you about your petit-bourgeois attitudes, then I know I should, but I can't."

Ellen and J were obviously coming from two completely different planets and I gave up. I gave her a really nice massage back at the dorm, but I knew it wouldn't ever get any better, really, and two days later I had her take me to the airport.

Ellen refused to acknowledge my leaving until the very last minute, when they started calling the standbys. "This is it, baby," I told her, holding out my arms. "You had your chance, now come kiss me goodbye."

She squeezed against me, still not saying anything. "Poor baby," I said, kissing her hair. "For all you know I may be back on the next plane. This could be just an excuse to get you to hold me."

"Don't go then, Frank," she said, resting her chin on my collar bone and speaking directly into my neck. "Don't make me say goodbye if you're just going to come back tomorrow."

I thought about changing my mind right then, and in New York, even after what Ellen said, I thought about turning around and catching the next flight back. But I didn't.

Instead I went up to Martha's Vineyard with my folks and met somebody on the beach. A women's libber, no less. We talked and I discovered that, besides the good body and healthy sexual appetite, Robyn had a decent line on the working class. We indulged in a lot of bourgeois decadent activities—sleeping, sun-bathing, fucking—and I managed to get over Ellen fairly quickly. Still, it was sort of sad.

Is it a million years since I was a Maoist? I wrote this story in 1982—back when I could remember shit, back when getting an MFA meant getting to hang out with Grace Paley. My successes have all been short-term; I write and perform solo theatre in Oakland, California.

18

"Princeton'll Straighten You Out!"

Henri Picciotto
(Princeton, UC Berkeley)

I grew up in Beirut, Lebanon. Many of my high school friends were radicals and communists, so I had mixed feelings about going to college in what they described as the belly of the imperialist beast. And in fact I almost didn't get to go, as I was initially denied a student visa. When I went to the US Embassy to ask why, the man I talked to claimed he had seen me throwing rocks at the Embassy as part of a demonstration. That was completely fabricated: I was not even in Beirut when that demonstration happened. The real reason was probably that I hung out with the wrong crowd. I arranged to see a cultural attaché. Upon hearing that I had been admitted to Princeton, he laughed, and said, "Princeton'll straighten you out!" He put in a good word for me, and the visa came through.

Princeton

I arrived at Princeton in the fall of 1967. SDS had a table at New Students' Orientation, or some similar event. I took one look at their literature and joined SDS on the spot. In the following weeks and months I was simultaneously introduced to the Princeton campus culture, the so-called counterculture, and the New Left—in addition to the broader US culture. That was a lot for me to take in, though American culture was already somewhat familiar, via American TV and *Mad Magazine*, both of which I had been exposed to in Lebanon.

Princeton was all-male at the time and seemed to expect hard study-ing during the week—and hard drinking on the weekend. As a teeto-taler, I didn't fit in. Moreover, I deemed myself a feminist and refused to attend the so-called mixers, as I felt the coeds that were brought in by the busloads were treated like cattle. The drug scene also didn't appeal to me. My fellow SDSers were amused by how straight I was.

Initially, my involvement consisted mostly of conversations with other SDSers. I also remember working on a flier about the corporate members of the university's Board of Trustees. I did attend demon-strations, but as a foreigner I avoided arrest.

My most daring (and pointless) action consisted of working with another SDSer to spray-paint a hammer and sickle with the dates "1917–1967" all over the campus walkways. We did this at night using a stencil on the anniversary of the Russian revolution. The next day, a history professor stopped by the SDS office and told us that this was the best thing SDS had ever done. Of course he was wrong: SDS that year was conducting a significant campaign against the university's complicity with the Vietnam War. This included a sit-in at the Institute for Defense Analysis and a demonstration that combined antiwar slo-gans with demands for changes in the dorm rules. That was attended by hundreds of students and was addressed by the university president, who agreed to set up a committee to investigate SDS's demands.

When Mac and Sally Smith, members of Progressive Labor, came to Princeton midyear, I felt that they represented a group I could relate to. They had a class analysis, were not seduced by the counterculture, and seemed more thoughtful than some of my other fellow activists. However, I didn't join PL. At that time, I thought of revolutionary communism as an important reference for a radical, but not something I would directly involve myself in.

A graduate student had taken me under her wing and invited me to her parents' home in Philadelphia at Thanksgiving. Later, she took me to a performance of the San Francisco Mime Troupe, which was on tour in New York (probably *L'Amant Militaire*.) At various antiwar demonstrations, I had seen street theater groups (the Pageant Players and the Bread and Puppet Theater). I was inspired to start such a group on campus. (I had starred in student-mounted plays back home in Lebanon, so I considered myself qualified.) Thus, the Radical Arts Troupe of SDS, also known as RAT, was born.

Perhaps half a dozen SDSers created the plays collectively. The women characters were played by some of the radical high school girls who hung around our chapter. One of our plays, *Strategic Hamlet*, told the story of how Corporate Claudius, having murdered Democracy, married Government Gertrude. His crime was exposed by a play within the play, which was presented by the Renaissance Arts Troupe. This was typical of the genre we developed: ten- to twenty-minute comedies, usually based on existing stories, with blatant advocacy of SDS political positions, typically ending with a call to action.

Even though I quite enjoyed all this, I never felt that I belonged at Princeton. Having seen movement newspapers with headlines like "The Day We Took Over the Streets of Oakland" (about the massive Stop the Draft Week demonstrations) and photos of the Black Panthers, I started to think about moving. The Bay Area in 1968 was attractive to a young radical. Putting that together with the knowledge that UC Berkeley was a co-educational institution made it easy for me to decide: I was going to transfer.

That summer, I was in Paris visiting family while the dramatic events that started in May '68 were still unfolding. I attended a mass student meeting that was addressed by Jean-Paul Sartre. I narrowly escaped arrest during a demonstration that was on a scale I had never seen before, and was never to see again: it seemed like all of Paris was in the streets. That experience convinced me that PL's worker-student alliance strategy made a lot of sense.

Berkeley

When I arrived at Berkeley, I immediately joined both SDS and the WSA. PL's emphasis on antiracism helped us participate earnestly in the campus struggles that were led by the Third World Liberation

Front: in the fall, a campaign to allow Black Panther Eldridge Cleaver to teach a course "on campus, for credit"; in the winter, a strike for the creation of an ethnic studies department and open admissions to the university. That spring, students and others occupied a university-owned vacant lot, calling it People's Park. One leader of that movement called for "taking over the means of leisure." (In other words, declaring that the Marxist concern with the means of production was now passé.) We were skeptical about this movement, which seemed frivolous when Vietnam was being destroyed and racism reigned.

But when mass student demonstrations were tear-gassed and shot at, the PL leadership correctly pointed out to us that this was an attack on the whole student movement, and it should not remain unchallenged. James Rector, a bystander on the roof of a movie theater, was shot and killed by the police. The next day, every other organization was running for cover and telling people to stay home, and National Guard soldiers were standing at every street corner. Undaunted, we printed fliers calling for a march on City Hall. We got up at the crack of dawn and distributed them in the dorms and at entrances to the campus. Thousands of students turned out and marched with us. The police and National Guard stayed out of our way. This felt important: we had helped the student movement refuse to be intimidated.

During that school year, I started a Berkeley Radical Arts Troupe, modeled after the successful Princeton experience. One of our plays, *Reserve Liberal Training Corps*, presented the university as an apologist for the war, one with a liberal veneer. (Students: "We deplore the violence on both sides!" while pointing at the Vietnamese peasant who shot back at a US bomber. Prof: "Well done! You have mastered the art of double-deploring!") Another play was about the university's Chancellor Heinz, who in one scene calls Governor Reagan to ask for more police. (At one performance, at that precise moment a phalanx of cops appeared. The actor ad-libbed, "Thanks for the quick service!") We staged dozens of performances on campus, always gathering substantial crowds, publicizing SDS actions, and handing out SDS literature.

Progressive Labor

Inspired by PL members' seriousness and courage and the coherence of their analysis, I ended up joining a PL study group, and later the party itself. I was a member for several years. I remember almost nothing from that experience, probably because the valuable work against war and racism gradually turned into mind-numbing and idiotic ultraleft sloganeering. After being in the thick of important movements, and contributing to them in not insignificant ways, my political work became increasingly irrelevant, if not out-and-out destructive. It consisted more and more of bizarre internal conversations (what would we do "after the revolution"?), selling the party's unreadable *Challenge* newspaper, opposing black nationalism and feminism.... Unfortunately, it's only in hindsight that I understood how toxic this was.

There were a few bright spots. At one point, I had been banned from campus because of my activism. I broke the ban and entered the university during a mass student antiwar rally. As I approached the microphone, the university turned off the sound system. They had underestimated me: I had a megaphone hidden under my cape. To much applause, I used it to start a chant and lead a demonstration across campus.

Another good memory: I wrote a review of a play by the San Francisco Mime Troupe for *Challenge*. This led to a short career as a theater critic for a free San Francisco monthly, which in turn led to being recruited to a playwriting team for the SF Mime Troupe.

Later, when some PL comrades were building support for Marines who were organizing against racism at Camp Pendleton, I organized a group to deface a Marines recruiting billboard by pasting a KKK hood on the face of one of "the few, the proud, the Marines."

What I Learned

On the one hand, what I learned from my student activism in and around PL was that it is right to stand up against injustice, and appropriate to take some chances when doing that. In the subsequent years and decades, I continued my political involvement by participating in the antinuclear movement, and later in efforts to support Palestinian rights and for peace in the Middle East. I participated in a Jewish sit-in at the Israeli Consulate, and in direct actions against both Iraq wars.

On the other hand, I also learned how to *not* follow PL's example. I advocate and practice nonviolence and completely reject PL's ridiculous armed struggle fantasies. In doing political work, I aim to build unity, not get into sterile ideological arguments. These lessons helped me immensely during my years as the first chair of the board of Jewish Voice for Peace, during which (with many others) I helped lead the organization from a small Bay Area group to a significant national activist nonprofit. The key was to bring together activists with widely different backgrounds and views around a political program all could agree to—quite a change from my PL days.

So yes, I learned more than mathematics at Princeton and Berkeley. PL and the broader movement contributed to my growing up, in both positive and negative ways. I have no regrets.

Henri Picciotto is a math educator (www.MathEducationPage.org) and the co-constructor of the cryptic crossword in The Nation. *He lives in Berkeley, California.*

19

Growing Up in the '60s:
From Introvert to Organizer

Frank Kashner
(University of Wisconsin, Cambridge, Mass.)

In 1966, I considered myself a liberal. I was against the US war in Vietnam because I did not want to go kill Vietnamese peasants or be killed by them. I was an undergraduate at the University of Wisconsin in Madison, where I joined the Wisconsin Draft Resistance Union. In the spring of 1966, students seized and occupied the administration building to oppose the school's participation with ROTC and the draft. I was there, scared of possible consequences, and it was by far the most politically radical thing I had ever done. A group of leaders, who had been selected by a process I did not understand, appointed one person to negotiate with the school. He made a settlement that others characterized as "a sellout." It was my first experience of direct action and contested leadership.

My local draft board withdrew my 2-S student draft deferment after I burned my card during an antiwar demonstration at the Pentagon. I then received a letter from the Milwaukee Army Induction Center ordering me to report there for my physical because I was being drafted. What happened there is a story for another time.

I graduated in the spring of 1967 with a bachelor's degree in philosophy. I was in philosophy because I, on the Asperger's end of the autism scale, wanted to find ways to understand people better (today

287

I might be called an "Aspie"). I was internally focused; my favorite expression was Max Stirner's, "All things are nothing to me." I had stopped using drugs only after coming within hours of dying from a dirty needle infection. It was only later that I saw that understanding people and learning how to conduct conflict required understanding society's institutions, how they affect our lives, and the roles we play in or outside them.

A friend and I moved to Boston, where we planned to make an antiwar movie. I landed a great job in a union film studio, Education Development Corporation (EDC), making educational films about social and scientific topics. I became a member of IATSE (the International Alliance of Theatrical and Stage Employees), and, while ignorant of the union's history, I enjoyed excellent pay and benefits with great co-workers and managers in a creative setting.

In Cambridge, I met people in the Progressive Labor Party. Through them and others I learned about Students for a Democratic Society and the Cambridge Peace and Freedom Party. I made many friends in what was a supportive and caring community.

PLers and other activists explained to me basic Marxist ideas: that there was a class of people, a ruling class, who gained wealth and power by exploiting workers and our resources. This class used their power for their own benefit and to the detriment of the working class and society. Over fifty years my social, political, and economic class views have become more subtle and textured. But like the spine in our bodies, a class view still forms the backbone of my worldview.

Many late-into-the-night discussions about US and world history showed me that social, political, and economic progress requires engagement and struggle by the working class and its allies. While I would like to say that we were equally focused on those facing racial, gender, and other forms of discrimination, much of that understanding came later.

The PL members advocated the need for a party to provide leadership for an inevitable revolution. I was intrigued, though I did not understand what they meant by a revolution and why it was inevitable, and I was wary of a party that seemed opaque and nondemocratic in its functioning. But the class view helped me understand why the US was in Vietnam, why rents were soaring, and more. These ideas were transformative for me, explaining much that had been previously inexplicable, like why there could be so much poverty in the midst of such wealth.

Between 1967 and 1970 I helped PL organizationally and participated with SDS in solidarity actions like campus worker organizing and strike support. We resisted the draft by getting on buses filled with recruits heading to the Boston Army Base to try to convince them not go into the army. One snowy day a small group of us "seized" the army base when they would not allow a friend to say goodbye to her husband, who was upstairs being inducted. The base guards called for help, and sounds of sirens filled the air. After about twenty minutes, the six of us were confronted by about two dozen riot police in full regalia, including clubs, shields, helmets, lights, and cameras, with their commander on a megaphone.

We were given "one last chance to leave," and to their surprise we took it, dashing down the stairs past the mass of police vehicles and off the base, checking constantly over our shoulders for pursuit. We were amazed that they seemed to have been convinced that we would fight them and that they wanted to capture on film the need to beat us into submission. They seemed so surprised that they did not even arrest us for trespassing. In struggles in Wisconsin, Cambridge, and Boston, I saw how confused and disorganized the authorities often were when confronted by determined, creative resistance.

The Maoist saying that our rulers are "paper tigers," meaning that they look more fierce and coordinated than they actually are, matched my experience and held true in my future conflicts, including those at General Electric. In light of all the exciting organizing work going on in political groups around me, I grew bored at EDC and wanted to get closer to the "real action," to bring my new ideas directly to workers. I then went to work for a third of my EDC pay at a local book publishing company, Riverside Press in Cambridge, supplying books to the women workers who put alphabetical tabs on them (the *American Heritage Dictionary*). I had just learned Karl Marx's labor theory of value, which states that the labor that it takes to produce a good or service determines the value of that good or service. I calculated that each woman, paid about $20 a day, added $300 of value by tabbing 300 books per day. (Tabbed dictionaries sold for $1 more than untabbed ones.) The women, native speakers of Portuguese, did not seem interested in my calculations, and as far as I know, never used them to request an increase in their pay.

Later I was assigned to work at the back end of a folding machine, a machine that folded printed pages into signatures as part of the bookbinding process. I got paper cuts, splinters from the boards that I inserted on the ends of the signatures, and rope burns from the rope that I used to tie the whole thing together. My co-workers, while friendly and tolerant of my views, were more interested in weekend skiing plans than in making a revolution. I was fired from Riverside Press after missing a month of work due to mononucleosis. There was no union and no long-term sickness benefit.

In 1969, I canvassed door-to-door for the Rent Control Referendum Campaign organized by the Cambridge Peace and Freedom Party. Many people, working class and poor, welcomed me into their homes, including those opposed to rent control; and I learned firsthand the effects of rising rents and uncaring, greedy landlords who sometimes refused to fix basic roof, plumbing, and electrical problems. I also saw firsthand that most ordinary people of all colors were willing to join hands with mainly white middle-class intellectual radicals to make social change. The campaign was successful, and Cambridge had rent control for twenty-five years until it was reversed by those who could benefit financially from Harvard and MIT expansion, whatever the fate of displaced tenants.

The Cambridge Peace and Freedom Party and the Worker-Student Alliance faction of SDS were accused by opponents of being front groups for PL, because some of their members were also in PL and because some of what they advocated was also advocated by PL.

To disorganized opponents, it seemed unfair that PFP and WSA members would come to meetings having already discussed and decided upon strategies that others had not considered or which they opposed. I could see that the PL way of operating was effective, but I also sympathized with some of the opponents. None of us, including those in PL, wanted to see broad-based organizations reduced to only those who agreed with PL.

I joined SDS and was included in discussions in the SDS office about the competing theories and strategies for SDS. Really, I did not know which were the correct theories. I was drawn to the WSA mainly because those were the people I had befriended. Also, WSAers seemed to make alliances and take real actions, while the Revolutionary Youth Movement seemed to be more talk and less action. Of course, it may have looked like a mirror image from where RYM members sat. In later years, I met many people who had been on other sides of political divides, and found them to be good people who basically wanted the same things that I did. At that time in SDS, the Left was riven with sectarian divisions that turned out to be more about "being right" than about being inclusive and effective.

In 1967 I attended an SDS meeting in Ann Arbor, Michigan, and then the 1969 convention in Chicago. In Ann Arbor, I sat near the speakers and, with my reel-to-reel tape recorder, I recorded the speakers in what I hoped would be historically vital discussions. The main thing I noticed was how mind numbingly boring they all were, RYM and WSA alike. Speaker after speaker, almost all men, would give endless speeches about how their approach was the truly revolutionary one that represented the true interests of the working class. I did not save the tapes because I thought that posterity would have no possible interest in them.

In 1969, I was on the SDS Credentials Committee of the National Convention in Chicago. I got to count the registrations as the Worker-Student Alliance faction won majority control of SDS from the Revolutionary Youth Movement faction. Afterwards, rather than concede defeat, RYM members seized control of all of SDS's resources, including its office and printing press. There wasn't much discussion or valuing of organizational democracy in those days. In the convention, RYM had threatened violence, but backed off knowing that the Chicago police would welcome an excuse to come and bust everyone's head, irrespective of factional politics.

In April 1969, I went to Harvard Yard to support the Harvard students when SDS and others seized the administration building. I did not enter the building because that role belonged to the students themselves. In the yard I heard from people in support, people neutral and open to learning about the issues, and people against the action. I guessed that these divisions are present to varying degrees in every conflict. Progress often requires organizing and conducting conflict, a skill not taught in our schools, either at a personal or a political level.

Due to my activism and association with PL, SDS, Peace and Freedom, and WSA members, I developed what were for me a new set of ideas and skills, including a class view of society, a recognition of the centrality of the working class, a principle that fighting racism is fundamental to bridging what would otherwise be destructive divisions, and a belief that ordinary people could change institutions and governments. I was also learning how to discuss difficult issues with people, how to write effective leaflets, and how to run printing presses and mimeograph machines.

My new outlook and skills, in the way that quantitative changes can become qualitative, were for me a change in my very being. My Aspie self had been internally focused, prone to moodiness, depression, and drug use. My new political self shifted from self-blame to anger at the ruling-class institutions, especially the government, and the many destructive manifestations of a class-based society. I became a different person, able to change my environment and society by interacting collaboratively with others and conducting conflict as needed and possible. That new way of being has served me and hopefully those around me in multiple careers and campaigns for fifty subsequent years.

After Riverside Press, I decided that I needed to be in a major factory with the "industrial" working class. I walked the picket line in solidarity with the 1969 GE / IUE contract strike, and then in 1970 I got myself hired at the highest paid GE piecework plant in the world, in Everett, Massachusetts, as a degreaser. I dunked parts into a large, poorly ventilated tank full of what I later learned was poisonous trichloroethylene. Workers would either bring their parts to me to be degreased, or I would go pick them up. I was in the International Union of Electrical Workers (IUE) Local 201, which had replaced the Union of Electrical Workers (UE) Local 201 in the 1950s after the UE local was destroyed by red-baiting McCarthy hearings and subsequent firings.

I did not know that there were already PL members working "under cover" at GE because I was on the periphery of PL and not privy to party doings. I was not sent to GE by PL, nor had I consulted with anyone in the party. Those party members already in the plant kept their politics secret from co-workers, perhaps fearing a negative reaction.

I did not keep my politics secret. I did not know to do so because nobody told me to (remember Aspies often take things literally and explicitly). Later, when I heard that there were already PLers in the plant, I thought, "How are we going to make a revolution if we keep our politics secret?" In the rent control campaign I had also been open with people and found that people are more open to new ideas than we often assume.

Even though it was a military plant, I handed out antiwar literature and sold the PL newspaper *Challenge* at the gate before going in for my shift. My co-workers seemed interested in the fliers, but not in the newspaper, which was strident without much content. ("Smash" this and that.) I heard that leftists had been assaulted in other area plants, and did not know until later why I was not. The plant guards would come out and photograph me at the gate.

During this time, I joined PL but only lasted a couple of months as a member. I saw that Leninist democratic centralism, their philosophy of leadership, meant in practice all centralism and no democracy. I was not a good order taker, so I told someone in the leadership, "I quit." They said that my quitting would demoralize others and asked if I would be a "secret nonmember." I agreed, and remained a secret nonmember of PL for more than four years, paying a high political price in the union for something I wasn't. A significant number of union members would never vote for me for union office because they thought that I was in a communist party, and I did not correct their misperception.

Early in my days in Everett, a welder came out and demanded to know what I was selling. At other plants, people were getting beaten up for selling *Challenge*. As was to happen repeatedly, I did not know what his reaction would be. Would he hit me? He had to know what I was up to since my openly selling "a communist paper" had to be the talk of the shop. Imagine my surprise when he reached into his pocket and pulled out a $5 bill. He turned to face the guards, handed me the bill, and as he took a paper, he said to the guards, "Now take a picture of this." We became friends.

Lest you think that I was tough because I was often in potentially dangerous situations, I have never been in a physical fight in my life and still do not know how to defend myself. Rather, I would attribute my adventures to curiosity and a willingness to take risks to accomplish my commitments.

I was befriended by several older workers, who seemed glad to see me in the plant. I learned that they had been members of the United Electrical Workers Union before it had been driven out of the plant by Joseph McCarthy's anticommunist crusade. Many people think that McCarthy was mainly about banning Hollywood writers and actors. Actually, he was first and foremost about smashing effective unions. His viciously anti-union hearings and other legislative actions cost union leaders jobs, livelihoods, and homes, and he and the government robbed union members of honest, hardworking, effective unions and leaders. In 1970, I was the first openly radical employee in Everett and Lynn GE since 1955. Many workers valued and supported me for that, unfazed by my public communist attachments.

When I had been in the Everett plant a few months, a woman was injured in the plant and the union was slow to respond. With a few other workers we put out a flier about the incident, which, based upon comments I got, was well received. The *Challenge* coverage of the incident, exaggerated and strident, perhaps designed to glorify the party, was insensitive to the needs and opinions of the woman and other workers. It convinced me to no longer give information to PL that could be misused. PL did give me a mimeograph machine that lived on my porch and which saw many workers produce many fliers over the years that changed both the company and the union.

After a few months on the job, I was called into the Everett GE personnel office. Over the low office partitions, I overheard a phone conversation in which one Human Resources person told another that "we'll get him up there [to the Lynn plant] where it will be easier for you to get rid of him." A few minutes later I was told that I was "bumped" up to the Lynn River Works Plant, where I became an "oiler," filling the individual oil cups in the ancient machines used by pieceworkers. Degreaser, oiler, and later, move man, were great jobs for me to have as an organizer, from since they allowed me to move around the plant talking with people. GE tried multiple times to fire me, but each time my friends and co-workers in the plant forced the union to defend me by talking to their shop stewards, calling the union hall, and coming to union meetings. Later, I was also brought up on charges for not saluting the flag and being a communist. The person charging me wanted me thrown out of the union. The membership did not agree.

I became active in the union, attended union meetings, and made friends with people interested in correcting company abuses and prodding the union to action. I was applying what I had learned in SDS, in the WSA caucus, in Peace and Freedom, and from PL friends.

I became aware of various factions in the local and district union. Late in 1971, I was approached by Angelo, a man who had been active in union politics at the local, district, and national levels for many years. He said to me, "Your newspaper talks about smashing racism. Is that all just talk or do you want to actually do something?" He said that several nonwhite workers had been fired in the past few months, and that the firings were part of a pattern. GE would hire nonwhites to satisfy federal requirements, but then those workers would invariably be fired within a year. I was grateful that he came to me and said that I would be glad to work with him.

Over the next few months we found other people, especially shop stewards, who wanted to do something about GE's racist practices and who also wanted to prod the local union to take action. With their help, we drafted a leaflet that we distributed at the plant gates in March 16, 1972. It was entitled, "GE — Equal Opportunity ???" Here are the first two paragraphs:

> GE spends a lot of $$$ to tell us how overly fair they are to minority workers. They have gotten millions of tax dollars for minority "training" programs like ST/EP. They have posters all over the place saying that they are an "equal opportunity employer." But what are the real facts?
>
> In this time of layoff, as the number of union cases against GE's harassment goes into the thousands, the worst of the layoff and Contract violations are against black and Spanish speaking workers. If GE gets away with it, you could be next!

The flier went on to list six workers who had been fired or harassed into quitting and particulars about each case. It encouraged recipients to attend union meetings to "join the fight to change [Local] 201 for the better." It was signed Members Against Discrimination (MAD).

We handed the flier out at the plant gates prior to starting our shifts. The company responded on March 20 by firing Charlie Murray, a white shop steward of long seniority. Their letter accused Murray of distributing a leaflet that was "disloyal and defamatory of the Company and its efforts to provide equal opportunity employment" and "defamatory, vile and abusive with respect to members of management."

Soon after that, another shop steward, Kevin Mahar, went to his manager and said, "I handed out the same leaflet. What are you going to do?" After his manager called Union Relations, Mahar was also fired.

Then a third steward, Richie Gallo, went to his foreman and said the same thing. Gallo's foreman returned after his call to Union Relations and told Gallo, "Nobody saw you handing out the leaflets so that is the end of it." Gallo got a few copies of the flier and, at the end of his shift, went to the gate, told the guard to watch him, and handed it out. He was fired.

The firing of three white stewards of long plant tenure and extensive family and social ties in the plant electrified the other workers. Many people who might not have taken action to defend nonwhite co-workers of short tenure and few plant social ties were ready to act. They came to union meetings and demanded action from union leaders who were used to doing little other than hobnobbing with company officials, and who were fearful and mistrustful of insurgent members. The stewards were returned to work with back pay, but it would take more to change management practices of open racism.

I had become friends with the other PLers in the plant. At that time PL and SDS/WSA members and friends, who were themselves from all walks of life, had ties to many other people interested in social change, including teachers, lawyers and reporters. The three stewards, Angelo, and many other shop activists were happy to see that some lawyers were willing to help us.

A case was brought against General Electric at the newly created Massachusetts Commission against Discrimination (MCAD). Ronnie Lee Loy, a man of Jamaican and Chinese descent, became the focus of hearings. He had been subjected to repeated open racial harassment by a foreman who had a history of abuse and drunkenness. Lee Loy was a rigger, balancing parts for a thirty-ton overhead crane. When the foreman wanted Lee Loy, he would march up and down the aisle demanding, "Where's the chink, I want the fucking chink." Whatever the official GE policies, racism was openly practiced in the shop, including a foreman with a wall plaque reading, "I like colored people, everyone should own one." A reporter at the *Boston Globe*, David Deutsch, did a great job of accurately covering the story through a series of articles.

Senior managers were subpoenaed to testify before MCAD as to what had happened and why they had allowed such practices. Chills must have gone through all of GE management, indeed, through managers all over the country, as the high-level GE managers squirmed under direct and well-informed interrogation. While nobody has done the research to prove it, I think that the Lee Loy case caused GE and other US corporations to change some of their most obvious and egregious racist shop practices.

PL did a good job covering the public story in *Challenge*, but I never told them about the internal strategy conversations, agreements, and disagreements among the shop activists who pursued both the Lee Loy case and improving the union leadership. Other PL people in the shop understood the need to keep secret from PL leadership information that was private to the internal shop and union struggles. By this time, I and others were knowledgeable about shop and union politics. PL did not provide useful leadership for us because they never seemed interested in learning from us. In those days, acting like they knew everything seemed to be more important to them than learning from others.

The next decade saw great and successful struggles to change both GE and the union. As an activist shop steward, I got to be part of several fascinating insurgencies. In 1975, I was part of the leadership of a strike around safety. New radio-controlled cranes had GE thinking that they could eliminate the job of crane operator. A run-away thirty-ton crane and several accidents convinced union members that we had to fight for life and limb. Each conflict with the company had an accompanying conflict with self-serving union officials. At one point, I got to be the prosecutor in the trial of the local's president on charges that he failed to support the members. On National Secretary's Day, two foremen took a woman to lunch and assaulted her in the car on the way back to the plant. Action by outraged workers, including picketing the home of the head of Union Relations, probably added chapters to management training manuals about avoiding overt racism and sexual assaults on women!

Despite several near-misses, I could not get elected to union office due to having been an open (and secret non-) communist and also due to my own failure to work closely with other progressives. I was infected with the "we're right so they must be wrong" disease (a.k.a. sectarianism). Other very fine progressives came into the plant, and many home-grown progressives emerged, thanks to mentoring. Through several elections, the union leadership was transformed to contain active, caring, class-conscious people.

By 1981, I felt that I had accomplished what I could at GE and the IUE, and that it was time to leave. I had become a machinist-all-around, but had no interest in running machines for the rest of my life. In evenings, I went to the Harvard Extension School and after completing four computer science courses, got an entry-level job with a small software company. I was interested in this evolving field, as well as in the role of leaders in progressive companies. Through two subsequent careers after GE, I was always, first and foremost, a shop steward in persona, putting co-workers' well-being and product and service quality first, even when it got me fired.

PL asserted that "all bosses are bastards," which had left me wondering both about party bosses and the origin and nature of good leadership. If humans build institutions, including political parties, where did good leadership come from and what did it look like? What kind of relations were needed to combat the common tendency of some to abuse their authority for self-promotion?

After GE, I spent nineteen years mainly in leadership roles for various software development organizations. In software engineering, I was able to be effective in my advocacy for those who worked for me and in product development. After the crash of 2001, I became a social worker, where my WSA learning and labor organizing skills were again put to good use. I finished graduate school in 2004, naively believing that "human services" would be humane, well-run organizations. Among social service agencies, I often found mean-spirited, self-serving managers running ineffective organizations. When I was able to practice independent of agencies, I went into local public schools, seeing students while working closely with their parents, teachers, and with school administrators.

In a local high school, a highly placed administrator ruled students by harsh discipline, intimidated their parents, and harassed and fired teachers. I listened to the students, their parents, and teachers and offered them ways to take action based upon my previous experience. Teachers got their union to pay attention and act. Parents, students, some caring administrators, and some members of the School Committee also took action. Three parents, four students, and eighteen teachers filed eloquent complaints and grievances about mistreatment and abuse. They got the abusive administrator out of the school, much to the relief of all. As a result, both the school and the union changed for the better, similar to what had happened at GE and in the IUE.

I am now retired and write this in the hope that activists learn that there is often room for action when they are faced with complex and dysfunctional corporations, government agencies, schools, unions, and other organizations. My personal and political transformation is an example of how being in struggles for social justice, collaborating and conducting conflict as needed, changes people. Our own growth, and the growth of those we influence, opens doors to building a new social order of greater justice, equality, and freedom.

I encourage you to learn how to both work collaboratively and to conduct conflict. I credit PL and its members for teaching me about ruling classes and the arc of history that brings us to today. The Lee Loy case could not have been won without their legal and journalistic help. At the same time, PL and the efforts of its members were hampered by sectarianism, by leaders giving orders with no democracy, and by thinking that leaders had to be all-knowing, thereby failing to learn from others.

Frank Kashner is retired after subsequent careers in software and as a social worker, where he applied some of the same methodologies for social change which he had learned at GE. He remains interested in social, economic, racial, gender, and environmental justice.

20

PL Reconsidered

Emily Berg
(Harvard University)

When I first heard about this proposed project, I was intrigued. Over the years I have maintained or resumed friendships with a few people I knew well and loved and worked with in those days—former PL members and friends—and from time to time we have talked about our shared pasts in SDS and PL. And I've wondered what happened to the many people I lost touch with, some of whom I remember very fondly, others not so much.

But I found that when I sat down to write, my interest drained away. I seem not to be really very interested in remembering and evaluating what I was involved in then. Why? My first answer to that question was that I don't think we were actually very important. We thought we were, and what we did and what happened were very important to us, in our individual lives, but especially when I look backwards now, we seem not to have been so important in the overall scheme of things. The civil rights movement has had lasting effects; the economic changes of the last fifty years have had enormous effects on people's lives and ways of thinking. But other than changing people's opinions about the war (and that was mostly done by the Vietnamese), our student movement never moved very far off campus. Of course it had zero effect on the changes in the economy that have so drastically impoverished so many people, and almost as little effect on working-class Americans' political opinions as they are becoming impoverished. Like progressives everywhere we have watched in dismay as the center has moved ever-rightward, to the point now that LBJ looks like a flaming radical.

A second reason I was reluctant to participate in this project is that I am not proud of many of the things I said and did while I was in Progressive Labor. PL was, by any useful definition, a cult, and the behavior of all of us who stayed with it past the earliest days, when it was weaker and less organized and thus more democratic, doesn't bear close examination without discomfort. As in all cults, loyalty to the leadership was the highest virtue, and open disagreement with party positions was aid and comfort to the enemy. Almost any tactic, including lies and violence, became acceptable in the service of the party line. We are lucky that there was never the slightest chance of PL's becoming an important force in the world.

The sad fact is that for nearly eight years I was a member of an organization that at first I did not understand, and as time went on and I understood it better, disagreed with more and more. But I kept my disloyal thoughts to myself—even kept them *from* myself—and over time got promoted to the local Boston leadership and the national Student Collective of PL. I was thus responsible not only for following but for winning people to PL's line and leadership. I did it primarily (I am glad I can say this) by political discussion and by being a nice person. I did participate in some of the shunning of "enemies" and even in some pushing and shoving in contentious meetings, but I was not asked to do more, probably because others knew I hated doing it. I think the Boston leadership (Jared Israel in particular) was good at knowing just how far people could be manipulated before they turned. There's no way to explain my longevity in PL except that I was in, and stayed in, because I didn't want to lose the friendship and respect of others; my place in PL was my place in the world.

I joined PL before it became a party, and before I had any idea of what a Marxist-Leninist party was. I had been active in the Harvard-Radcliffe SDS labor committee and met PL people there; they seemed to me to be the smartest, most committed and analytical, and the hardest workers of the people there. I joined PL on the philosophical grounds that communism was something entirely new and entirely necessary in the world, and that you couldn't not be a communist if you had any integrity. Did I really believe this, or even think that it made sense? It's hard to imagine that I did, especially since I had other friends who did not like PL who I respected, but I chose the new friends over the old, joined a study group, and soon joined PL. I don't remember when PL became a party; I don't think I even noticed.

I don't remember a lot about what we did in those days, except for a victorious struggle to form a union of hospital workers at a small hospital in Roxbury; I remember tremendous moments of solidarity when the workers (led by PL members) sat down on the job and we on the outside supported them with pickets and leaflets; I remember being inspired by the meetings of workers in a church basement, and noticing how the very best is sometimes brought out in people in the moment of struggle. Other things too ... but I felt at that time that I was in the right place, with the right people. Discussions of utopia, or warnings from anticommunist SDSers, seemed silly and unnecessary. It is interesting to me that I remember this period best of all, although it was longest ago. I felt then and still feel that it was mostly positive for the people I worked with and for me.

I graduated that summer (1966) and was slated to go into trade union work for some reason ... maybe the hospital union work? But at the last minute for reasons I either don't remember or never knew, I was assigned to Boston University to work in the SDS chapter there. I was at BU, I think, for the next three years, maybe four, where I participated in first building and then helping to destroy the antiwar movement there. As SDS moved toward a split, our chapter became very factionalized, primarily I think because of us. I don't mainly blame PL for the national SDS split, which was orchestrated by the Weatherman/RYM people, but I think at BU we were much more sectarian and argumentative than the other side—Eric Mann in particular, but also kids who were around the student newspaper and student government as well as non-PL SDS members. We had nothing but contempt for them, and they did not deserve it. I wonder sometimes how it would have been if PL had had a weaker presence at BU; I have the impression that at some campuses where there were fewer of us we therefore had to be less sectarian and thus did much better work.

During this time I also was co-opted (never elected, of course, that's not Leninist) onto the Boston leadership and the Student Collective. My memories are episodic and amazingly few; what was really going on for me during that time was maintaining and navigating friendships, going to jail, and falling in love and getting married. But I do remember when my best friend was hounded out of PL for organizing a faction of the UMass club; they didn't agree with the campus worker-student alliance strategy and wanted to continue focusing on the antiwar movement instead. I could not endure the contradiction between my agreement with her—and my attachment to my PL world, so I broke off our friendship. That still stands out in my mind as one of the worst things I ever did. The hiatus lasted many years, and was only ended when she called me up after PL was a distant memory.

It is hard to square my actions at the time with my self-concept as a person of some integrity, intelligence, and compassion. But there it is, and it will never go away. I think … I hope, that I learned a few things, primarily that I will always struggle with my need to be liked, as opposed to my desire to be honest. Some of the less personal things I've learned are: 1) The idea of a vanguard party is elitist and self-serving (for the vanguard) and discourages independent thought, eventually leading to either splits and the Moscow Trials, or just the regular old cult of personality —and always to condescension or contempt for regular people; 2) Ditto for democratic centralism, in which centralism will always trump democracy, especially since the vanguard of the vanguard (the leadership) must be right by virtue of being the vanguard, sort of like papal infallibility; 3) What history teaches will always be debatable, but the present-day results of the successful Marxist-Leninist parties, and the record of what they have done, should at least give us pause.

Like a lot of people, I did not leave PL in a clear and honest way. I got depressed, became less active, got involved in raising children, stated a few doubts to leadership in a friendly, self-deprecating way, and was therefore asked to … become a secret member! Which I did, and which meant nothing at all except that I met with a few other secret people at nice restaurants and discussed their mostly nonexistent work. I don't remember ever actually quitting—maybe I didn't, because of course it was Boston PL that split from national PL, I think because Jared Israel (the leader in Boston) was being ousted by the rest of them, so he took the offensive and took us with him in January 1974. I went along, participated in a few chaotic but weirdly fascinating meetings where all the pent-up disagreements and questions that people had suppressed popped out, as though we were suddenly catching up with the intellectual fads and fashions of previous decades. The disintegration of the Party for Workers Power (the Boston party) happened very fast, because there was actually very little that united us by that time, except for organizational loyalty, personal history, and friendship ties.

A not very consoling thought that occurs to me, when I feel a rush of shame about my behavior throughout that time, is that my actions were not very different from most people's, including those of people I love and respect. Even those who did break decisively and honestly with PL only did so after a period of going along to get along and trying not to think too hard about what they were doing. This makes me realize that my behavior was typical human behavior, which is cold comfort as far as self-esteem goes, but to my mind adds force to all the caveats about Leninism listed above. Leninist organization relies on human weakness.

Some people in this project have talked about lessons that we can draw from our experiences, ones that we can pass on to the present generation of activists. I have to say that I don't think they need any of that kind of help from us. The new labor movement of low-wage workers, the housing activism around gentrification, movements against the school-to-prison pipeline, the blooming of feminism—as well as the Occupy movements and Black Lives Matter, and all the other ferment up to and including Sanders and even Clinton activists, have so far done all right without our lessons. Their evolving ideas about leadership are a lot more interesting and positive than ours were. I hope they figure it out and not become isolated from the mainstream of people, though we did not.

A long time ago, a comrade joked that some friends of his were into "anarcho-cynicism"; I don't want to be cynical so I think I would classify myself as an anarcho-skeptic. I'm still politically active, much more interested in the details of how things can be made better and a lot less interested in large concepts, and forever suspicious of leaders although aware that they are necessary. And a lot more humble about my—our—importance as activists or organizations, when compared to the large forces that are actually shaping our world. Also, like most people after the disastrous and lethal failures of socialist revolutions, a lot more humble about big solutions. It's not at all clear to me that there is any real workable alternative to "democratic socialism," which is really just managed capitalism, except for very small societies. And *nothing* is guaranteed or permanent; it seems obvious to me that there is always a tendency toward some form of class rule, and that the best activism consists in always trying to empower those at the bottom. All of which only leads me to the conclusion that I don't know what the "answer" is; I even suspect that there isn't one; but I usually can know which side I'm on. It may be that that is all that can ever be done; in any case it's the best I can do for now.

Emily Berg is a retired social worker and lives in Boston.

Harvard students confront Robert McNamera, Lyndon Johnson's secretary of defense, 1966.

kers' Power button.

Harvard SDS blocks McNamera's car, 1965.

Anti-ROTC demonstration, Harvard, 1969.

STRIKE FOR THE EIGHT
DEMANDS STRIKE BE
CAUSE YOU HATE COPS
STRIKE BECAUSE YOUR
ROOMMATE WAS CLUBBED
STRIKE TO STOP EXPANSION
STRIKE TO SEIZE CONTROL
OF YOUR LIFE STRIKE TO
BECOME MORE HUMAN STR
IKE TO RETURN PAINE HALL
SCHOLARSHIPS STRIKE BE
CAUSE THERE'S NO POETRY
IN YOUR LECTURES
STRIKE BECAUSE CLASSES
ARE A BORE STRIKE FOR
POWER STRIKE TO SMASH THE
CORPORATION STRIKE TO MAKE
YOURSELF FREE STRIKE TO
ABOLISH ROTC STRIKE BECAUSE
THEY ARE TRYING TO SQUEEZE
THE LIFE OUT OF YOU STRIKE

Harvard University strike demands, 1969.

Anti-ROTC demonstration at Fordham University in New York.

Fordham SDS.

Antidraft demonstration at the Chicago Induction Center; Earl Silbar is in the center.

People in Harlem protest Columbia's expansion and displacement of their community, 1968.

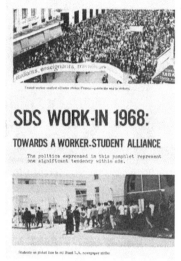

SDS WORK-IN 1968:
TOWARDS A WORKER-STUDENT ALLIANCE

The politics expressed in this pamphlet represent one significant tendency within sds.

WSA promotes the Work-in project, 1968.

Columbia University strike sit-in, 1968.

STRIKE IF WE MUST

Columbia strike button, 1968.

Anti--Apartheid demonstration at Columbia.

A copy of *Fight To Win*, a free WSA/SDS broadsheet distributed before the SDS National Convention in 1969.

CCNY SDS.

STRIKING STUDENTS SEIZE U
AFTER CONFRONTING PRE
SENATE PASSES MOTION

Wood Warns
The Students
On Effects
Of Action

by Paul Tooher

Between 250 and 300
angry UMass/Boston students
led President Robert C. Wood
from his office back to the
Boston campus Monday
demanding that he end the
University's complicity in the
Vietnam war.

A small contingent of the
group broke into the
President's offices at 85
Devonshire Street, smashing a
receptionist's window to gain
access to the suite. They
demanded that the President
accompany them as they
marched back to the Sawyer
Lounge.

Demands

They also demanded that
he set up their position that he
end all military recruitment on
all UMass campuses
permanently, that ROTC be
banned from the Amherst
campus, and that all defense

UMass Boston: SDS antiwar demonstration.

New York City cops monitor protests at Columbia, 1968.

Antiwar protest, UMass Boston, 1970..

WSA supports striking campus workers, Boston, 1970.

Columbia SDS button

Bill Lyons, president of the IBEW, speaks at a WSA rally, Columbia, 1972.

Campus Worker-Student Alliance button, 1970.

Lee Loy wins discrimination case

12/7+SpARl

Ronnie Lee Loy won his three-year-old anti-discrimination case last month, with GE paying $20,000, the most ever. A victory for all working people.

Lee Loy supporters demonstrate at MCAD headquarters.

Jamaican-born Ronnie Lee Loy was fired Jan., 1971 from the GE Riverworks Plant in Lynn, Mass. As Lee Loy proved at hearings before the Massachusetts Commission Against Discrimination, he'd been hit by a foreman after refusing to obey an improper work order. GE then covered up for the foreman by firing Lee Loy for insubordination and accusing *him* of assault.

So Lee Loy filed with the Massachusetts Commission Against Discrimination (MCAD). This agency claims to be a great friend of the little man, a real liberal agency in a real liberal state. But the fact is, MCAD has never made a final finding of race

over the plant. Lee Loy's witnesses had to come in day after day but weren't allowed to take the stand. Time after time, the Commissioner would insist that a witness who wasn't present on a particular day was the only one she wanted to hear. Unlike GE's witnesses, Lee Loy's witnesses were in danger of losing their jobs from having constantly to take off work.

Even though the MCAD was running the hearings like an obstacle course for Lee Loy, GE wasn't satisfied. There was still too much publicity in the wrong places, *bad* publicity.

GE fears light of day

For one thing, Lee Loy and his lawyer and the witnesses got a lot of

contributing $1500 at plant gate collections to cover legal costs.

GE puts foot in mouth

During the hearings, Lee Loy and his lawyer, Steve Kehoe, used GE's own prize witnesses to expose the company. This was easier than you'd think, because these guys are real dumbbells. Take this example. Last May, Ray Holland, Employee Relations Chief at the Riverworks plant attacked minority workers in the

hearings room in Lynn courthouse, the MCAD lawyers and hearings commissioner Regina Healy dined with — you guessed it — GE managers, at Anthony's Hawthorne Restaurant (very posh!).

A tricky maneuver...

So GE and MCAD agreed: the hearings had to go. First the MCAD pulled a little magic trick: they joined their own anti-discrimination suit

General Electric loses an employment discrimination case, 1974.

PL March for Jobs, 1970.

UMass Boston antiwar demonstrators.

WSA with striking GE workers, Boston, 1970.

21

Global Boston

Debbie Levenson
(UMass Boston SDS and PL)

UMass Boston opened to 1,227 undergraduate students in September 1965 at 100 Arlington, the old fourteen-story Boston Consolidated Gas building (with a terrible elevator) in the then rundown Park Square–Stuart area of downtown Boston, full of bars and cheap lunch places, not far from the Combat Zone and its strip joints. It aimed to offer a top-quality inexpensive education to students from urban poor and working-class and middle-class families; professors were recruited from top-name universities; classes were kept small; and course offerings ranged from seminars on Shakespeare to one on E. P. Thompson's *The Making of the English Working Class.* New to a new school, the professors seemed excited to work there. Faculty were beyond progressive: I remember Ron Schreiber, who taught a popular poetry class and came out of the closet before he got tenure, just to be clear about what counted in life. That was the tone of the place. They went there to teach—it was not a place to get a book done—and students wanted to learn. Simple as that sounds, it was key.

It was a privilege to go to UMass Boston. The students tended to be older, they often worked part-time or full-time—there were immigrants, and daughters and sons of immigrants; there were young parents, welfare recipients, cab drivers, waitresses, you name it—and they came from Boston's working-class neighborhoods, like South Boston,

Jamaica Plain, East Boston, Roxbury, Dorchester, Allston, and towns
on the North and South Shores. An unusually large number of Vietnam vets enrolled at UMass, since as vets they were entitled to free
schooling and a stipend. I've heard that as much as 20 percent of the
student body by 1970 was composed of Vietnam vets. A Vietnam veteran, an ex-marine who had joined Vietnam Veterans Against the War
(VVAW), organized campus vets with a passion and energy that pulled
others into the organization. The vets brought urgency and a sense of
history to campus.

The student movement at UMass Boston quickly became very
strong. Between 1967 and the end of 1970 there were three building
occupations, one to win back the job of a fired professor and two
about Vietnam and the demand that ROTC be thrown off all UMass
campuses in the state. When we learned in May 1970 about the US
bombings of Cambodia, a majority of students went on strike and
hundreds of us marched to an office building where the Board of
Trustees met and hauled the chancellor back to campus to address
our demand about ROTC. In addition to these antiwar activities, there
were feminist and gay and lesbian rights groups and a Black Students
Organization (BSO). Students and faculty promoted programs in
Women's and Black Studies. The large school lobby had a steady buzz
about politics, with literature tables, leaflets, and the accompanying
arguments.

The SDS membership reflected the city and campus: working class,
some Vietnam vets; brother and sister from "Southie" (an area that
was Irish white working class, and one stereotyped as completely racist); second-generation Syrians, Portuguese, and Italians; immigrants
from Honduras, Ecuador, Brazil, and Mexico; and others including a
few middle-class Jews, such as myself and Aaron Cohen. (I don't mean
that as a putdown, or to say we were slumming at all. In-state tuition
at a fine school was a dream come true.) All these young women and
men, the discussions and the fun we had, those moments of "speaking
truth to power" confrontations with authority when one has a forceful
voice out there in the world, our commitment, the risks we took—all

those times that belonged to us gave me my best moments of the 1960s and early 1970s—hands down.

I started at UMass Boston part-time in 1967, stayed for several years, and helped build a solid SDS chapter on campus. I was also an SDS regional traveler, and I had been a member of PL since the Boston chapter started in 1964. At UMass, PLers in SDS were genuinely friendly, and we enjoyed meeting people and talking over ideas. We were fairly articulate about the nature of capitalism and the state, the idea of proletarian power, the imperialism of the Vietnam war, the perils of liberalism, how a Black "riot" was a rebellion for liberation and justice, and how racism divided people. Nothing wrong with all that: However, what we talked down or walked past were key questions about the meaning of liberation and respect. We virtually opposed feminism, gay and lesbian rights, "Third World" revolutionary groups, the push for black studies, student power, and among much else; Progressive Labor implicitly or explicitly opposed the leadership of any group that wasn't ... PL.

In 1968 school officials announced that UMass would be moved from downtown to an isolated landfill peninsula on Dorchester Bay. Stuck at the end of what was an otherwise barren expanse lived hundreds of black and white families in a housing project called Columbia Point. PL, SDS, and many other campus groups, such as the VVAW, argued against The Move—as we called it—for many reasons. The Move to Columbia Point removed students from the lively downtown; it was not located near public transportation; and above all, it threatened the existence of the housing project. On campus we PLers had a substantial part in a large campaign that informed students about, and pulled them into, the fight against The Move. This was our Worker-Student Alliance (WSA). As significant as it is to make the argument about the historical force of the working class, our WSA was one-sided: because PL had no community work in Dorchester, there was presumably no one with whom to "ally," and it never entered our heads to look for leadership to the Dorchester activists who were already trying to deal with the UMass administration. The party really wanted us to sell

Challenge everywhere we went, including the Projects, which I don't recall ever doing, since the paper was so turgid and unrelated to the issues at hand.

At least we UMass PLers/SDSers had the good fortune of being at a distance from the party leadership, which was obsessed with Harvard. No one noticed if we played down the party line. Why explain to white students that the Black Panthers were "wrong," or that African independence leaders were all "sellouts," especially when many students had tremendous curiosity about world revolution? We even managed to avoid trashing the Mobilization Against the War with the vigor PL did elsewhere when the Mobilization called what became the largest ever demonstration against the war in Boston.

Turning to the more general topic of Boston PL, I hope it is useful to make very critical remarks about it. It encouraged arrogance. We had a political opinions about everything—based on what? Even through there were people in PL who had studied rural revolutionary movements, we learned little about these within the party. We never read anything about African colonialism, much less the struggles against colonialism. We never read a book about Cuba, and I never read the Panthers' 10-point program. Boston PL encouraged dependency. A leadership group chosen by the national leadership ran PL from top to bottom, and it relied on the time-tested tools of personal manipulation. We never elected leaders, and one's "place" in the party depended on "favoritism" of various kinds.

In addition, people who disagreed with the party line were cajoled or humiliated until they supported it. We were either "good" members who defended the party line well, or weak, "bad" ones if we didn't. There was little to no horizontal discussion (that was considered "factionalism"). Sections of the party did not know those in other sections. Everything was a secret. It was textbook authoritarian control. My worst experiences in the 1960s/early 1970s were PL meetings, and they brought out the worst in me, the deep wish to be "right" and "liked." My relationships with people in the party were rocky, and at some point I started to oppose the idea of democratic centralism. I was eventually kicked out, together with an undocumented Mexican national whom the PL leadership threated to turn over to Immigration authorities.

All this is *not* to say that most of us who joined PL had bad intentions at all. We were part of the times of the late 1950s and 1960s. We wanted a just and better world, and believed it could happen. World War II had a huge impact on me, and the narratives of that war and the civil rights movement were the overriding "big events" of my youth. I grew up with the ethic, almost a command: "don't be a good German"—that is, don't be passive when others are hurt. I did not participate in the civil rights movement, but at the same time my understandings of it had distinct authority in my life. My mother was from Texas, and on several occasions she drove my older brother and me from New Jersey, where we lived, to see her parents in San Antonio. We stopped in segregated motels, restaurants, and gas stations, and saw all those "No Colored People" and "Whites Only" signs. My grandparents in San Antonio raised the standard for me. They were white theosophists from Missouri farming families, and they lived in a small rented bungalow with a pear tree in the back, and a distinct cultural atmosphere inside. Their eclectic radicalism was a powerful crucible of nonconformism and leftist thinking. They believed in reincarnation, the Bhagavad Gita, Henry Wallace's Progressive Party, FDR, and an end to Jim Crow.

I was probably seven when I tagged along with my brother to a public swimming pool in San Antonio one day and he got into a big argument with our Texan cousin about the "Whites Only"/"Colored Only" sections that had two sets of thick tall metal chains between them, and he and I stood there and didn't go swimming. When I was around nine or ten I saw a photo of what I think could only have been Emmett Till's face all bloated and mangled, his skin twisted up. I never forgot that photo.

Altogether, there was some sort of youthful conflation of the materiality and physicality of racism and anti-Semitism; segregation, concentration camps, torture, and fences that you couldn't jump over.

These were not really equivalents, yet the almost photographic quality of this composite pushed me in the direction of activism.

Later on, when I was in public high school in New Jersey, my brother and I went to the August 1963 March on Washington. I don't remember what the speakers said. It was just *huge, solemn,* and *important.* That I got. It was around that time that someone explained to me what Robert Williams wrote about in *Negroes with Guns,* which was published in 1962, and it made sense to me. Maybe militant self-defense was my first serious political strategic thought.

The Harlem Rebellion was a major reason that I got involved with what was then the Progressive Labor Movement. Obviously, I was distant from the rebellion, but I was in New York City that summer when Harlem exploded after a policeman named Thomas Gilligan killed James Powell, a fifteen-year-old African American. PL put out a poster headlined "Wanted for Murder: Gilligan the Cop." The murder and the poster hit me hard: a horrid murder; a really strong answer. I heard about Bill Epton and read his fantastic speech "I Have Been Found 'Guilty.'" Hanging around New York, I also heard that PL had sent arms to the miners on strike in Hazard, Kentucky. Around that same time, the students who had broken the US government's travel ban, including many from PL and the May 2nd Movement, were hauled before HUAC. My brother and I went to Washington on a bus to support them, and they were heroes to me. I still have a clear picture in my mind of Vicky Ortiz and Conrad Lynn, heads up, shoulder to shoulder.

The same summer of the Harlem Rebellion and the May 2nd Movement antiwar demonstration in Times Square, I attended a New York City meeting of PLM that was, as I recall, a founding meeting of the Progressive Labor Party. I absorbed some of what was said, but not much. Nonetheless, if one wanted to change the world, here was a group that could. It had the fire, and it talked about world revolution. The people there appeared smart and daring, and many were, such as Bill Epton, who was later expelled from the party.

At that time and for a long time after, I did not know much about any of this: the Student Committee for Travel to Cuba; the Kentucky miners' strike; or the response to Harlem Rebellion. PL always presented all this as all accomplishments of PL. The inability to realize that many different people and the dynamics of many events were part of this history guaranteed that arrogance was foundational to PL. And PL always talked about PL. The Cuba trips stand out to me in this regard because, like many in the USA, I was fascinated by Cuba and impressed by those who went there. But the students who broke the ban basically talked about breaking the ban, as important as that was, and not about *Cuba*. And in no time at all, PL was claiming that the leaders of the Cuban Revolution were just a "Merry band of Robin Hoods" who had no idea what they were doing—and in fact we had no idea of what they were doing.

In addition, for all the militancy PL projected in 1964, Boston PL wasn't really that militant. Harvard students took over a building, fine; but when a party member suggested that we very carefully do something about the tires of the National Guard tanks when there was a threat that they would be used against Roxbury in 1967, he was ignored. That whole spirit of the 1964 Harlem Rebellion was over and done. And I don't think that Boston PL consistently engaged in large-scale grassroots campaigns, although the Peace and Freedom Party in Cambridge is a major exception to this; no doubt the excessive compartmentalization of PL limits my knowledge and I know little about the party's trade union work. It certainly seemed that PL had no significant part in the city's largest grassroots organizations or in the important successful community fight against a proposed highway that cut through white, Latino, and black working-class neighborhoods in the South End, Roxbury, Jamaica Plains, and Roslindale. PL was decidedly not part of any African American or Latino/a initiatives.

As I noted above, many memorable, brave, and thoughtful people joined Boston PL and changed the course of their lives to fight for justice and change. PL was the catalyst for this activism. But being that initial catalyst was not enough. The leaders huddled around one another instead of opening the door to broader healthy discussions and projects, the life blood of which needed to come from that famous group "the people." In its anti-intellectualism, Boston PL ridiculed nuances and stifled those who pushed back against the leaderships' brand of pseudo working-class "Marxist-Leninist" pragmatism. To one extent or another, many of us were accomplices in that process of sorting out the "right" people in the party from the "wrong" ones, of cold-shouldering the latter, and of accepting the party's lack of transparency and accountability.

Much about me got choked up, for lack of a better way to express it. One was intellectuality. We had a narrow reading list. I read that monotone *State and Revolution* at least three times. And when I first joined PL, I read Stalin's clumsy *On the National Question* and Marx's *German Ideology* as well as *The 18th Brumaire*. It is no joke that while PL still "approved" of the Chinese Communist Party I read *Peking Review*, and stuff like "How to Be a Good Communist" and the *Little Red Book*. "On Contradiction" was a party favorite. I did not read any of the amazing texts being written in the US by women in radical black and Latina groups. Every leftwing white woman in Boston was talking about *The Golden Notebook* except for women in PL. Fanon was being read widely, especially by black and Latino activists, and we never discussed his work. We did not read James Baldwin, much less W.E.B. Du Bois. I could go on.

There was *zero*, in fact markedly *subzero* discussion about gender, sex, or sexism, or racism within the party—except for rote statements like "women and black workers suffer special oppression," and "male chauvinism and racism divide the working class." In addition, PL was homophobic, and at a time when that was being challenged in the streets. Stonewall took place in 1969 and it was a nonevent for PL. Talk about self-suppression! By a series of co-incidences, as a kid I knew many gays and lesbians without giving it a second thought. They were friendly adults in my adolescent world, yet I lost touch with that part of my own experience, those friends and my own thoughts about them. I must have forgotten that teenager who thought Baldwin's *Giovanni's Room* was the greatest novel in the world.

After I got kicked out of PL and socially blacklisted by the "comrades," life went on. A certified ESL teacher in the Boston Public Schools, I taught at a school in Jamaica Plains and then worked for CETA, teaching English to Spanish-speaking immigrants on the North Shore. I went back to my old habit of reading good books. At night I got an MA in history at UMass Boston, Columbia Point, and wrote an MA thesis on workers councils in Chile during the Salvador Allende era that discussed how workers and community residents could make history without vanguard parties. I won a fellowship at NYU to pursue a PhD in Latin American history. I lived in New York City, then traveled to and lived in Guatemala and wrote a dissertation on the Guatemalan urban labor movement (available as the paperback book *Trade Unionists against Terror*).

I taught at Columbia University for eight years, then got a job in the history department at Boston College, where I taught for two decades. Boston College was a wonderful experience in many ways, but it made me appreciate again and again and again the UMass Boston of the 1960s. At seventy-one, I retired. I have kept writing, and I am working on a colleague's online project called "Global Boston" about Boston's immigrants. You can check it out at https://globalboston.bc.edu/.

Debbie Levenson lives in Boston.

22

The Harvard Strike of '69
and What Happened Next

Mary Summers
(Harvard University)

I have a vague memory of my pacifist father muttering darkly about Harvard as the home of the architects of the Vietnam War, militarists and their apologists (McGeorge Bundy, Walt Rostow, Robert McNamara, Arthur Schlesinger Jr.), when I received my acceptance to Radcliffe in the spring of 1966. But I told him that I wanted to go to the university that I had heard about for years, from him, my mother, and their friends. I loved their stories about working with F. O. Matthiessen, who wrote foundational books in American Studies, while organizing the Harvard Teachers' Union, campaigning in support of the leftwing dock workers' union leader Harry Bridges, giving one of the nominating speeches for Henry Wallace's campaign for president, and fighting hard against the blacklisting of communists in organizations like the ACLU. That was the Harvard that I wanted to go to, where my parents and their friends had learned to love history, literature, and the arts in ways that they saw as profoundly connected to living lives of principled engagement with the wider world.

In large part because of my parents' influence, I was already a supporter of the civil rights and antiwar movements when I arrived at Harvard in the fall of 1966. I was also, however, at least equally concerned with pursuing their passion for poetry. Getting a C– on my first paper on Robert Frost's "The Oven Bird," in Hum 6, a course where we had to write on a different poem each week, is still one of the sharpest memories of my freshman year. After that, I became known as the girl who would stay up all night, typing away in the Briggs Hall basement, writing and rewriting that week's assignment, especially loving Yeats' "On a Political Prisoner" and "Easter 1916" and T. S. Eliot's "Four Quartets."

While I was working so hard academically, I was also trying to find my way socially. I made some friends in my dorm, but as a Midwestern public school girl who had spent her high school Saturday nights folk dancing and who had never had a real boyfriend, I was intimidated by mixers and somewhat put off by students from wealthier and more worldly backgrounds. I socialized most with the few friends from St. Louis who had also come east to college.

Over time, however, I got more involved in antiwar activities both on and off campus. I remember going to antiwar teach-ins that gave us a wide range of activities to sign up for. I tried many of them, rang-ing from training sessions for draft counselors to picketing the army base where draft inductions were taking place (which somehow always involved the early morning and the freezing cold), to canvassing Cam-bridge neighborhoods with an antiwar petition. I was outraged when I heard that Harvard intended to institute disciplinary proceedings against the students who had blocked Dow Chemical from recruit-ing on campus. *Dow Chemical.*[1] All of us had seen the pictures of the children in Vietnam burning from napalm. Apparently the Harvard administration thought that Dow Chemical was critical to the life of the university, but that students who believed strongly in stopping the murder of Vietnamese children were not. I remember calling my par-ents in tears to say that if Harvard wanted to expel students who pro-tested Dow Chemical's recruiting on campus, then I didn't want to stay at Harvard. Hundreds of us turned in our bursar's cards to say that we wanted to be counted as having been at the demonstration.

---

1 "Study Examines Dow Protesters," *Harvard Crimson*, March 12, 1969.

In the course of my sophomore year, I was especially attracted by efforts to reach out to a broader public, as opposed to spending my time talking to other students who already agreed that the war was wrong. I then got involved in volunteering for Eugene McCarthy's "Clean for Gene" primary challenge to LBJ. With many others, I got rides hours north on the weekends to trudge door to door in the snow in towns like Littleton, New Hampshire. At that point I despised LBJ's voice so much that I could barely stand to listen to his press conference in March 1968 announcing that he would not seek another term, after McCarthy did surprisingly well in New Hampshire. On spring break I went with some friends to Indianapolis to campaign for McCarthy after Robert Kennedy had entered the race. After knocking day after day on doors in black neighborhoods, asking people to listen to Mc-Carthy in a televised speech before making up their minds, I remember being heartbroken by that speech myself. It was all about "appealing to youth" and "healing the generation gap," nothing about poverty, or race, or who had been fighting and dying in this terrible war.

That experience made me more open to SDS's anti-ROTC campaign when I returned to campus. I still remember—and am grateful for—the willingness of SDS friends (who were later associated with both sides of the growing split in SDS) to engage in long, thoughtful arguments about their decision to focus their antiwar efforts on Harvard. It took a lot of arguing to convince me that organizing to get ROTC off campus was a significant strategy for working against the war. They walked me through the facts about how ROTC trained men to become second lieutenants, officers who led search-and-destroy missions in Vietnam. Strategically, they argued that it made sense to focus on how our institution contributed to the war effort. This was the place where we could hope to make a difference that could have an impact on the wider world. Once convinced, I found that knocking on dorm doors and approaching people in the dining hall with petitions made me feel less alienated on campus. I looked for common ground with everyone I spoke to and enjoyed conducting friendly arguments with many of my classmates.

At this point, I had started going to some SDS meetings, though for the most part I have only vague memories of them. I liked the small working groups better, where we hammered out the language of leaflets and petitions. Meanwhile, the general body meetings grew from back rooms to large lecture halls. At these bigger meetings, I was put off by some of the posturing of the (mostly male) speakers on both sides of the SDS split and found the passion invested in their differences hard to follow. I had "non-leader" (at least in the sense that they were not among the main speech-givers) friends on both sides of these arguments. The doctrinaire language of some of the grad students whom I knew to be in PL put me off, but I appreciated the hard, patient work that WSA members did to introduce the rest of us in SDS and the wider campus to issues faced by workers on campus. Allying with these workers made more sense to me than glorifying the "youth movement," much less the macho posturing of the Weathermen. As a result, over time I became a tentative supporter of the Worker-Student Alliance side of SDS while holding on to my friendships outside that fold.

I still missed meetings and demonstrations if I had a paper due, but the arrogance of the Harvard administration made me an ever-stronger supporter of the anti-ROTC campaign. Harvard's administration defended its "right" to train second lieutenants for Vietnam as fiercely as it had defended Dow Chemical's "right" to recruit on campus, arguing that officers who were trained at Harvard would be more intelligent and humane than your average blue-collar draftee. They ignored petitions to abolish ROTC, signed by a majority of Harvard students and many faculty.[2] They threatened to suspend and take away the scholarships of students who participated in a sit-in at Paine Hall, demanding that the faculty vote on a motion to abolish ROTC.[3]

In short, while I was put off by some of the rhetoric, I appreciated the ongoing opportunities SDS gave me to participate both in mass

---

2 William R. Galeota, "Negotiators to Heed Faculty ROTC Edicts," *Harvard Crimson*, April 7, 1969.

3 Robert Krim, "Pusey at SFAC," *Harvard Crimson*, April 9, 1969.

organizing efforts on campus and significant debates about the substance and the strategies of our campaigns. What I did not agree with was the push to escalate to the building takeover strategy that had taken place at Columbia and some other universities around the country. I rushed back to campus from spring break a day early to attend the meeting where that tactic was voted on—and defeated.[4]

Those of us who had voted against the takeover were not happy when the students who had lost that vote (who were for the most part associated with PL and WSA) decided to take over University Hall anyway. I remember walking around in the confusion inside University Hall, until I found someone I knew well enough to question why they had decided to take this action. I don't remember much of what he said, but I still value the spirit with which he stepped aside from the strategizing going on among his comrades to answer every question I wanted to ask. I finally decided, like many others, that while I still did not like the tactic of the building takeover, I would show my support for the SDS demand to get ROTC off campus by standing on the steps of the building. I rushed back to my dorm to get some blankets, preparing to stay overnight, before Harvard locked its gates.

The rest to some extent is history. Harvard President Nathan Pusey proved himself to be the university's equivalent to Bull Connor: a man so ready to unleash police brutality against his own students that he won virtually the whole campus' support for the strike that followed.[5] At 3 a.m. more than four hundred police officers from every surrounding community massed in Harvard Yard.[6] At that moment, I was still prepared for what I had seen in civil rights demonstrations. I envisioned my fellow students and I standing on the steps, refusing to

---

4 William R. Galeota, "300 Storm Pusey's House after Anti-ROTC Meeting," *Harvard Crimson*, April 9, 1969.

5 "Cordier Discusses Unrest on Campus at Conference," *Harvard Crimson*, March 20, 1969; Krim, "Pusey at SFAC"; "Who's Lying about the Original Demands?" *Harvard Crimson*, April 15, 1969; "Statement by the Harvard Corporation on Strike Issues," *New York Times*, April 19, 1969.

6 "Police Raid Sit-in at Dawn; 250 Arrested, Dozens Injured," *Harvard Crimson*, April 10, 1969.

respond to their orders to disperse, and being carried away in a classic model of civil disobedience. Instead, the police rushed the building, clubbing everyone in their path.

Who knows what would have happened if Pusey had decided to wait us out, as so many university presidents do in similar situations today? As it was, the whole world, including my parents, saw the images of the "bust," many of us with our heads bleeding, on the news that night. The administration's expectation that many students would be injured was underlined when we made our way to the Student Health Center. It was typically closed at night. But there it was with all the lights on and a somewhat hostile staff awaiting our arrival. It was the sympathy of the doctor who took my stitches out the following week that made me cry.

What came next was the transformative experience of seeing the entire university with all its experts, its think-tanks, its professors shuttling back and forth to Washington, brought to a halt by the strike that followed. The more the demands of the students who took over University Hall were debated and discussed on campus, the clearer it became that most of us agreed with them. The sharpest debate occurred at a mass meeting at Memorial Church, where a strong majority voted down a proposal that we focus on demands for a change in university governance. Ending Harvard's contributions to the war and its expansion at the expense of neighboring communities mattered more to us than procedural negotiations about our voice, or the faculty's voice in running this elite institution. We voted to continue the strike around our substantive demands.[7]

After that meeting, the key questions discussed, from the freshman dorms to the most advanced scientific laboratories, were the strike demands.[8] There were no more classes, no more exams. For those few weeks, students and sympathetic faculty succeeded in taking the university away from the administration and creating a school for study-

7 "SDS Statement," *Harvard Crimson*, April 10, 1969.
8 William M. Kutik, "Teaching Fellows to Go on Strike," *Harvard Crimson*, April 12, 1969.

ing justice and what it should be. The entire campus debated the issues that first led me to join SDS: the war in Vietnam and how men from Harvard had helped to plan and justify it; the role of ROTC and the second lieutenants who were leading troops into battle. We studied how Harvard operated as one of the biggest landlords in Cambridge and on Mission Hill, treating the residents of these neighborhoods as if they were so much dirt to be swept out of the way whenever necessary.[9] We studied the nature of a Harvard education, and the stereotypes and lack of attention to the experience of working and poor people that pervaded so much of our curriculum, as well as the history of the war itself and its context in the broader issues of imperialism and colonialism. We also studied the choices that were before each of us as students at Harvard: whether to accept the elitist view of the world that developed and justified search-and-destroy missions, pacification programs, and the destruction of neighborhoods; or to insist that we could no longer allow activities like these to go on in our name.

Two weeks after the bust I think it was the Harvard faculty who called for a meeting of the entire university community in the football stadium, where we proceeded to pass votes in support of every one of the strike demands.[10] To end our strike, Harvard ultimately had to agree to abolish ROTC on campus and to replace ROTC scholarships with university aid. Harvard also restored the scholarships of students who had been placed on probation for protesting ROTC, and made a commitment to build low-income housing in neighborhoods that had been disrupted by university expansion.[11] The university further agreed to form a Department of African American Studies.

Many of us were so distrustful of the administration that we left campus that spring and returned the following fall, far from realizing

---

9 Ruth Glushien, "Cambridge Residents Hear SDS Speakers," *Harvard Crimson*, April 14, 1969; Adele Rosen, "City Asks More Say in Housing," *Harvard Crimson*, April 14, 1969; "A Concession," *Harvard Crimson*, April 15, 1969.

10 "Stadium Meeting Set for Friday; Buhl Will Chair," *Harvard Crimson*, April 17, 1969; "Stadium," *Harvard Crimson*, April 19, 1969.

11 "SFAC to Study Apartment Rents; Will Wait to Act," *Harvard Crimson*, April 22, 1969.

all that we had won. I spent much of the next academic year writing my History and Literature senior thesis on Thomas Moore's *Utopia*. I would occasionally join one of the small picket lines at University Hall, organized by what remained of the Worker-Student Alliance, which now focused only on specific worker grievances in ways that made few connections with students' interests in the antiwar, women's, and Black Power movements on campus. I graduated the following spring, still inspired by the strike, and still alienated from the university as an institution.

I did not learn that Harvard had actually built low-income housing on Mission Hill until twenty years later, when I decided to do a little research on the strike and its aftermath after I agreed to give a speech at a Harvard Strike reunion in the spring of 1989.[12] There at a rally on the steps of University Hall in solidarity with students who were then fighting for divestment from South Africa, I underlined what to me was still the heart of what we had won:

> The Harvard strike taught us a great deal about how political leadership and argument can tap the values that each one of us is trying to express in our daily lives and help us organize together for our common goals. It taught us to focus on institutions where we could make a difference, and each of us has continued to do that in a thousand ways, whether as professionals or organizers, in businesses and unions, government and grass roots politics, in our neighborhoods and our families. When the media asks "Are we still crazies?" our answer is "No. We never were." When they ask, "Have we sold out?" our answer is, "No. We never will." Our everyday lives involve all kinds of struggles over values and goals and what our society should be about—and from time to time, these struggles erupt in amazing ways. No one can predict when or how some job action, some routine election, some seemingly random act of protest will suddenly become something much bigger. Then we get a major chance to transform our world.

12 An Open Letter From the Student Strikers of 1969," *Harvard Crimson*, April 11, 1989.

That was the speech that I gave at a time when it still seemed possible to repeat with confidence what I thought I had learned from the Harvard strike of 1969.

This confidence was due in large part to the fact that in 1989 I was still living my life on a trajectory that (to me at least!) was profoundly shaped by my Harvard strike experience. What had continued to give meaning to my life was finding people to work with on strategies to change the world around us. I found such people in a wide range of places: a collective of women connected to *Our Bodies, Ourselves* making a movie on abortion and birth control immediately after graduation; the Medical Committee for Human Rights and union organizing efforts, when I was working as a nurses' aid and a ward secretary for a few years after that; Boston's Neighborhood Health Centers after I became a physician assistant; and Boston's Progressive Labor Party, which split from the national organization, renaming itself the Party for Workers' Power in the early 1970s. Then in 1979 Bruce Allen, whom I had not actually known at Harvard, but was the SDS speaker at the 1969 graduation, convinced me to move to Cleveland, where then Mayor Dennis Kucinich was giving speeches about "the corporate vampires sucking the blood of American's cities."[13]

Allen saw Kucinich's war with Cleveland's banks and utility companies as evidence that electoral politics represented an arena in which we could engage in political (and class) struggle in ways that many more Americans recognize and participate in than was the case when we were selling communist papers, or organizing May Day rallies, or engaged in single-issue campaigns. He therefore decided to run for City Council as a supporter of Kucinich. When I arrived, the campaign I found myself immersed in was as sharp as Allen had promised: "Stand Up [to business elites] with Kucinich" was the slogan of the mayor's campaign for reelection, versus the "Together [with the corporations] We Can Do Better" of his opponent, George Voinovich. After weeks

---

13 For an account of Kucinich's battles as mayor of Cleveland, see Todd Swanstrom, *The Crisis of Growth Politics: Cleveland, Kucinich, and the Challenge of Urban Populism* (Philadelphia: Temple University Press, 1985).

of knocking on doors and making phone calls, debating what were essentially the pros and cons of class struggle with the city's residents, I thought leftists throughout the country should be inspired by the fact that 40 percent of the city voted for class struggle! The fact that Voinovich felt compelled to run on a platform of preserving Muny Light, the public power company established by the city's populist Mayor Tom Johnson, which had been the focal point of Kucinich's battles, signaled how powerfully Kucinich had succeeded in transforming the city's political landscape.

As the city's mayor, Kucinich had also played a significant role in making Cleveland the one city in the country with a court-ordered busing plan that did not result in white violence. His leadership—and that of the Stokes brothers—had been such that it was possible to build a serious interracial campaign for the open City Council seat in Ward 4, the Buckeye-Woodland, Shaker neighborhood on Cleveland's East Side where Allen lived. Once the largest Hungarian community in the United States, the ward had become primarily African American. Allen, his law partner Blair Hodgman, and I learned as fast, and as much, as we could, meeting people, recruiting volunteers, and speaking to organizations. Like the Kucinich campaign, the experience of knocking on doors, learning the neighborhoods, figuring out how to speak to what people had in common in their concerns with issues like crime and abandoned homes was compelling political work, even though Allen failed to win enough votes to beat Ken Johnson, the African American candidate he ran against.

After winning respectable vote totals in another campaign for City Council, followed by one for state representative, we had to retire from the expensive business of running campaigns, but stayed involved in the 21st Congressional Caucus, an organization built by Congressman Louis and former Mayor Carl Stokes that dominated the East Side's politics and held regular meetings. We also began to get more engaged in environmental organizing around acid rain, a deeply controversial issue in Ohio, whose coal plants were a key contributor to the effects of acid rain on forests, lakes, fish, buildings, and monuments throughout the Northeast. Our 21st Congressional Caucus connections eventually led to my getting a job as "the office manager" (and for many weeks the only paid employee) of Jesse Jackson's 1984 campaign in New Hampshire. Before I had even set out for New Hampshire, Bruce Allen and I had volunteered to write a speech for Jackson to give at a national acid rain conference, when we learned that he was the only presidential candidate who had not committed to be there. We succeeded in crafting an appeal on an important issue that was new for Jackson in language that he said "had my rhythm." (Meaning, I think, that we had a good feeling for the religious/social justice language of the civil rights movement; and that I tend to write in iambic pentameter.)[14] The result was that Jackson decided that it was useful to have a speechwriter for white audiences. He asked for new speeches whenever he returned to New Hampshire, and I delivered on the dangers of nuclear power and throwing tax payers' dollars in a hole called Seabrook. After hearing George McGovern speak in one of the presidential debates, I also decided to try calling for cutting the military budget by a third and investing in roads and bridges and decent schools and housing.

Shortly after the Michigan primary, Jackson hired me to go on the road as a full-time speech writer. As hard as it was to live in a 24/7 campaign environment, I loved reaching out to local organizations in whatever state Jackson would be campaigning in next to learn about the issues that mattered most to them. I wrote about black lung disease and losing fingers, limbs, and family members in the mines for West Virginia, farm bankruptcies for the Midwest, the conditions faced by farm workers in Vineland, New Jersey, and what hard-pressed communities were paying into the federal defense budget versus what they were getting in return, everywhere we went. For the most part Jackson worked with whatever I gave him. When he found that a theme struck a chord with his audiences, he spoke to it all day long. He was, however,

---

14 Coverage of the speech and conference: Philip Shabecoff, "Acid Rain Is Theme of Gathering in New Hampshire Political Test," *New York Times*, January 7, 1984, sec. US.

clearly convinced that white people did not want to hear about racism. The only time I could get him to talk about race, outside of the context of the achievements of the civil rights movement in Greenwood, Mississippi, was a speech for the Commonwealth Club in San Francisco, where he wanted to talk about the economy. In that setting, I wrote him a speech about the auto companies' efforts to blame their own failures on the Japanese, and the impact of the anti-Asian sentiment they stirred up across the whole country. That speech, a friend later told me, was featured on NPR.

Writing speeches that appealed to people's shared aspirations for good jobs, safe streets, and clean air was an exhilarating experience. At the same time, however, I was disappointed (if not, given his history, surprised) by Jackson's failure to support any serious organizing efforts for the agendas that he spoke to. After the national election was over, he also started to miss payrolls. At that point, I headed back to my former job as a physician assistant in a community hospital in Cleveland. I continued, however, to be on the lookout for speechwriting jobs. I was now convinced that putting good words into the mouths of politicians was a way that I could have some impact on national political debates.

The working conditions were much better with the 1986 Harriett Woods campaign for an open Senate seat in my home state of Missouri, and the campaign itself should have been an exciting one. Only four years earlier Woods had surprised everyone by running a "Give 'em Hell" campaign against Reagan's cutbacks with strong support for women's (and abortion) rights that lost by less than 2 percent of the vote (the closest Senate race in the country) to incumbent John Danforth, even though her lack of financial support from the Democratic Party meant that she had to pull her very effective TV ads in the last weeks of the campaign.[15] When running for an *open* seat in 1986, however, the full support of the Democratic Party may well have been

---

15 Adam Clymer, "Danforth Appears to Lead in Missouri Senate Contest," *New York Times*, October 13, 1982, sec. B.

her greatest liability. Their consultants told her that she should run on only three issues: trade, competitiveness, and the farm crisis.

I did love the chance the Woods campaign gave me to write speeches for and about the family farm movement. I struggled to learn the ins and outs of why they supported supply management programs and higher commodity prices rather than farm subsidies and lower prices, but once I came to understand their commitment to working with environmentalists around a vision for a more planned agricultural economy that would allow farmers to make a living (both in this country and around the world) *and* protect watersheds, soil, and wildlife, I was hooked. Here were the kind of movement I had been looking for ever since I had first gotten involved in electoral politics: people committed to building effective local organizations and actions *and* winning elections; people with a political agenda that challenged Ronald Reagan's commitment to "free markets" so effectively that Democratic politicians, who ran from the word "planning" on every other issue, flocked to their cause. The speech I wrote for the three-day United Farmers and Ranchers Congress in St. Louis in September 1986 was a triumph. For Woods's more routine appearances, however, I could never figure out how to write speeches about trade and competitiveness that did not bore me, the candidate, and her audience.

The results spoke for themselves. Woods lost that open Senate seat by a 47 to 53 percent margin to Kit Bond, who proceeded to serve as a deeply conservative Republican in the Senate for the next twenty-four years. On that gloomy Election Day in 1986, I was on the phone with Adolph Reed, Jr., a political scientist at Yale, with whom I had become friends after reading his critical book about Jesse Jackson, which a friend from the Jackson campaign had given me, saying, "This says everything that we think."[16] It was during that conversation that I decided to apply to graduate school in political science, inspired by Reed to think

---

16 Adolph L. Reed, *The Jesse Jackson Phenomenon: The Crisis of Purpose in Afro-American Politics*, 2nd ed. (New Haven: Yale University Press, 1986); Mary Summers, "The Front Runner: Jesse Jackson in Black and White," *Nation* 245, no. 18 (November 28, 1987); Clymer, "Danforth Appears to Lead."

this was a field that would allow me to speak about politics in my own voice, as well as potentially continue to work as a speechwriter.

When I arrived in New Haven in the fall of 1988, Reed and other members of the Political Science Department got me interested in supporting the African American State Senator John Daniels's decision to challenge the city's five-term mayor, Ben DiLieto, who had not faced a close election since he took office in 1979. I was soon deeply engaged in writing Daniels an announcement speech, voicing the disgust of the black community—and many allies—with an administration that had consistently prided itself on its programs for "economic development" (tax abatements and special favors for the developers of office towers, condominiums, and shopping malls) in a city with the second highest infant mortality rate in the country.

Daniels's challenge to what so many had assumed was an invulnerable incumbent encouraged testimony from more and more people about corruption and incompetence at City Hall. Just a couple of weeks before my Harvard Strike reunion, DiLieto announced that he would not be running for reelection. For me, this sudden decision was one more affirmation of everything that I had learned from my experience at Harvard. You may begin with only a handful of people, but if you are serious about developing a strategy to win, to reach out to others in every way possible, you can change the world. And that was the message I gladly delivered at that Harvard Strike reunion.

But that was then, in 1989 when experiences like the Daniels campaign, the response to Jackson, the family farm movement, and the years in Cleveland all suggested that it should be possible to reach out to people around the country with a political agenda that spoke to all that so many of us want for ourselves and our children: a time when it did not even occur to me that Ronald Reagan might be the last president in my lifetime capable of speaking with seeming conviction about the working people who built this nation. In 1989 I had not yet lived through decades of Bushes and Clintons, decades of growing inequality, decades of neoliberals taking over the Democratic Party, and Tea Partiers organizing so effectively against them. I had not yet seen a man like Steve Bannon put to work all the lessons I had learned—about the possibilities of putting words into the mouth of a candidate capable of appealing to and mobilizing a significant electorate—to upend the world. And all in the wrong direction.

Close to thirty years later, we now have to come to terms with living in a country where Donald Trump was elected president: a man whose administration may well succeed in dismantling many of the rights and protections that Americans have fought for since before the New Deal. These are, in short, years when those of us who identify with progressive movements need to offer serious critiques of these movements' failures, sober advice instead of cheerleading. I will, therefore, do my best to briefly summarize what I see as the lessons from my experience with the Progressive Labor Party and the Worker-Student Alliance, as requested by the editors of this book, as well as the organizing efforts I have been involved in since then.

1. Leadership, Outreach, and Organizing

Many of my classmates and I benefited from the hard work of those members of PL and WSA (and other factions of SDS) who saw themselves as organizers. They succeeded in engaging a significant number of us in ongoing outreach, debate, and discussion, looking for common ground, as well as opportunities for sharp debates. Looking at today's world, it may sound old-fashioned, but blogging, social media, and starting another nonprofit are not enough. There is no substitute for "mass work" and relationship-building: door knocking, and phone calls, reaching out to people in one-on-one conversations, learning what people are thinking and how to appeal to them.

For me the key lesson of Trump's election was how much most politicians and left/liberal social movements have failed to reach out to people who feel deeply threatened by a wide range of economic, demographic, and cultural change. Outside of the Sanders campaign and a handful of other candidates, we have seen too little in the way of serious efforts, either from the Democratic Party or the leaders of social movements, to speak to people who do not automatically agree with their ideas and issues. Writing off millions of Americans as racists and misogynists, without even trying to conduct serious arguments or find common ground, is a betrayal of everyone in this country, and around the world, whose lives can be so profoundly impacted—for better and for worse—by decisions made by the US government.

2. Organizing for Your Principles, Ideas and Values within Broader Movements and Institutions

PL's commitment to fighting racism and allying with the working class could come across as sloganeering. But PL and WSA members' efforts to follow through on those commitments made a big difference in building coalitions that avoided the worst consequences of self-congratulatory cultural leftism. Harvard PL and WSA's alliances with campus workers and neighborhood communities on explicitly antiracist terms, as well as their efforts to recruit African American students, played an important role in formulating the demands of the student strike at Harvard, where we did not see the kind of split between white antiwar and Black Power student groups that occurred on many other campuses. PL's position against nationalism meant that they opposed the strike demand for a Black Studies Department, but they did not walk out of SDS—or drive out the supporters of that demand—over their differences.

In the year after the strike, however, Harvard PL/WSA followed a new party line and abandoned engagement with the wider antiwar and women's movements to focus *only* on student-campus worker organizing. This was a significant loss for everyone involved. Similarly, the disinterest to outrage that many of our old PL/SDS friends expressed in the decision of a few of us to become involved in electoral politics short-circuited what might have become useful discussions about how to engage in national political debates more effectively.

3. Democratic Practices and Decision-Making

One of the factors that made PL and WSA, along with other factions in the leadership of Harvard SDS, effective in the years leading up to the strike was a commitment to building SDS as a democratic organization that took votes on its positions and strategies. The result was ongoing debate, discussion, and recruitment of large numbers of people (like me), who developed more of a stake in the issues involved. The movement that resulted was far stronger, I would argue, than those of later organizations that chose to avoid the inevitable problems associated with electing leaders and having divisive debates by taking positions only by consensus. Such efforts to avoid conflict and the responsibilities of leadership inevitably resulted in the drifting away of anyone who did not want to attend endless meetings.

It may well be the case that PL's increasingly centralist organization (like that of several other radical Left sects) with a handful of leaders, in love with their own line and rhetoric, denouncing any questions or disagreements and learning less and less from anyone actually trying to organize, bears some responsibility for subsequent generations' distrust of leadership and passion for consensus. I myself heard or saw too many instances where political zeal became an excuse for bullying: some that I deeply regret participating in myself. Nonetheless, I still see trying to take political leadership as important and try not to be too judgmental towards those who do, even when I wish they could be kinder and happier, as well as more effective.

4. Having a Base, Seeking Power, and Wanting to Win

If you want to consider yourself an organizer for any cause (other than reveling in your own identify and values), you need to develop a clear sense of what you want to win and a strategy for doing so. You should want to take and use the power necessary to achieve concrete demands. Whether you are on offense or defense, working for new priorities or to prevent terrible harm from the inside or the outside of the institutions you seek to change, you should be deeply interested in finding allies and building coalitions to achieve results that matter to real people and our planet.

My greatest regret is that so much that was so positive about the experience of the Harvard strike of '69 for so many of us was channeled into the idea that we could only change the world by assault from the outside, or at least from the bottom up. What we missed was what teachers like Matthiessen gave my parents and their generation: the conviction that we could pursue big goals in a big way in a wide variety of arenas. We failed to learn that movements that succeed have insiders and outsiders, people working within institutions that hold power, as well as people working on the outside, mobilizing the disenfranchised, the marginalized, and the pissed off.

I am proud of all us who participated in the Harvard Strike, those who became teachers, nurses, lawyers, doctors, social workers, researchers, and bus drivers, those who went to work in factories and became union organizers—people who played remarkable roles and sometimes organized important struggles in all these settings. But I wish that it was not Al Gore, with his careful, wooden, moralizing appeals to elites and all that they represent with regard to the Democratic Party's failure to develop compelling progressive, antiracist, pro-labor political leadership in the United States, who became the most politically prominent graduate of the Harvard class of 1969. Almost fifty years later, it is getting too late to hope that one of the rest of us will succeed in putting what we learned from that experience to work in a more powerful way. But at least I continue to hope that as teachers and organizers, we can help younger generations to do better.

Mary Summers is a senior fellow and lecturer at the University of Pennsylvania. She teaches academically based community service courses on the politics of food and agriculture and on public education. She has been published in The Nation, Urban Affairs Quarterly, Political Science and Politics, Agricultural History, *and several edited volumes. mysummer@sas.upenn.edu*

23

A Texas Republican's Path
to SDS-WSA and PL

John Mitchell

The 1960s movements against the Vietnam War and for civil rights grew to hundreds of thousands—maybe even a few million. How did a clean-cut Republican kid like me, who grew up in segregated Texas believing that everyone should volunteer to fight if there was a war, become a radical activist? Why did my beliefs briefly go as far as Marxism and revolution? Old friends from fifty years ago asked me to write about my (our) experiences with an eye to learning from mistakes. This is my story.

When I was in high school, everyone I knew liked the sound of John F. Kennedy's "Ask not what your country can do for you, ask what you can do for your country"—even my Texas Republican family. My grandfather fought in the trenches of France in World War I. And my father made the Norden bombsights that enabled 85 percent of our bombers to return from missions over Germany (up from 50 percent when hitting targets meant they had to fly lower).

In 1963 a scholarship enabled me to go from small-town Texas to Harvard. My life had been summer jobs since age fourteen and dancing to great music from Elvis Presley to James Brown. Life was good and relatively carefree. The Cuban Missile Crisis came and went, but very few of us really worried about "the Bomb." Didn't everyone know that a nuclear war would have no winner? I figured that politicians were reading just like I was, and they were guarding against the possibility of a nuclear war starting by mistake as depicted in the book *Fail Safe*.

Many of my friends thought that Martin Luther King's "I Have a Dream" speech in Washington had been a signal that the South's Democrats (called Dixiecrats) would finally be pushed aside and confined to the dust bin of history. My neighborhood football game included a black kid. Many, like me, had worked with people of color from an early age and had positive relationships with them despite segregation.

Within a few years life went from the *Sea of Love* to a sea of change—murders of civil rights workers, JFK's assassination, Martin Luther King's assassination, riots in over 100 cities, more assassinations—while a "police action" in Vietnam became a war killing over a million people and a protest movement grew to hundreds of thousands—some of whom would be killed right on their college campuses.

Money was the only thing that kept me from joining ROTC at Harvard. The dorm crew paid more, and I needed every penny I could scrape together on top of my scholarship and loan. I loved science and majored in chemistry. Science was what I'd do for my country! We had to improve our scientific capability to beat the Reds, who had beaten us by launching the first satellite, Sputnik. I trusted the government. After all, Eisenhower had protected the world from Hitler and years later had protected black students integrating public schools in Little Rock.

I began worrying a bit in 1964 when Barry Goldwater started talking about using nukes in Vietnam because the government had been telling us that we were just advisers in a police action to protect a tiny country from a few commie criminals. In some ways the movie *Dr. Strangelove* reassured us. None of our leaders could be that crazy! When Lyndon Johnson trounced Goldwater in November 1964 I thought, "Worries over."

But conventional bombing of North Vietnam began in 1965, and antiwar demonstrations got big enough to be taken seriously, even by apolitical science majors like me. Maybe it would blow over quickly. Most of us at Harvard barely noticed when Harvard SDS led a confrontation with Secretary of Defense Robert McNamara. Most of us weren't informed enough to know that he had said we would be out of Vietnam by the end of the year. We didn't even know that he had refused to debate opponents of the war during his two-day visit to Harvard's Kennedy Institute of Politics.

I was immersed in chemistry. I was looking forward to my professor's special, optional lecture on napalm—after all, he was its inventor! Napalm was fascinating scientifically– neither a solid nor a liquid. A gel with a geometric molecular structure just unstable enough to combust upon impact! When Professor Fieser concluded his talk saying something like, "I have no right to judge the morality of napalm just because I invented it," I was troubled.

I just couldn't see myself working for the rest of my life with people who thought this way. While trying to dissuade me from changing majors, the head of the department stood behind Fieser's statement. I wasn't somebody who thought about morality more than the next guy, but I had been influenced by a number of novels focusing on moral dilemmas as well as religion. I remembered seeing *Judgment at Nuremburg* in high school, and the horrific consequences of napalm use in Vietnam had become public knowledge. I switched my major to English. Hadn't Hitler's Germany taught us what happened when scientists put their heads in the sand?

Meanwhile, the threat of the draft was heating up. During summers in my hometown my noncollege buddies and I asked each other, "Should we should all join up together?" We wondered why nobody's parents were pushing us to enlist despite all the World War II stories we had grown up hearing, ones where guys went to other states to enlist if they flunked a physical in their own state. We were pro-military. We weren't afraid of guns—we shot them in Boy Scouts, for chrissakes! Growing public ambiguity, plus things that weren't said, even among my parents' Republican friends, made me think twice. I wasn't going to kill anyone before I was sure about this war.

The son of a prominent wealthy hometown family dropped out of Duke to join the Marines. (He was killed in Vietnam near the end of

1966.) The son of another prominent family dropped out of Caltech to join the civil rights movement (where he was almost killed by racists). Most of us held off doing anything—wondering and waiting.

1967

The summer before my senior year at Harvard I got a part-time internship at Boston's ABC-TV News. The station's editorial policy never distorted war casualty numbers, but it encouraged reporters and editors to omit them. We discovered that management was trying to fire a reporter (not an opinion writer) because he reported *all* the casualty numbers from the wire services (AP and UPI). His contract protected him, and the grapevine told him to be careful—although most reporters supported the war. I found out for certain that every single script he wrote was scrutinized in the hope that he would make even a typo in reporting casualty numbers. I began to question the reality of freedom of the press, thinking that management had the right to control opinions in editorials, but not to omit obviously important facts.

I sought out books like *Vietnam! Vietnam!* by Felix Greene and *Vietnam: The Logic of Withdrawal* by Howard Zinn. I went to an antiwar teach-in. I reread the books and talked to friends about them. My disillusionment grew. Demonstrations in Washington became larger, and protests spread to many cities and campuses across the country. I was now certain that the government was systematically lying to us. How could we determine the reality? It wasn't until four years later that the *Pentagon Papers* revealed internal government acknowledgments "that South Vietnam—unlike any of the other countries in Southeast Asia—was essentially the creation of the United States" and that the secret bombing of Cambodia and Laos had begun in 1967. In other words, we began bombing adjacent countries two years after our defense secretary had promised that the US "police action" would be over.

Government assurances that "victory is around the corner" grew increasingly hollow. Nobody knew how long the war would last or how big it would get. Some newspapers suggested that civilian casualties now totaled over 100,000. From 1963 to 1965, US casualties jumped to 11,153 from 1,863, and US troop levels more than doubled to just under half a million. Terms like *butchery* began to appear in the mainstream media. In April, Muhammad Ali, one of the most popular and charismatic figures of our time, refused to be drafted.

Virtually every young guy began making plans to face an insatiable draft. Some paid shrinks to declare them unfit. Some planned ahead to flee to Canada. Many enlisted in the navy or the coast guard to avoid the army. We felt powerless. Most considered demonstrations useless, but better than nothing. My friends and I avoided them. Why would the government listen to us if it wouldn't listen to one of its own— Arkansas Senator J. William Fulbright, chair of the Foreign Relations Committee and a prominent Dixiecrat segregationist? (His book *The Arrogance of Power* attacked the Johnson administration's justification for the Vietnam War.)

I thought of myself as a doer, not a talker. And I got sick and tired of bullshitting with friends "sittin' on the pavement thinking about the government" (as Bob Dylan's *Subterranean Homesick Blues* had it).

Walking down River Street in Cambridge one day, I saw a poster saying something like "From Protest to Resistance, October 16: A Day of Conscience. Turn in your draft card, burn your draft card, renounce the war in whatever way your conscience tells you to." Sounded good. This was what I would do for my country! More than talk. If enough of us did it, the country would wake up. A couple of days later I got handed a Harvard SDS leaflet calling for protests against Dow Chemical (the manufacturer of napalm) for October 25. I decided to do that, too.

I wanted to be effective, get taken seriously—prove that I was patriotic, that I understood the issues, and that I wasn't a coward. I wrote a letter to my draft board saying that the Nuremburg principles required me not to serve in Vietnam because the war was illegal and immoral. I promised to serve if the government successfully defended the war in court. On October 16, 1967, I mailed my letter as part of a New England Resistance action in Boston's Arlington Street Church. Yes, I really imagined that the government would put the war along with me and others on trial—that they would be fair to us in our difference of opinion about something so important.

A week or so later I joined the SDS demonstration against Dow Chemical. I was eager to oppose the immorality of US napalm bombs, but I didn't know anyone in SDS. We sat down in the hallway outside the Dow recruiter's interview room. SDS leaders began talking about a history of indigenous resistance against French colonial rule, coups and puppet governments, and lies our government was spreading. About a hundred of us stayed for the day, not obstructing—but definitely embarrassing the recruiter and Harvard. Thinking back about this time in my life, I thought of both the government and the university as virtual parents who had fallen asleep with a lit cigarette between their fingers. We would wake them up. It was clear that the SDS core thought differently, but they didn't impose their views on the group. What happened over the next month or so woke *me* up.

I lost my student deferment. I lost my internship in television news. I was put on probation by Harvard. And I lost my parents and grandparents because they stopped speaking to me. The hometown guy who left Caltech for civil rights work in Mississippi arrived in Cambridge after narrowly escaping being killed. I was terrified as well as emotionally isolated. I dropped out of school. Most of my friends were shocked. I was the guy with a scholarship and Republican parents who never got in trouble. One or two of my friends joined me in protest, so I wasn't completely alone. I made a lot of new friends, some in organizations like the American Friends Service Committee and the Boston Draft Resistance Group. One thing was for sure—in recognition of growing discontent, the government didn't waste time making draft resisters' lives difficult.

Being fired from my intern job was unexpected and revealing because my boss, the news director, was mentoring me toward a journalism career. I had set up the news department's film library for him, and when the FBI asked to see our footage of the Arlington Street Church draft protest, my boss told me not to worry. When they asked if I had been a participant, I didn't hesitate to say, "Yes, my boss knows about it but doesn't agree with me." After all, this was my "strategy"— shock them into rethinking what they are doing.

The next day, my boss asked me to lunch at a fancy restaurant. While waiting for our meal he began to cry. He had told the FBI that I was harmless. But they wanted me gone. They went over his head to the station president, who then told my boss, "Fire the kid or you will get fired and blacklisted from ever working in TV news again." He wasn't supposed to tell me any of this, but he couldn't help himself. He was shocked and liked me enough to let me know what I was up against. He was in his late forties with three kids, and he wasn't about to fight.

Over the next few months it became clear within the draft resistance network that the FBI had initiated a nationwide campaign of harassment against protesters and their families. People weren't charged with crimes, just harassed with visits and phone calls. The government was afraid to face us in public—in the courtroom. Naturally my image of government as parent was shattered. Free speech and freedom of the press meant nothing to them. They would suppress it at will. The message from almost everywhere, including Harvard, the paragon of academic freedom, was "my country right or wrong." What happened to integrity and the search for truth? The "Great Society" began to look mentally ill. Many of us, including me, thought it needed electroshock therapy.

Draft resistance kept lots of us busy counseling, leafleting, picketing the army base, and sometimes sneaking in to disrupt, but our numbers weren't growing enough to impact the war in a big way. Our actions meant that newspapers found it harder to spread the stereotype of a few cowards burning fake draft cards in the shadows, but there weren't enough of us to make "suppose they gave a war and nobody came" a reality.

At draft resistance meetings we discussed various theories, but we shied away from talking about imperialism and class analysis, terms emerging in some SDS literature. I, like most draft resisters, was unaware that there had already been years of student groups working hard to change the government's foreign policy. We knew little or nothing of liberal organizations like SANE (National Committee for a Sane Nuclear Policy). Most of us hadn't even heard of the US Communist Party, the Industrial Workers of the World, the Progressive Labor Party, the Socialist Workers Party, or the Spartacist League.

SDS was pretty absent from draft resistance events, except for a few people distributing or selling literature. I had been to an SDS meeting, but it turned me off. A lot of the discussion lost me. There were two hotly debated issues—whether large demonstrations in Washington were worthwhile and whether SDS should explicitly demand "immediate withdrawal" rather than "peace now." Marxist views, almost absent from the draft resistance, were often visible within SDS. In virtually every organization I encountered, anger was bubbling up just beneath the surface. Later I learned that SDS leadership was migrating from espousing "participatory democracy" to talk of revolution.

As widespread worry about the future spread, frustration entered popular music—for example, Arlo Guthrie's *Alice's Restaurant Massacree*, which highlighted a guy getting his physical exam at the New York army base telling an army psychiatrist, "Shrink, I want to kill."

One night a few friends and I had fun with this song. Dialing 411 in those years could get almost anyone's number. (Only a few were unlisted.) We cued up *Alice's Restaurant* right to "Shrink, I want to kill" and called General Lewis Hershey, the head of the draft. After ascertaining that it was really him, we played the verse and hung up. Then we sat around paranoid, thinking the FBI might be coming for us— feeling safer in an apartment than on the street. No, I wasn't smoking pot. In fact, I was carefully avoiding it because the FBI was interviewing half the people I hung out with.

As the death count grew, the government had no idea that they were screwing up big time! You had to laugh because you knew their days were numbered. The insanity couldn't continue. Yes, there were just too many people in government with a pre–Civil War mentality, like the one wacko history teacher in my Texas high school. But they couldn't last. Democracy would work. People would purge them from the government, educated by and hastened by us! We might be jailed, but then released when the insanity ended. So we hoped....

I, like most people, didn't know much history. High school classes didn't cover World War II's extensive fire-bombing (almost a hundred cities in Japan and several in Germany). And until the 1980s historians didn't have access to the classified documents in which our military explicitly called the strategy "terror bombing"—documents revealing that our government understood that Japan had been defeated by the blockade and bombing before Hiroshima, that the Japanese people were starving, and that their manufacturing had been brought to a standstill. We didn't need to drop the Bomb to save our troops from needing to invade Japan; Truman dropped the Bomb to terrify the Soviet Union, against the advice of all his senior military staff.

I kept reading and began asking questions of anyone who would talk to me. Most of the SDSers I met were astounded at how little I knew, but nobody I met wanted to spend much time explaining. Some were insistent that draft resisters were "playing into the hands of the ruling elite." They argued that we should build a mass movement, but they hadn't been able to do anything that impressed us. Sure, demonstrations were good, but they didn't really hurt the government any more than we did with our draft resistance—probably less. What did a movement mean? What could or should it do?

At least we draft resisters put a drag on the war itself and built a mutual support network that maximized that drag. Why were the Left groups reluctant to picket the army base with us every time one of us got a notice for a physical—or worse, a notice that we had been drafted? They were probably right that the military-industrial complex had lured Congress and the State Department into this folly. That if we were Vietnamese, maybe we would be rebels, too. Yes, we were naïve about how strongly our government would resist logic and public pressure. And we were ignorant about the prevalence of authoritarian regimes globally. Either half a million troops would end the war quickly, or the lunacy would be terminated because the cost would be too great...

1968

As 1968 began, public awareness of the deep flaws in US foreign policy and civil rights was growing fast. Only a hard core of radicals even imagined what we would see. Most of us still thought we would help the system come to its senses. But events made this one of the most tumultuous years in the twentieth century. The most critical events include the following.

The Boston Five conspiracy indictment. The year began with conspiracy charges against Benjamin Spock (a world-renowned pediatrician who had spoken out publicly against the war, William Sloane Coffin (Yale's chaplain, a former member of Yale's Skull and Bones, and a former CIA employee), Mike Ferber (an organizer of Boston's draft resistance events), Marcus Raskin, and Mitchell Goodman. Immediately, many began make comparisons to the internal repression in Nazi Germany.

The Tet Offensive. At the end of January, surprise NLF attacks against thirty-six of forty-four South Vietnamese provincial capitals and another fifty cities made it obvious that opposition to the South Vietnam government was widespread, not a tiny group that needed "policing." Either our government was completely incompetent, or it had lied to us about popular support for the rebels to get us involved and to make it impossible not to escalate!

The Orangeburg Massacre. The South Carolina Highway Patrol killed three demonstrators and wounded twenty-seven others in response to an unarmed demonstration on the South Carolina State campus demanding desegregation of the community's only bowling alley.

The My Lai Massacre. Stories were emerging about killings of unarmed Vietnamese civilians. However, it took two years for the details of My Lai to become public despite efforts by a helicopter crew that had witnessed the massacre. In late 1969 photographs by a veteran hit the papers, accompanied by a story revealing the murder of about five hundred unarmed men, women, and children.

LBJ announces he will not seek re-election on March 31.

Martin Luther King, Jr. is assassinated on April 4. Whoa! The government didn't care enough to protect its most inspiring civilian leader—a Nobel Peace Prize–winning preacher who espoused nonviolence. Photos of the scene made it obvious that even minimal protection would have prevented this atrocity.

About a hundred inner cities explode into massive riots in response to King's assassination.

Columbia University is shut down by protests and building occupations that conclude with a student strike opposing the university's involvement in the war and expansion into Harlem.

Robert F. Kennedy is assassinated on June 5.

The Democratic National Convention rejects Eugene McCarthy, the peace candidate who won its primaries. Television outside the convention captures thousands of mostly peaceful demonstrators being beaten. They had come to Chicago hoping to celebrate McCarthy's nomination. They chanted "The whole world is watching!" still hoping, like so many others, that the government would wake up.

The Chicago 8 conspiracy indictment was intimidating to the many academics who had begun speaking out about social issues, because it focused on "incitement to riot" for the demonstrations outside the convention. On the one hand, they became more careful; on the other, they carefully organized many moderate petitions and demonstrations that free speech court rulings would most likely protect. They were especially cautious to reiterate that they were not encouraging anyone to break the law. Historical comparisons emerged that educated many like me—the Palmer Raids against socialists and anarchists in 1919/20, the Sacco and Vanzetti case, the Hollywood 10 blacklist of the McCarthy era in the 1950s, the investigations and hearings of the House Un-American Activities Committee.

The first six months of 1968 transformed the beliefs of many, including me. After Tet, I began attending almost any public meeting about the war, and I read any Left literature I could get my hands on. I invited any Marxists (if they saw the Soviets as an enemy) to join me for coffee and talk about their theories. I didn't see elections as a solution anymore, at least not without a long-term, grassroots movement first. The problems were embedded in Washington in both parties.

I read a Progressive Labor pamphlet on the war. Wow! Marxists who talked about how the so-called communists in Vietnam were selling out a grassroots revolt. They argued that the war was the inevitable result of capitalist imperialism. The arguments were convincing, especially given available alternative explanations. Saying that the war was a tragic mistake was no longer an acceptable explanation. Washington knew from the beginning that it was up against a popular rebellion but didn't want admit that. Now the government had no choice but to increase the repression of its critics—silencing them to keep the war machine running smoothly. They knew that defeating the Vietnamese would take years. Now we knew that defeating Washington would take years, too.

Despite growing anger and frustration, the draft resistance avoided heavy internal conflict because it was characterized by an instinctive dislike of theory and because it stayed loyal to every resister—from the many religious pacifists to the few self-proclaimed anarchists. Most of us didn't know that the frustrations we felt had been simmering within SDS for several years and were beginning to sharpen differences of opinion among its leaders from Columbia University to San Francisco State. In the national leadership of SDS, the early participatory democracy concept was being replaced by a revolutionary youth concept. In what seemed to contradict their own principles, that leadership advocated expulsion of the Progressive Labor Marxists at a national meeting. They were unsuccessful. In this environment of faction fighting and increasing revolutionary posturing by the SDS National Office, it became harder for moderates within SDS to be heard or participate.

US bombing in Southeast Asia was approaching World War II levels, total casualties were too large to get accurate counts, the draft had grown to hundreds of thousands a year, and cities here at home were in turmoil. The Associated Press quoted a US Army major about a battle in Vietnam: "It became necessary to destroy the town to save it." Didn't that make it clear just how wrong we were? The machine was eating up our friends and families. My kid brothers were now at risk. Maybe it wasn't crazy to talk about revolution when our military leaders sounded genocidal. What could we do to be effective? Few of us were Marxists, but we knew playing the standard political game wasn't working. However, revolution was a serious, long-term proposition.

The New England Resistance organized some sanctuary events— guys being inducted forcing the government to come and arrest them inside churches rather than tamely showing up at army bases. Cool. Make it harder on the government. But this wasn't a growing trend, and it didn't make it that much harder. If the church filled up with a lot of people, the government would wait until the numbers diminished, and the result would be the same. Jail for refusing induction. I planned to make it even harder, to hide here in the States if I got drafted so they would have to look for me.

One guy I knew set up a meeting with a dozen hard-core draft resisters. He wanted to plan derailing a munitions train. Two of us walked out. The others said no a few meetings later. We needed to get the American people to stop the war, not become vigilantes. Nobody bought into the argument that we would be punishing war criminals— that anyone having anything to do with a munitions train was a war criminal, from the people who loaded it to the engineer. On the West Coast some activists were going to airports and confronting returning vets with "Baby Killer" signs—embarrassing most activists, but getting tons of press. Frustration at what most historians now describe as pointless slaughter led to self-righteousness. Unfortunately, the self-righteousness eventually would lead to horrible vigilantism by a tiny, but extremely visible part of the movement.

When Columbia University was shut down in April, SDS's credibility shot way up among those of us whose anger and frustration was nearing the boiling point. The university cut its ties with the Institute for Defense Analysis. This would hurt the war effort. Could this victory be duplicated?

The month of May saw events in France that shocked the world—demonstrations, strikes, and the occupation of factories and universities across the country—bringing the entire economy of France to a virtual halt. More than 20 percent of the entire population got involved in factory strikes for a period of two weeks. France's President De Gaulle retreated to a military base in Germany to plan a NATO military invasion to break the workers' occupations and strikes, but managed to defuse the situation by dissolving the National Assembly and scheduling new elections. (Talk about a way to end the war! Why couldn't we build a general strike here?)

Protests were mainstream now, and virtually every campus had at least a "peace" group. But "the Movement" was incapable of uniting the discontent under an organizational umbrella. It was now okay for people to say we needed to consider ideas about revolution in movement meetings. Consider FBI harassment, conspiracy indictments, police murders of civil rights protesters, police repression, a daily barrage of lies, and to top it all off—shocking stories from veterans who returned and not only joined protests but organized some of their own. There were revelations that low troop morale was widespread, and there were even reports of officers being fragged (blown up with fragmentation grenades by their own troops). (See the movie *Sir! No Sir!* for more on the movement within the military.)

After the Democratic Convention, talk about persuading people in power often got laughs. But it was a big leap to organize for massive militant actions that were against the law. Was Chicago the last big tantrum to get our parental government to fix things? After all, they created this world for us, didn't they? It wasn't turning out to be what they said it was. Elections? The Democratic Party didn't even honor the victory (that is, actually nominate) the man who had won its own primaries.

At this point, many of us understood that only a massive movement way beyond college campuses had any possibility of bringing the Vietnam conflict to a close and bringing racial justice to our society. Nobody I knew was really reaching out to entire working-class communities. Then I met people in the Cambridge Peace and Freedom Party who had put an antiwar referendum on the ballot and were running an antiwar candidate for state legislature. In addition, they were organizing a referendum that would put rent control into law. This group was a coalition of different opinions brought together by the Progressive Labor Party. I was impressed. I reread their Vietnam pamphlet and sought them out. They encouraged me to join SDS and become a regional traveler to build new chapters on other campuses, focusing on a national campaign to abolish ROTC.

Hmmm. Depriving the army of a major source of officers! That would make more of a difference than more demonstrations in DC or a draft resistance movement that wasn't growing. But what would it take? Events at Columbia suggested that abolishing ROTC was possible. We had to canvass dorms, get petitions signed, confront college administrators, and "build a base" that was prepared to take over buildings until our demands were met.

The San Francisco State strike lasted for months starting in the fall of 1968. Students and faculty demanded Black and Third World ethnic studies, increased minority admissions, minority faculty hiring, and an end to ROTC. SDS and PL played a major role in this struggle, which was largely a success.

Around this time, I joined the Worker-Student Alliance Caucus, which PL had organized within SDS. It had become obvious that it would take more than college students, more than young people, to make any real changes. I was impressed that PL was working in unions, organizing welfare mothers, and had forced the local Stop and Shop to stop carrying nonunion grapes.

Everything I grew up thinking about America's role in the world as a defender of freedom had been turned upside down. Had the military industrial complex Eisenhower had talked about taken over? Was revolution the only way to remove them? It was obvious that neither mainstream political party was interested in changing things on the home front or abroad. Globally prominent scientists in a world-renowned university had told me that I should put my head in the sand. The government was interfering with the free press. Police were murdering peaceful protesters. The Democratic Party wasn't democratic. I personally knew about a dozen guys who were tied up in the courts, about to go to jail, or going to Canada. Most of them (and often their families) had suffered FBI harassment. Many had lost jobs. And many had been abandoned by family and friends. On top of this I knew that my brothers and many of my friends would end up in the armed forces, and most of those enlisting were doing so to avoid becoming "boots on the ground."

Was the problem capitalism? I wasn't sure, but I wasn't sure it wasn't. PL's analysis explained that Vietnam was bigger than we realized, with significant resources including bauxite, rice, and rubber. Only imperial ambition could explain the folly of an escalation against an overwhelmingly popular uprising—one not unlike our own against the British—an uprising that had kicked the French out of Vietnam in 1954. Only imperial ambition explained rationalizing the criminality of defoliating thousands of miles of peasant farmland with Agent Orange (a deadly dioxin) and napalm, indiscriminately killing civilians. Yes, the government said we were fighting the Reds, but weren't we really pushing peasants into the Soviet sphere by opposing what was really an anticolonial revolt? We hadn't intervened in Hungary where supporters of our "way of life" were far more numerous, so why intervene in Vietnam? Did the Cold War mean setting up puppet governments in Cambodia and Laos while claiming to spread freedom and democracy? Doing the same in Latin America? When nobody in the government spoke out against the concept of destroying a town in order to save it, it seemed like territorial expansion was the path the government was intent on.

Whatever the case, abolishing ROTC looked good to me. This would hurt the war effort more than anything else I had seen proposed, depriving the armed services of its main source of officers. I'm not a theory guy. I'm a get-it-done guy. I wanted to help abolish ROTC at every college in the country. I could think about the rest later. I knew the people I was working with were serious about building mass support. They weren't going to go off half-cocked. And the PL brand of Marxism was adamant about the Soviets' betrayal of Marxist ideals, clearly seeing the USSR as an example of state capitalism with imperial ambitions of its own. Were they naïve to think they could organize a different kind of egalitarian revolution? I'd figure that out, but first win some victories!

1969

When the government started another conspiracy trial in 1969, it not only reinforced the need for action that would materially affect the war effort, but also got more people, including me, thinking that the government needed complete replacement. Eight people (David Dellinger of the National Mobilization Committee, Rennie Davis and Tom Hayden of SDS, Abbie Hoffman and Jerry Rubin of the Yippies, Bobby Seale of the Black Panthers, Lee Weiner, and John Froines) were charged with conspiracy to cross state lines with intent to incite a riot in Chicago during the Democratic National Convention.

I joined PL and continued to organize SDS chapters in the Boston area while maintaining a close relationship with Harvard SDS. The logic of Marxism, the long-term approach, and the practical effectiveness of abolishing ROTC gave me some comfort in the middle of abandonment by my family and every institution I knew. We were principled, disciplined, and hard working—the way I was brought up to be.

Within SDS, arguments about strategy started heating up. Initially any talk about reaching out to working people's communities was met with ridicule by some SDS leaders. Forget about workers; they're the problem. Think young people. Look around at the counterculture—sex, drugs, and rock 'n' roll. I had many friends who had "tuned in, turned on, and dropped out." I knew they weren't going to do anything to hurt the war effort other than not participate. Some of them were going off the deep end. Relatively harmless pot usage had migrated to LSD for many and with devastating personal consequences for some. It hardly seemed that making the Rolling Stones'

"Street Fighting Man" an SDS theme song was the best way to go.

The WSA caucus and friends wanted to focus on organizing to abolish ROTC on campuses, not street fighting fantasies. Slowly, but surely, we were building SDS. Around Boston there were significant SDS chapters at Boston College, Boston State, Boston University, Brandeis, Harvard, MIT, Northeastern, Tufts, and UMass Boston. We didn't focus on demonstrations. We tried to build campaigns—canvassing dorms and setting up tables outside dining halls. We developed leaflets with explanations of things rather than short moralistic statements. We shared books and various pamphlets that were available. This methodical approach worked.

We had some impact on racism as well. On some campuses, we raised the issue of universities divesting in South Africa in order to defeat apartheid. This campaign developed strength two decades later. To help defeat racist ideology, we created leaflets and pamphlets to discredit academic "theories" that encouraged bigotry. For example, in 1969 Berkeley Professor Arthur Jensen ignited a firestorm with an article suggesting that the gap in IQ scores between blacks and whites was rooted in genetic differences. Worse was Nobel Prize–winning physicist William Shockley, who espoused a philosophy of "retrogressive evolution," arguing that genetically inferior blacks were reproducing faster than whites—thereby creating retrogression in human evolution. He actually advocated eugenics, specifically calling for replacing the welfare system with a "Voluntary Sterilization Bonus Plan," which, as its name suggests, would pay women to undergo sterilization.

Our commitment to a long-term approach was sometimes marred by frustrations that threatened to tear us apart. One night a close friend in the PL leadership asked me to meet him outside the Harvard ROTC building. He had a can of gasoline. I insisted on approval from the entire leadership and managed to shut him down. Whew! We were able to police ourselves. Our patience paid off a few months later with a Harvard student strike.

By 1969, the angry tone of Credence Clearwater Revival's "Fortunate Son" stood in sharp contrast to the Beatles' release of "Give

Peace a Chance." This trend continued to echo for several years afterwards.

By now I had been arrested several times inside the Boston army base and at demonstrations—and received more visits from the FBI. And my phone was tapped. I'm sure of this because one night a buddy and I provoked the listener so much that he got mad and broke into our conversation to tell us off. I was now convinced that the government was controlled by a ruling capitalist elite whose self-interest required expansion into and control over Third World countries. I believed nothing short of revolution could stop them.

Within SDS these ideas began to consume more and more time in meetings. Yes, we discussed the war and the campaign to abolish ROTC, fight racism, and push various efforts to end discrimination against women, and stop environmental pollution; but we became increasingly insensitive to people who still believed that protest could force the electoral process to work. We spent too much time discussing political differences between the various groups vying for leadership. And these discussions became way too hostile—after all, a wrong position on revolution was counterrevolutionary. We lost much of our focus on winning civil rights and stopping the war while we in PL consumed too much time critiquing the Vietnamese National Liberation Front and the Black Panthers.

Despite our insensitivity and weakened focus, by the spring of 1969 we had at least five hundred students at Harvard (about 10 percent of undergraduates at the time) willing to commit a strong action to abolish ROTC—enough people to justify taking over the administration building, an action that went beyond more passive civil disobedience. We had several thousand petition signatures, but SDS as a whole wasn't ready to support this type of action with a vote. The most vocal opponents said that they supported the goal while arguing that the university would seal off the building the minute they heard about our vote. PL had a small meeting of about a dozen people. We decided to spearhead a takeover and reached out to some of the WSA leaders to finalize a plan.

Here's what happened. We called a rally at a class-change time in the morning in front of the administration building. Once a crowd had gathered (many of whom had been called the night before) the WSA Caucus speaker called for people to go inside and occupy the building. A group of preassigned guys walked the deans and staff out of the building. They were equipped with bicycle chains and locks in order to be able to seal doors just before the inevitable bust came. Almost everyone in SDS and many others joined this action.

There was no violence in the takeover; however, one dean asked to be escorted out with one of us on each arm as a symbol of passive resistance. When the police bust came at 4 a.m. there were hundreds more students outside supporting the occupation but unwilling to participate in the takeover. They took the brunt of police beatings. The police were so brutal that the majority of students voted to strike a few days later even though they didn't agree with the occupiers on some issues. Ironically, the university administration, thinking they would defuse things, managed this meeting, inspecting student IDs and verifying the vote; so all we had to do was talk to people, leaflet, and then make our case at the meeting. The resulting strike vote was "Harvard certified!" Two years later, Harvard sent the two guys who had escorted the passively resisting dean out of the building to jail. They served nine months of a one-year sentence for assault and battery. We found out years later that the university threatened to fire the dean if he didn't testify against them.

Sometimes we compared ourselves to the resistance movements against the Nazis in Europe, thinking that a series of invasions of Third World countries was imminent. Today, I still believe that abolishing ROTC on so many campuses, resistance within the military, and protests by veterans were huge factors in forcing the US to stop waging war in Vietnam. I'd like to believe that we were wrong to anticipate additional invasions of Third World countries. However, the number of clandestine interventions and the massive incursions into Laos and Cambodia still makes me wonder.

SDS Splits

SDS held a national convention that summer. The national leadership remained hostile to PL and WSA. They and their supporters had many different points of view, held together by a belief that young people, rather than working people, would be at the heart of any successful movement. They had morphed from talking about young street-fighting men breaking windows to talking about a revolutionary youth movement. The original "participatory democracy" concept had now completely disappeared. Breaking windows outside the Democratic Convention in 1968 had seemed childish to most of us. Now we weren't sure what to expect. They were vociferous about the shortcomings of working-class people, sometimes seeming to blame workers more than the government for racism and the war.

As the convention began it became apparent after informal counts that the WSA might be able to win votes on some issues. We had grown and were the largest single group present. After denouncing WSA for not agreeing to unconditional support for the Black Panther Party and the Vietnamese National Liberation Front, the impromptu creation naming itself the Revolutionary Youth Movement (RYM) walked out and declared WSA (including PL) expelled from SDS. They then proclaimed themselves to be the real SDS. About a third of the people who came to the convention went home when this happened. And in the aftermath, with two organizations claiming to be SDS, thousands across the country began looking for another vehicle to continue to protest the war.

Did this split destroy SDS? I suspect it was just the final nail in the coffin. The first nail was impatience with people who came to SDS looking for an effective protest organization but who weren't interested in talking revolution. Faction-fighting was the second. The final nail was the split—a nail driven home when the RYM-SDS destroyed the membership lists and then splintered off into the Weather Underground. For me, as my incredulity grew and my beliefs moved leftward, my anger and frustration isolated me from many potential allies who didn't share my new beliefs. And any talk of revolution began to seem childish at best after the Weather Underground appeared on the scene.

The largest action the Weathermen ever mustered was the "Days of Rage" in Chicago—three hundred people breaking glass, throwing trash cans, and fighting with the cops and their tear gas. Later a smaller group became the Weather Underground, carrying out a few bombings. Several of them accidentally blew themselves up in New York's Greenwich Village.

At Harvard, about twenty Weatherpeople showed up at the Center for International Affairs. There were no faculty members available to discuss the war machine, so the pseudo-militants chanted "Off the pig!" while the action's leader threatened a secretary with scissors for "supporting the pig war machine." As you might imagine, the media paid no attention when WSA-SDS called a press conference to explain that this cowardly pseudo-radicalism represented a tiny minority of what had been a massive, broad-based organization.

Today history has succeeded in portraying "the movement" as degenerating into the Weather Underground. Media sensationalism and poor research has allowed a minuscule aberration to taint the hard work of hundreds of thousands of people who made tremendous sacrifices in hopes of getting our country to do the right thing. I was one of the more naïve. A friend recently reminded me that people who took buses to Mississippi as part of the "Freedom Rides" wrote out their wills before going.

None of the Left's splintering and the Weather sect's insanity kept public sentiment against the war from growing. The remaining WSA-SDS chapters continued actions against the war and racism and mobilized public support for the 1969 General Electric strike. WSA-SDS continued a past project, the Summer Work-In, with radical students, especially those from more affluent backgrounds, taking factory jobs, leafleting factory gates, and talking about the war and racism. The reception they got was more positive than most expected, and in some cases led to long-term relationships as working people joined the movement.

Various groups including SDS continued for several years despite the intimidating 1970 murders of protesters at Kent State and Jackson State. Several extremely committed SDS and PL individuals attempted to organize within the army when drafted. One guy came close to organizing a work stoppage against the war in US bases in Korea. Another was put in solitary confinement for close to a year before being discharged. A third was tortured with sleeplessness until he became seriously ill before being discharged. My Texas friends reached out and thanked me when they got home from 'Nam. Our youthful bonds survived the media portrayal of the movement as insane bombers. They knew me better than that.

It is worth noting that the WSA-SDS did continue various activities against racism during this period as well as begin organizing relationships with their colleges' workforces. At Harvard there was a notable victory against the university's racism toward campus workers. Blacks were hired as apprentices in the skilled trades, but never promoted to the journeyman level after appropriate experience—a racist practice that kept Harvard's costs down. With publicity and demonstrations, students enabled workers to overturn this practice. During this period WSA-SDS mistakenly neglected antiwar campaigning, focusing primarily on relationships with working people, especially campus workers. PL was the driving force behind this priority, abusing the trust they had earned and antagonizing many who disagreed.

As we graduated and entered the work force, many of us continued to organize in our communities and on the job. I am proud to have been associated with efforts of hundreds of thousands of very different people who put their lives on hold to end the war and defeat racism. I am proud to have been one of many who worked hard to discredit any kind of anti-egalitarian thinking. I still listen to Marvin Gaye's songs "Inner City Blues" and "What's Going On" and the words to Curtis Mayfield's "We People Who Are Darker Than Blue" still ring true.

Looking Back and Forward

Today the arguments about race echo the arguments back then. The "white skin privilege" view of racism survives and is now espoused widely throughout academia. Is it a "privilege" to be less oppressed? Racism is against the interest of working people, undermining the unity needed to build an effective grassroots movement.

Marx suggested that capitalism would mold "the proletariat" into communards. The human condition is better than that. Plenty of non-proletarians have made tremendous sacrifices to defeat social injustices and create a more egalitarian world. Unfortunately, PL became preoccupied with class background, often treating academic intellectuals as useless except as sources of funds and improved writing—especially ironic given the backgrounds of many of PL's leaders.

Revolution. Were we way off-base to think a revolution would be needed to stop what the US was doing in Southeast Asia and elsewhere? There were substantial reasons to think the country was pursuing an imperialist path toward the acquisition of territory. On the other hand, the US withdrew from Vietnam and abstained from major military action until 1990. After US withdrawal, the amorphous anti-war movement saw no reason to exist. And those of us on the Left had isolated ourselves from the possibility of creating a long-term grassroots movement that was independent of the political parties. The movement of the sixties proved the old adage that you can't tell truth to power. And this turned out to be true within SDS and PL as well as the society at large.

Grassroots movements have always been the most important force for social change. Grassroots organizing can force the political parties to make improvements and ensure that hard-won improvements are not reversed. But it would be a mistake to see political parties as grassroots organizations. They exist primarily as cliques between elections.

Has there been progress? One might argue that the Iraq War "mistake" cost fewer lives than the Vietnam War. One can also argue that the "n" word is banned and segregation is illegal. But the black–white income disparity hasn't changed significantly. And half of all families have experienced a decline in their real net worth. That decline is far greater among lower-income families. And these realities only scratch the surface of social problems we face. Our culture is facing them with materialism and drugs rather than a grassroots movement that unites all of us who are not part of the ruling wealthy elite.

Lessons

"Don't follow leaders, watch the parking meters" (Bob Dylan). Seriously, movements are groups, not leaders—mutually supporting communities, not cliques. We should learn to articulate, not worship the articulate. Organizing should rotate leadership, favoring integrity, hard work, teamwork, and positive energy over charisma.

Focus on useful improvements, not pie in the sky. Rather than focusing on perfect positions, we should organize coalitions of many opinions united around shared purposes. Should energy protests focus around an end to all fracking and pipelines or less of both with better, safer practices?

Believe in people. We should listen to and learn from people, asking what they believe and why before suggesting why they might consider thinking differently. Any change worth making can be explained, and we should make the effort to communicate these explanations—avoiding the self-righteousness that often accompanies legitimate anger at injustice—remembering that we ourselves have changed our minds about things. People are dynamic. Their instincts support equality and solidarity; their beliefs are not intractable.

Look at yourself. Clean up the world but start in your own room.

Acknowledgments

We would like to thank everyone who made the production of *You Say You Want a Revolution* an unalloyed pleasure. Foremost among them is Steve Hiatt, copy-editor and book designer extraordinaire, who took our manuscript and graphics and shaped it into a book. We are also indebted to Robert Plone for additional copy editing and our research director, Alan Ginsberg, who ferreted out comrades from fifty years past so we could importune them to contribute a memoir. During the two-year period of putting this collection of memoirs together we contacted over a hundred people who were either members of Progressive Labor Party, the Worker-Student Alliance Caucus of SDS, or both. Of the group we contacted, about half said they would contribute a memoir. In the end we received the twenty-two memoirs representing universities from most every region of the country.

We also want to thank both individuals and institutions who helped us locate documents and other material that were instrumental in creating the book. Ken Epstein turned over four moldering boxes of documents, old magazines, newspapers, and photographs that had been stored in his garage for decades. Pat Foreman, Ernie Brill, Joe Berry, Polly Levin, and Jeff Gordon gifted us with yellowed copies of *New Left Notes*, *PL Magazine*, leaflets, posters, and buttons, and images of many of them found their way into the book. The Marxist Internet Archives

(Marxists.org) was invaluable in locating key documents and verifying fifty-year-old memories. The San Francisco State University Library Archives, the Taminent Library of New York University, the archives of the University of Washington, Harvard University Archives, Columbia University Archives, UC Berkeley, and Bolerium Books in San Francisco were resources for additional research.

Paula Braveman, Margaret Leahy, Joe Berry, Ellen Israel, Eric Johnson and Chris Raisner, Dick Reavis, Paul Yamasaki, Tom Flusty, Ed Morman, John Pennington, Michael Sacco, Max Sklar, Ruhama Veltfort, Mike Pincus, Vivienne Bailey, Bob Biderman, and others provide encouragement and feedback as the manuscript progressed. The photographs came from multiple sources, but we were extremely fortunate to have the contribution of El Puente de Claudio, whose photos appeared in PL publications in the mid-sixties. He graciously went through the negatives he had saved and produced fresh copies, and a number of them are included in the book. We also want to thank Jeff Blankfort, Nacio Jan Brown, Steve Ludwig, Stuart Solloway, and Meredith Eliassen, curator of the SFSU Photographic Timeline Collection for additional photographs. For additional technical support we relied on Carolina Vallejo of Copy Central, Gustaf Engstrom, and Joanne Rosen.

We also would like to thank numerous friends and family who put up with us and offered sage advice through the two years of putting the book together, especially our partners, Paula Braveman and Sue Schultz, as well our daughters, Jennifer, Rosie, Sara, and Sulyn. Most of all we want to thank the twenty-three men and woman whose memoirs are this book.

Resources

Adelson, Larry. *SDS*. New York: Scribner's, 1972.

Ali, Tariq, and Susan Watkins. *1968: Marching in the Streets*. New York: Free Press, 1998.

Barlow, William, and Peter Shapiro. *An End to Silence: The San Francisco Student Movement in the 60s*. New York: Pegasus, 1971.

Bradley, Stefan M. *Harlem vs. Columbia University: Black Student Power in the Late 1960s*. Urbana and Chicago: University of Illinois Press, 2009.

Buhle, Paul. *History and the New Left: Madison, Wisconsin, 1960–1970*. Philadelphia: Temple University Press, 1991.

Buhle, Paul, ed., with Harvey Pekar and Gary Dumm. *Students for a Democratic Society: A Graphic History*. New York: Hill & Wang, 2008.

Elbaum, Max. *Revolution in the Air: Sixties Radicals Turn to Lenin, Marx and Che*. 3rd edn. London: Verso, 2018 [2002].

Foley, Michael S. *Confronting the War Machine: Draft Resistance During the Vietnam War*. Chapel Hill: University of North Carolina, 2003.

Gornick, Vivian. *The Romance of American Communism*. New York: Basic Books, 1977.

Gosse, Van. *The Movements of the New Left 1950–1975: A Brief History with Documents*. New York: Bedford/St. Martin's, 2005.

———. *Rethinking the New Left: An Interpretive History*. New York: Palgrave Macmillan, 2005.

————. *Where the Boys Are: Cuba, Cold War America and the Making of a New Left*. London: Verso, 1993.

Leonard, Aaron J., and Conor Gallagher. *Heavy Radicals: The FBI's Secret War on America's Maoists*. Alresford, UK: Zero Books, 2015.

Levy, Peter B. *The New Left and Labor in the 1960s*. Urbana and Chicago: University of Illinois Press, 1994.

Lewis, Penny W. *Hardhats, Hippies and Hawks: The Vietnam Antiwar Movement as Myth and Memory*. Ithaca, NY: Cornell University Press, 2013.

Lieberman, Robbie, ed. *Prairie Power: Voices of 1960s Midwestern Student Protest*. Charlotte, NC: Information Age, 2010.

Rossinow, Doug. *The Politics of Authenticity: Liberalism, Christianity, and the New Left in America*. New York: Columbia University Press, 1998.

Sale, Kirkpatrick. *SDS*. New York: Vintage, 1974.

Schultz, Bert. *Fordham SDS* [video]. Cominsane Press, 2015.

Sonnie, Amy, and James Tracy. *Hillbilly Nationalists, Urban Race Rebels, and Black Power: Community Organizing in Radical Times*. Brooklyn: Melville House, 2011.

Tucker, William H. *Princeton Radicals of the 1960s, Then and Now*. Jefferson, NC: McFarland, 2015.

CPSIA information can be obtained
at www.ICGtesting.com
Printed in the USA
BVHW071139131218
535235BV00016BB/860/P

9 780578 4065